The Civilian Conservation Corps

Duke Historical Publications

The Civilian Conservation Corps, 1933-1942: A New Deal Case Study by John A. Salmond

Duke University Press *Durham, North Carolina* **1967**

 L.C.C. card no. 66-30206

Printed in the United States of America by the Seeman Printery, Inc.

Preface

This is the life story of a federal agency. It is also the chronicle of a successful experiment. The plan to put unemployed young men to work on the conservation of natural resources, conceived amid general skepticism in the first fruitful weeks of Franklin Roosevelt's first administration, flourished to become one of the most popular of all the New Deal measures. It was also one of the most successful. During its life span of nine years more than 2.5 million young Americans passed through the Civilian Conservation Corps. In so doing, they benefited both themselves and the nation. These benefits were immediate, obvious, and well distributed. Farmers were assisted by soil erosion camps and by work in reforestation and fire control; local businessmen received an economic boost from their participation in the camp trade. The families of the enrollees were aided by the monthly allotment checks which they received. The youths themselves gained both physically and in outlook from the camp experience. The purpose of this book is first to examine these matters at greater length.

These practical benefits account, to a degree, for the CCC's extraordinary popularity. Even without them, however, the Corps would probably have touched a responsive chord in American hearts. For it appealed to one of the most durable of American folkways, the mystique of the forest. In an age of rapid urbanization, the CCC boys made one think of the frontier. This appeal was, in a sense, nostalgic; the boys re-created the spirit of an heroic age now past. Moreover, in a predominantly pacifist society, perhaps the CCC's military connection had some special meaning for those who still valued martial virtues. These, too, are themes which I have considered.

This book does not pretend to be a comprehensive history of the Civilian Conservation Corps. My concern, primarily, is with the central organization, not the thousands of camps. I have tried to explain how the Corps was developed and operated, I have discussed both its successes and its failures, and I have identified the reasons for its widespread popular appeal. But I have not been able to examine the Corps at the grass-roots level to any great extent. This, therefore, is a history of the Civilian Conservation Corps as seen, in large part, through Washington eyes.

Many people and institutions have aided in the making of this book, and I can mention but a few by name. I must thank, first of all, the Duke University Commonwealth-Studies Center for financing my researches. My greatest academic debt is owed to Dr. Richard L. Watson, Jr., chairman of the History Department at Duke, who first suggested the subject to me, and whose advice, encouragement, and criticism have been the formative factors in this work. Dean Snyder, formerly director of CCC Selection, graciously took the time to discuss aspects of his work with me, while my research would have taken far longer, and been much less enjoyable, had it not been for the constant assistance and attention of Mr. Stanley Brown, National Archives, Washington, and Messrs. Jerry Deyo and Joseph Marshall, Franklin D. Roosevelt Library, Hyde Park, New York. To all these gentlemen, I owe my thanks.

My friends and colleagues, Mr. M. W. Raffel, Victoria University of Wellington, New Zealand; Dr. M. E. R. Bassett, University of Auckland, New Zealand; Dr. Lynn L. Marshall, University of California at Santa Barbara; and Dr. Bruce L. Clayton, Allegheny College, have each read the manuscript, either whole or in part. Their textual criticisms have been invaluable, while, with great fortitude, they have also acted as sounding boards for my ideas. Mesdames C. van Ginkel and M. Firth, secretaries in the History Department of Victoria University of Wellington, have typed the complete manuscript, saving me much time and tedium. I wish to thank, too, the Editorial Board of the *Journal of American History* for permitting me to use in Chapter V material which first appeared in that journal as part of an article. My greatest debt is to my wife, Barbara Ann Salmond. She has assisted me in my research, in formulating my ideas, and in setting them on paper. This book is dedicated to her.

All the people mentioned above have helped give this book whatever merit it may possess. For its defects, I alone am responsible.

John Salmond
July, 1966

Contents

The Civilian Conservation Corps

1. *The Creation of the CCC*

In March, 1931, a handful of young Negro tramps were arrested in Scottsboro, Alabama, and charged with rape. The sheriff's office alleged that, while riding a freight train from Chattanooga, they had brutally assaulted two white girls, also hobos. The boys were duly tried and convicted, though the evidence against them was, at best, unconvincing, and the case developed subsequently into an affair of national importance, a rallying point for liberals, and an opportunity for Communist exploitation. The fate of these boys became a symbol of Southern injustice and of white indifference to Negro despair. The Scottsboro trial was seen as illustrating aptly the brutalizing aspects of racial discrimination in America.[1]

The racial implications of the incident served to camouflage the fact that the very situation of the Scottsboro boys illustrated equally well another of the urgent problems facing Americans. In the chaos of depression America, almost two million men and women had abandoned all pretense to a settled existence and had simply taken to the road, traveling in freight cars or on foot, sleeping in caves or in shanty towns, aimlessly drifting in search of vanished security. Among them were about 250,000 young people, "the teenage tramps of America" as they were sometimes called, all, like the Scottsboro boys, wandering the land looking for a future. The need to rescue them was crucial.[2]

Moreover, these juvenile drifters were but a tiny fraction of the total of jobless youth. Most of these unemployed youngsters, indeed, never left their home environment. Figures of unemployment among young people during the depression decade are incomplete, but George Rawick has calculated that in 1932, of those between the ages of fifteen and twenty-four who were in the labor market, perhaps one in four was totally unemployed. A further 29 per cent worked part-time only.[3] This was an Ameri-

1. Arthur M. Schlesinger, Jr., *The Age of Roosevelt*, III, *The Politics of Upheaval* (Boston, 1960), 428-429.

2. Schlesinger, *Age of Roosevelt*, I, *The Crisis of the Old Order* (Boston, 1956), 251.

3. George P. Rawick, "The New Deal and Youth: The Civilian Conservation Corps, the National Youth Administration, the American Youth Con-

can crisis. These young people, endlessly tramping city streets or stagnating in country towns, were in a situation not of their own making. Bewildered, sometimes angry, but more often hopeless and apathetic, they were a generation already deeply scarred. The government could no longer afford to ignore their plight.

The federal government had also to cope with scars of a very different kind, the disfiguring marks which three generations of waste and ill-usage had left on the American landscape. Forests had once covered 800,000,000 acres of the continental United States, but by 1933 there were a mere 100,000,000 acres of virgin timber left. Much of the nation's timber resources had thus been brutally squandered. Moreover, wanton forest destruction had compounded the crucial problem of soil erosion. Each year water washed three billion tons of the best soil away from American fields and pastures, and wind accounted for a like amount. Indeed, by 1934, more than 300,000,000 acres—a sixth of the continent—had gone, or was going. Deserts of dust were replacing the grasslands of the Great Plains, the once verdant Texas hills had become stunted tufts, as erosion galloped through the land.[4]

The Civilian Conservation Corps was thus, in one sense, a catalyst. Through it, a new and vital president, Franklin D. Roosevelt, brought together two wasted resources, the young men and the land, in an attempt to save both.

The idea of putting young men to work in the woods was scarcely new. Many men in many places had played with the notion at some time or another. Nevertheless, a number of people have tried to trace the CCC to a single source, the great Harvard philosopher, William James. In 1912 James had published an essay entitled "The Moral Equivalent of War," in which he had advocated "the conscription of the whole youthful population to form, for a certain number of years," a part of a great army "enlisted against nature." This force, he contended, would bring

gress" (unpublished Ph.D. dissertation, University of Wisconsin, 1957), pp. 18-29.

4. Kenneth Holland and Frank Ernest Hill, *Youth and the CCC* (Washington, 1942), p. 12; Stuart Chase, "Where the Crop Lands Go: Spendthrift America's Dwindling Estate," *Harper's*, CXXXV (Aug., 1936), 225-233.

countless benefits both to the youth and to the land.[5] Many people simply interpreted the CCC as being the application of James's suggestion to depression America. Roosevelt, however, could not remember having read the essay and certainly denied ever consciously connecting it with the Corps. "But," he admitted, "it is a very interesting thought."[6]

Interesting it may have been, but there were certainly other influences which must be considered. In the first place, relief work in the forests had begun on a limited scale in parts of the United States even before Roosevelt was elected. In both California and Washington, for example, the Forest Service co-operated with state and county officials in running subsistence camps for the unemployed in forest areas. The local authorities clothed and fed the men, while the Forest Service sheltered them and directed the work. Similar schemes were being operated or at least planned in other parts of the country, and Roosevelt was aware of most of them. They undoubtedly influenced his thinking on the CCC to some degree.[7] Then too, there were the overseas examples to follow. By 1932 the governments of Bulgaria, the Netherlands, Norway, Sweden, Denmark, Austria, and above all, Germany, had established conservation camps for the unemployed. The German Labor Service was to become by far the best known of these and the one most easily comparable to the CCC. Under Adolf Hitler, the Labor Service, as shall be discussed in a later chapter, had a distinctive militaristic and authoritarian flavor. It developed into a vehicle for Nazi propaganda, and because of this Roosevelt always warmly denied that it had ever influenced his thinking on the CCC. The two bodies, in his view, simply could not be compared.

5. William James, *Memories and Studies* (New York, 1912), pp. 290-291.

6. Roosevelt to Prof. I. C. Keller, Nov. 15, 1934, in Franklin D. Roosevelt Papers, Official File 268—Miscellaneous (hereinafter cited as Roosevelt Papers, O.F. 268), Franklin D. Roosevelt Library, Hyde Park, N.Y.

7. R. F. Hammatt, "The Forest Service and Emergency Conservation Work" (typescript in National Archives), pp. 1-3. Records of the CCC, Chronological Reference Material by Subjects (hereinafter cited as C.R.M.), No. 782(a), in National Archives. See also R. L. Deering, "Camps for the Unemployed in the Forests of California," *Journal of Forestry*, XXX (May, 1932), 554-557; F. A. Anderson, Executive Committee, Mississippi Forest Service, to Roosevelt, Nov. 5, 1931, in E. B. Nixon, ed., *Franklin D. Roosevelt and Conservation, 1911-1945* (New York, 1957), I, 49.

This, of course, is partly true, because the CCC never developed the German Labor Service's frankly political functions. Nevertheless, a connection can perhaps be discerned. The German camps were originally the creation of the Weimar Republic. In 1931 when they began, their functions were to check unemployment among young men and to perform useful conservation work. They were voluntary in nature, the young men enrolling for six months at a time and receiving a token wage. So similar are all these provisions to those eventually adopted by the CCC, that it seems at least possible that, despite Roosevelt's energetic disavowals, prior German experience could have influenced the specifics of the American development.[8]

Though one can indeed find a wide variety of possible sources for the idea of the CCC, it nevertheless remains true that more than any other New Deal agency it bore the personal stamp of President Roosevelt. Without him, relief work in the woods may have remained only an idea. Roosevelt's love of the land was both passionate and total. His own Hudson Valley estate, at Hyde Park, was a constant source of the profoundest delight to him, and driving his specially appointed automobile he would spend hours exploring its giant forests, its gentle hills, its streams and glades. The new President was a strict Jeffersonian in his belief that a rural existence was the best of all possible worlds. In his view, nothing benefited soul, mind, and body more than a life lived close to nature. It is in this context that his long-term interest in relief schemes involving the moving of urban dwellers back to the land must be understood. This passionate belief, too, can be seen in the concept of work in the forest for young men.[9]

Roosevelt's feeling for the land did not stop at Hyde Park, but rather embraced the whole continent. No feature of American life disturbed him more than the callousness with which the national heritage was being destroyed. As Arthur Schlesinger, Jr., has written, "he felt the scars and exhaustion of the earth almost

8. The best book on European labor camps is Kenneth Holland, *Youth in European Labor Camps* (Washington, 1939); see also Stephen H. Roberts, *The House That Hitler Built* (London, 1937), pp. 211-218.

9. Schlesinger, *Age of Roosevelt*, II, *The Coming of the New Deal* (Boston, 1959), 335-336; Frank Freidel, *Franklin D. Roosevelt*, III, *The Triumph* (Boston, 1956), 224-225.

as personal injuries."[10] Roosevelt, a long-time disciple of Theodore Roosevelt's Chief Forester Gifford Pinchot, had been a fighter for conservation for most of his adult life. He knew what must be done and was acutely aware that action had to be taken immediately.

Roosevelt's experiences at Hyde Park pointed the way, in his view, to a national solution. When he took over the estate in 1910 the once fertile soil was virtually exhausted. Where corn had formerly grown, he planted great trees and loved them both for their majesty and the hope of renewal they gave the earth in which they stood. Reforestation, he believed, could save the nation's natural resources as it had saved Hyde Park.[11]

From the time he first entered public life in 1910, Roosevelt fought for conservation measures. As chairman of the New York State Senate's Fish and Game Committee, he tried to develop a comprehensive reforestation scheme, and he even made conservation an issue in his unsuccessful campaign for the vice-presidency in 1920. He retained—indeed, he strengthened—his conviction during his long period of convalescence from polio.[12]

When he triumphantly returned to public life as governor of New York in 1928, Roosevelt seized every opportunity to translate his ideas into action on a statewide basis. The most important of these efforts was his successful sponsorship of an amendment in 1931 to the constitution of New York state. This amendment gave the state government authority to purchase marginal land and reforest it, the money to be provided by a bond issue. It was a policy directly in line with Roosevelt's deepest convictions, and his open support of it won him national recognition among conservationists.[13]

As governor, Roosevelt lost no time in using these new powers, and, at his direction, the New York conservation commissioner, Henry J. Morgenthau, Jr., introduced a broad reforestation scheme. In 1932 Roosevelt was able to develop it as a

10. Schlesinger, II, 335.
11. Freidel, III, 232; Schlesinger, II, 336.
12. Freidel, *Franklin D. Roosevelt,* I, *The Apprenticeship* (Boston, 1952), 136-138; II, *The Ordeal* (Boston, 1954), 84, 149; see also Nixon, I, 38-41.
13. Freidel, III, 231; see also Bernard E. Bellush, *Franklin D. Roosevelt as Governor of New York* (New York, 1955), pp. 94-98.

part of New York's unemployment relief program. The men required for tree-planting were all taken from relief rolls, and 10,000 people were thus given temporary employment. Morgenthau later alleged that the CCC was simply an extension of the New York development.[14]

Of course, this was not so. The New York plan was but one of a number of streams contributing to the eventual creation of the Civilian Conservation Corps, and it is impossible to single out any one source as being of prime importance. What can be said, however, is that Roosevelt breathed life into a scattered collection of ideas. Of all the New Deal agencies, it was his personal creation.

It was during his speech accepting the Democratic presidential nomination, on July 2, 1932, that Governor Roosevelt first hinted at the outlines of his national plans for conservation. He called for "a definite land policy" to fight "a future of soil erosion and timber famine." "In so doing," he said, "employment can be given to a million men. That is the kind of public work that is self-sustaining. . . . Yes, I have a very definite program for providing employment by that means."[15] Here, in generalized form, was the idea of the Civilian Conservation Corps. The problem now was to give it substance.

Although the reforestation-employment plan was attacked derisively by President Hoover's secretary of agriculture, Arthur M. Hyde, professional foresters and interested laymen praised its farsighted aims.[16] Throughout the election campaign, Roosevelt conducted a vigorous correspondence with men such as Gifford Pinchot, now governor of Pennsylvania, gathering their views.[17] In his campaign speeches Roosevelt referred from time to time to his idea of providing work in the forests for the unemployed, but he showed no evidence of having thought the plan through in any detail.[18] Not until mid-November was the Forest Service even brought into the picture. Then, the secretary

14. *Congressional Record* (hereinafter cited as *C.R.*), 73rd Cong., 1st Sess., Vol. 77, Pt. 3, pp. 3004-3005, where a speech by Morgenthau to the twenty-first annual meeting of the U.S. Chamber of Commerce is reprinted.
15. Nixon, I, 112.
16. New York *Times*, July 6 and 7, 1932.
17. Nixon, I, 119-126.
18. C.R.M., Appendix I, Documents 3 and 4.

of agriculture-designate, Henry Wallace, and Roosevelt's economic adviser, Rexford Tugwell, called on the chief forester, Major Robert Y. Stuart, and instructed him to develop plans for putting 25,000 men to work in federally owned forests. Stuart, a career forester, ardent conservationist, and a protégé of Pinchot, was certain that the Forest Service could handle such a number easily, but he must have had his doubts a month later when he was told the number to be expected was 250,000. The Forest Service had done little enough to prepare for such an expanded role. True, it had recently completed a survey of work needing urgent attention, but this was confined to federal forests only. Such information as it did possess on the condition of state forests was spotty and inaccurate. Though the survey provided at least an indication of where camps could profitably be established, there was obviously much more information needed before the scheme could be developed properly.[19]

In January, 1933, an event of some importance, in view of the way the CCC eventually developed, took place. Senator James Couzens, the liberal Republican from Michigan, introduced a bill in the Senate authorizing the Army to house, feed, and clothe unemployed young men from the ages of seventeen to twenty-four at military posts. The measure was bitterly opposed by military authorities and was soon quietly shelved. Nevertheless, it served to introduce the concept of Army assistance with relief schemes into top-level thinking, and it also forced Army officials to realize that, whether they liked it or not, they might have to fulfil such functions in the future. Consequently, base facilities were checked, and, where necessary, strengthened.[20]

Such developments, however, hardly constituted specific planning for the work relief scheme. The economic crisis worsened in the opening months of 1933, and the President-elect was too involved with matters pertaining to it, as well as with the process of Cabinet formation, to devote much thought to his conservation plans. He made only indirect reference to the idea in his inaugural address of March 4, 1933, and not until March 9

19. Hammatt, pp. 1-3.

20. *Ibid.*, pp. 3-6; see also John Jacob Saalberg, "Roosevelt, Fechner and the CCC—A Study in Executive Leadership" (unpublished Ph.D. dissertation, Cornell University, 1962), pp. 9-10.

did he outline what was in his mind. Then, at a conference attended by the secretaries of agriculture, the interior, and war, the director of the budget, the Army judge advocate-general, Colonel Kyle Rucker, and the solicitor of the Department of the Interior, Edward Finney, Roosevelt sketched out a plan to put 500,000 men to work on a variety of conservation tasks. He asked Rucker and Finney to prepare a draft bill, to be in his hands that same evening.[21] Working frantically throughout the day, they had an outline ready for the President by 9 P.M. and discussions on it were held immediately. This original draft proposed the recruitment of 500,000 men a year, to be employed not only on conservation tasks but on public works projects as well. It was intended to be a basis for discussion only and was certainly treated as such. Few details of this preliminary meeting were made public, but it was rumored that the Army would be used to organize the camps and to recruit enrollees. The Chicago *Tribune* reported that the President would attempt "to swing the efforts of three departments—War, Agriculture and Interior—behind his idle relief project."[22]

Roosevelt, for the first time, gave the conservation project some serious and sustained thought. On his own he drew up a more detailed plan for putting an army of unemployed young men to work solely in the forests and national parks, and on March 14 he outlined his idea to Raymond Moley. According to Moley, he announced, "I think I'll go ahead on this . . . the way I did on beer."[23]

"Going ahead" meant rushing a message over to Congress without consulting anyone further on either the wider implications of the CCC idea or specific details of its prospective operation. Moley, therefore, urged delay, both to check impulsive action on the President's part, and also to give Cabinet members and congressional groups a chance to fit the proposal into a wider scheme of unemployment relief. It seems that Moley's advice was heeded. At least Roosevelt abandoned his plan for immediate

21. Finney to K. Rucker, March 11, 1933, Roosevelt Papers, O.F. 268, Box 1; see also Nixon, I, 138n.

22. Chicago *Tribune*, March 11, 1933.

23. For details of this important interview, see Raymond Moley, *After Seven Years* (New York, 1939), pp. 173-174.

action on the reforestation proposal and instead sent a memorandum to the secretaries of war, interior, agriculture, and labor which read:

> I am asking you to constitute yourselves an informal committee of the Cabinet to co-ordinate the plans for the proposed Civilian Conservation Corps. These plans include the necessity of checking up on all kinds of suggestions that are coming in relating to public works of various kinds. I suggest that the Secretary of the Interior act as a kind of clearing house to digest the suggestions and to discuss them with the other three members of the informal committee.[24]

The way was left open for consideration of the CCC within a wider framework of far-reaching public relief proposals.

The four secretaries met on March 15, 1933. After a wide-ranging discussion they forwarded a joint memorandum to the President which made it quite clear that they had considered the CCC both as a self-contained agency and also as an integral part of a three-pronged attack on the problem of industrial unemployment. Furthermore, they thought that the CCC should be "strictly limited to works which are not available as projects for public works. . . . and that it is highly desirable that they should be specifically confined to forestry and soil erosion projects in the Bill."[25] By confining it to these specified works, it was hoped to relieve the fears of those who believed that such an agency would depress wage levels and, by impinging on work normally done by free labor, limit job opportunities even further. Roosevelt decided to incorporate most of the points covered by the

24. Roosevelt to Secretary of Agriculture, March 14, 1933, Files of the Secretary of Agriculture—Conservation, in National Archives. The memorandum is also printed in Nixon, I, 138. The secretary of labor was now included in the discussions, partly because of the new approach to the CCC as part of a general scheme to relieve unemployment, but also to forestall opposition to the Army's recruiting of the men. This job was now to be done by the U.S. Employment Service. See Francis Perkins, *The Roosevelt I Knew* (New York, 1946), pp. 178-179.

25. *The Secret Diary of Harold L. Ickes*, I, *The First Thousand Days* (New York, 1953), 7. The other prongs were (1) federal appropriations for grants-in-aid to the various states for direct relief work, and (2) "A measure for a large, practical, labor-producing program of public works, under the control of a board which can allocate them in such a manner as to drain the largest pools of unemployment in the country. . . ." See Nixon, I, 141-142.

memorandum into his forthcoming message to the Congress on relief.[26]

At his third press conference, held the same day, the President talked at some length about his plan for work in the forests. He covered the need for such work, the number of men who could be usefully employed, and the proposed wage rate of $1 a day, indicating that action on the scheme was imminent.[27] The next few days were spent composing and discussing the President's relief message and in preparing the final draft of a bill for the establishment of the Civilian Conservation Corps.[28] On March 21, 1933, the President's message on the "Relief of Unemployment" went to the Congress. It outlined a diverse attack on the problem, to be fought on three specific fronts:

> The first is the enrollment of workers now by the Federal Government for such public employment as can be quickly started and will not interfere with the demand for, or the proper standards of, normal employment.
> The second is grants to the states for relief work.
> The third extends to a broad, public works, labor-creating program.

The President asked for quick action on the first of these measures. He proposed, he said, to create a civilian conservation corps to be used in simple work, primarily confining itself to forestry, erosion, flood control, and related projects. Such works would be controlled by the existing machinery of the Departments of Labor, Agriculture, War, and the Interior, and would be financed initially, not by new funds, but by "the use of unobligated funds, now appropriated for public works." Provided that the measure became law within two weeks, Roosevelt estimated that 250,000 men could be given temporary employment by early summer. He concluded his message by pointing out the

26. Moley, p. 174.

27. Samuel I. Rosenman, ed., *The Public Papers and Addresses of Franklin Roosevelt* (New York, 1938-1950), II, 69-71.

28. A memorandum from the chief forester, Major Stuart, forwarded by the secretary of agriculture, Henry Wallace, to the President on March 20, 1933, foreshadowed much of the eventual organization of the CCC, including enrolment and conditioning by the Army, a director, and an advisory council composed of one representation for each department involved. Stuart suggested Frederick A. Delano as a possible director for the work. See C.R.M., No. 780(a), Organization.

benefits of such work to the national domain and to the moral and spiritual welfare of those employed in it: "We can take a vast army of these unemployed out into healthful surroundings. We can eliminate, to some extent at least, the threat that enforced idleness brings to spiritual and moral stability. It is not a panacea for all the unemployment but it is an essential step in this emergency."[29] Following the message, identical bills for "The Relief of Unemployment Through the Performance of Useful Public Work and for other Purposes" were introduced into the Senate and House.[30] Both were committed without debate, the Senate bill to the Committee on Education and Labor, the House bill to the Committee on Labor.

The main provisions of the original measure are important in view of subsequent criticisms and modification. The bill gave the President authority to enlist a civilian conservation corps from among the unemployed to be enrolled for a year, with no discharges "to be permitted except under such rules and regulations as the President may direct." Remuneration was to be not more than $30 monthly, and if an enrollee had dependents he was to be compelled to make a monthly allotment to them. No age limit on enrolment was set, nor was there any provision against enrolling married men.[31]

Reaction to the measure in the nation's press, preoccupied by the struggle over the Administration's contentious farm legisla-

29. For the message, see Rosenman, ed., *Papers*, II, 80-81.

30. *C.R.*, 73rd Cong., 1st Sess., Vol. 77, Pt. 1, pp. 650-651, 701. The Senate measure (S. 598) was introduced by Sen. Joseph T. Robinson (Ark.), the House measure (H.R. 3905) by Rep. Joseph W. Byrns (Tenn.). Charles Price Harper, in *The Administration of the Civilian Conservation Corps* (Clarksburg, W. Va., 1939), p. 9, says that the "original bill, introduced in Congress March 13, by Senator Costigan, evolved much criticism," and he cites *C.R.*, 73rd Cong., 1st Sess., Vol. 77, Pt. 1, p. 247, as his source. Here Harper is clearly in error. No such bill was introduced that day; indeed, at that early date very little had been made final about the CCC. Sen. Costigan did introduce S. 325, "To Provide Emergency Financing Facilities for Unemployed Workers, to Reduce Their Distress, to Increase Their Purchasing Power, and Employment, and for Other Purposes." This bill had nothing to do with the CCC and was referred to the Committee on Manufactures without debate.

31. For the original bill, see *Unemployment Relief: Joint Hearings Before the Committee on Education and Labor, United States Senate, and the Committee on Labor, House of Representatives, 73rd Congress, First Session, on* S. 598, March 23 and 24, 1933 (Washington, 1933), p. 1. Hereinafter cited as *Unemployment Relief, Joint Hearings*, 1933.

tion and by the signal events in Germany where Adolf Hitler was beginning his persecution of the Jews, was muted and mild. Only the New York *Times* of the major newspapers commented editorially on the bill. The paper thought there could be no doubt about the enthusiasm and sincerity of the President in urging the scheme, but it was less certain that Congress shared his conviction as to its practicality.[32]

It was among the ranks of organized labor that the proposal provoked the strongest reaction. As soon as the content of the bill was known, William Green, the cautious, usually circumspect president of the American Federation of Labor, issued a blistering protest against many of its provisions. He was particularly opposed to the Army having any part at all in the scheme. Such a connection, he argued, would lead to the "regimentation of labor" under military control and to Army wage rates. The bill, he thundered, had awakened "grave apprehension in the hearts and minds of labor." A. F. Whitney, president of the Brotherhood of Trainmen, was similarly condemnatory. Passage of the measure, he complained, "would place Government's endorsement upon poverty at a bare subsistence level."[33]

The Socialist party, with Norman Thomas its spokesman, had previously declared its opposition to the proposal, arguing that the camp plan could have no lasting effect on the unemployment problem and that far wider measures were required. When the specifics of the bill became known, the Socialists supported organized labor in its opposition to the wages and recruitment provisions. Thomas warned that "such work-camps fit into the psychology of a Fascist, not a Socialist, state."[34]

The impact of labor's criticism was not lost on the members of the House and Senate committees, who were to begin joint hearings on the bill on March 23. Several members, particularly the chairman of the House Committee on Labor, the liberal William P. Connery, Democrat of Massachusetts, shared labor's apprehensions. In order to calm these fears, the President called the committee members to the White House on the evening of

32. New York *Times*, March 22, 1933.
33. *Ibid.*, March 22 and 24, 1933.
34. *Ibid.*, March 15 and 24, 1933; *Literary Digest*, CXV (April 15, 1933), 6.

March 22. There he explained the intent of his measure, described it in more detail, and denied the validity of labor's objections. His persuasive argument won over most of those present, though Connery remained unshaken in his opposition, particularly to the $30 monthly wage rate.[35] The President's intervention made possible the beginning of the joint Senate and House hearings the next day in an atmosphere of co-operation. The presiding officer was Senator David I. Walsh, Democrat of Massachusetts, chairman of the Senate Committee on Education and Labor, who set the tone immediately by urging that the matter be expedited as much as possible in accordance with Roosevelt's wishes.[36]

Major Stuart, the chief forester, was called early and examined at length on the need for forestation work. When questioned on how the Forest Service proposed to operate the camps, Stuart described to the committee the way the Forest Service was helping to run the California subsistence camps; he expected the new scheme to follow a similar pattern, he said. His statement was, for the most part, non-contentious, though he did make a successful plea to have the scope of the proposal broadened to include work in state and private as well as national forests. If this were not done, he argued, there would have to be a mass movement of men from states east of the Mississippi River, where about 70 per cent of the unemployment was located, to states west of the Rocky Mountain region, where 95 per cent of the public domain lay. He wanted co-operative agreements made with the states to allow work in state forests and parks, explaining that the Forest Service had made many such agreements in the past.[37]

The most trenchant querying of Stuart's testimony was not on the need for conservation, but on the propriety of paying men only $1 for a day's labor. Connery and Representative Richard J. Walsh, a California Republican, contending that the regular wage paid to forestry workers was $3 a day, inquired how conflict could be avoided, especially if the new $30-a-month men were

35. New York *Times*, March 23, 1933; see also *Time*, XXI (April 2, 1933), 11.
36. *Unemployment Relief, Joint Hearings*, 1933, p. 3.
37. *Ibid.*, pp. 9-14.

put to work beside permanent foresters receiving the higher wage rates. Stuart explained that he considered the President's bill to be a relief measure, and that comparison with regular wage schedules was beside the point. Furthermore, he believed that regular Forest Service employees could be used as supervisors, and thus there would be a clear distinction of function between the "$1 and $3" men.[38]

It had become obvious, however, that Connery was still far from satisfied about the effect of the $30-a-month rate on the general wage level, and thus the testimony of the next witness, the secretary of labor, Miss Frances Perkins, assumed added importance. In a succinct statement, Miss Perkins emphasized that the Administration regarded the bill as a relief measure and that it was expected the bulk of the workers would come from the ranks of the young, unmarried men "who had been left out of calculation by most relief agencies." The Corps, therefore, was definitely not to be viewed "in the sense of providing real wage-producing employment." Questioned by Connery, she denied that the wage rate could be compared with that paid to "sweat-shop work," if only because in the camps the men would be provided with food, housing, and work clothes as well. Miss Perkins vigorously opposed his contention that private industry would adopt the $1-a-day wage scale as a standard throughout the country if the bill were passed. Stressing the voluntary nature of enrolment, she claimed that there was nothing in the bill to suggest that labor would be regimented in any way.[39]

The Secretary's lucid testimony in support of the bill meant that the first day's hearings ended on a note favorable to the Administration. It was likely that the bill would be accepted without drastic modification. That feeling was heightened when on the same day the secretary of war, George Dern, held a press conference. He discussed the limited role of the Army in the recruiting program and pointed out that the Department of Agriculture would actually administer the camps.[40] The charge of "militarization of labor" seemed to be untenable.

38. *Ibid.*, p. 19.
39. *Ibid.*, pp. 22-27.
40. New York *Times*, March 24, 1933. The role of the Army was to increase greatly in the following weeks.

When the hearings continued on March 24, the director of the Bureau of the Budget, Lewis W. Douglas, explained that the financing of the Corps through the use of unobligated funds would not mean the sacrificing of alternative public works projects,[41] while the Army's chief of staff, General Douglas MacArthur, was definite that he contemplated "no military training whatsoever."[42] Moreover, MacArthur, amplifying Dern's statement, insisted that individual selection would be in the hands of the Department of Labor. The Army's role would be confined to collecting the selected men, clothing them, giving them a physical examination, conditioning them for about two weeks, and then transporting them to the various camps, where the Department of Agriculture would take them over.

The next witness, President William Green of the American Federation of Labor, changed the whole temper of the hearing.[43] After paying tribute to Roosevelt and "the sincere and humane considerations which have inspired all those who have sponsored this measure," he proceeded to attack it bitterly on three counts: that its provisions admitted the principle of regimentation of labor, that the proposed wage rate would inevitably have a depressing effect on general wage standards, and, less important, that the use of unobligated funds could deprive some free laborers of their livelihood. Green contended that the regimentation of labor was implicit in the use of the Army, in the "involuntary allotment" provision, and in the strictures against discharge until after a year's service had been completed. To him, the measure indeed "smacked of fascism, of Hitlerism, of a form of Sovietism . . . ," an ideological potpourri very much to be deplored.[44] On the wage rate, Green was similarly scathing, claiming that:

> As soon as this bill is passed by the Congress of the United States, it will go down in history as a Congress that has established a dollar a day wage for the payment of labor on the public domain. . . . The masses will lose sight of the relief feature, but they will remember this Congress deter-

41. *Unemployment Relief, Joint Hearings*, 1933, pp. 34-36.
42. *Ibid.*, p. 41.
43. For Green's testimony, see *ibid.*, pp. 44-61.
44. *Ibid.*, p. 46.

mined that a dollar a day was the pay that should be given to men working in the forests . . . of the richest, most powerful nation under the sun.[45]

In response to questioning, Green suggested that a bill be introduced providing for the payment of standard rates of pay under voluntary conditions of employment. He considered an amendment formulated by Connery, which provided for thirty-day, voluntary enlistments at wage rates of $50 a month for single men, and $80 for married, to be "a great improvement of the proposed measure." Neither Green nor Connery would accept the principle that a relief measure could not be considered in the context of providing employment at regular rates. At the end of his testimony Green made sure that the whole country, and not just the committee members, knew what he thought of the bill. Dexterously questioned by Connery on a coast-to-coast radio network, he left no doubt as to how bitter was the AF of L's opposition to the proposed agency.[46]

Green's views were reinforced by M. J. McDonough of the Building Trade Department of the AF of L, and Herbert Benjamin, representing the national committee of the Unemployed Council of the United States, a Communist-controlled organization. Benjamin was also most concerned that sending the head of a family to camp would cause "the violation and destruction of the families of American workers."[47]

With Benjamin the hearings ended, apart from the brief consideration of a letter from an acerbic-sounding gentlemen who opposed "this plan for putting gangs of helots to work in the national forests" because of the "inevitable ruination" of these areas.[48] Green's testimony had shattered the optimistic note of the earlier discussions. By opposing the bill so bitterly, the AF of L had probably insured a long and contentious debate should the measure be reintroduced into Congress in its present form. Though Green's objections were ridiculed by newspapers of all

45. *Ibid.*, p. 48.
46. *Ibid.*, pp. 53, 61.
47. Schlesinger, II, 295; see also *Unemployment Relief, Joint Hearings*, 1933, p. 72.
48. *Ibid.*, pp. 72-73.

political complexions, his point was well taken.[49] If the President was to get his conservation corps quickly, the need for compromise was apparent. It was up to the committee members to suggest what could be done. When an amended S. 598 was reintroduced into the Senate on March 27, 1933, it was obvious that the House and Senate committees had wrought well. Senator Walsh, in comparing the substitute with the original bill, explained how the changes had been made:

> After the committee heard these objections [of the AF of L], the committee met in executive session and reached an agreement that there were two features of this bill to which no-one objected, namely the opportunity to engage in forestation work as a means of relieving unemployment, and secondly, the use of unobligated funds.
>
> When the committee reached the agreement that these two provisions of the bill were non-controversial we proceded to redraft the original bill, and have submitted to the Senate an amendment in the nature of a substitute which does practically nothing more than authorize the President to go into the public domain, carry on forestation, and employ citizens from among the unemployed.[50]

Walsh was not exaggerating. Gone were the restrictive provisions concerning enrolment and discharges; nor was the highly controversial $30 monthly wage rate mentioned. The President was simply authorized "under such rules and regulations as he may prescribe, and by utilizing such existing departments or agencies as he may designate,"[51] to run the CCC relatively unhampered by statutory fetters. Prompted by Stuart's suggestion, provision was made for work on state forests and parks, and, in some instances, on private lands. The committees, convinced of the need for haste, had provided a bill aimed at keeping debate to a minimum.

The bill's passage through the Senate was further facilitated by the political acumen of Senator Walsh, who guided the measure through two days of debate with expert skill. He constantly stressed the need for quick, positive action, dissuading senators

49. See Chicago *Tribune*, March 27, 1933; New York *Herald Tribune*, March 23, 1933; St. Louis *Post-Dispatch*, March 25, 1933.
50. *C.R.* 73rd Cong., 1st Sess., Vol. 77, Pt. 1, p. 862.
51. Nixon, I, 146-147.

from adding amendments because of the delays involved and the limitation of presidential authority which could occur, and calming fears and apprehensions about some of the bill's implications.[52] Walsh emphasized the emergency nature of the legislation and the consequent need to make certain allowances for its provisions. The "whole bill is permissive" he said at one point:

> and that is what all this emergency legislation is. Each bill that we have passed here has given the President permissive authority. It has not been compelling and controlling, as it should be if it were urging a permanent policy. That is why I asked the Senators at the very beginning to keep in mind three things: emergency, relief work, and unemployment.

The only way for Congress to deal with the problem, he believed, was to give the President both the authority and the means to work out the details of administration, and not to attempt to do so itself.[53]

Partly because of Walsh's tight hold on proceedings and partly because of the broad provisions of the measure, what little opposition there was to the bill in the Senate was itself of a general nature. Predictably, it came from a few Republicans who protested, not against specific aspects of the legislation, but against the increasing tendency to concentrate power in the Executive, which they profoundly deplored. In their view, the establishment of the Civilian Conservation Corps under the conditions outlined in the bill would be an unjustifiable acceleration of this trend.

The leader of this small group was Senator L. J. Dickinson, an Iowa conservative. He bitterly opposed the granting of further authority to the President, grimly warning that "we will see the time when we will rue the day when we put so much power into one man's hands."[54] Dickinson was ably supported by Republican Senators Arthur Robinson, of Indiana, and Henry D. Hatfield, of West Virginia. Referring to Green's earlier state-

52. *C.R.*, 73rd Cong., 1st Sess., Vol. 77, Pt. 1, p. 864. The only amendment of any importance which was added in the Senate extended the President's authority under the act from one to two years; see *ibid.*, p. 929.

53. *Ibid.*, p. 863.

54. *Ibid.*, p. 934.

ments, they both pointed out, quite reasonably, that the amended measure gave the President even more power over wage rates and employment conditions than had the original bill. Thus, the belief that the new measure satisfied, in large part, labor's demands seemed clearly erroneous.[55]

The majority who favored the amended bill, however, was overwhelming. Influential Republicans praised it. Senator William E. Borah of Idaho, for example, asserted that the bill was quite constitutional and, indeed, represented "the mildest form of delegation of power" that he had seen since the session began. It was passed by voice vote on March 28 after the adoption of a few minor amendments of a permissive or clarifying nature and sent to the House.[56]

Opposition to the measure in the House was much more vigorous and sustained than in the Senate, and criticism ranged over a far broader spectrum. Groups in both parties opposed the bill for widely divergent reasons. The amended bill was reintroduced on March 27, together with the majority and minority reports of the joint hearings. Connery, as chairman of the House Labor Committee, immediately announced that though the committee had approved the amended measure, he personally intended to fight it and would endeavor to have adopted an amendment laying down wage rates of $50 monthly for unmarried enrollees and $80 monthly for married enrollees. He took this stand, even though a letter from Green had made it clear that the AF of L had reversed itself and had indorsed, albeit reluctantly, the amended bill.[57]

On March 29 the House resolved itself into the Committee of the Whole to consider the bill as amended and passed by the Senate on the previous day. Connery, in offering his amendment, repeated most of the arguments which Green had developed at the hearings. He insisted that the bill, if passed, "would tag labor at $1 a day throughout the entire U.S.," and that the President could pay workers fifty cents a day "if he so wished." Then he announced, rather dramatically, that Green had once more shifted his position and again stood opposed to the measure, a

55. *Ibid.*, p. 936.
56. *Ibid.*, pp. 929-936.
57. *Ibid.*, pp. 876-878.

switch which probably did little for Connery's case as it made Green seem more of an opportunist than a man of abiding principles.[58] Connery received strong support from Representatives Marion A. Zioncheck, Democrat of Washington, and Glenn Griswold, Democrat of Indiana, both of whom claimed to speak as friends of labor.[59]

From the opposite wing of the political spectrum came a vigorous attack by a group of House Republicans, aided by two Southern Democrats. Like their Senatorial counterparts, they viewed with grave alarm the granting of such wide powers to the President. Representative Caroll L. Beedy of Maine epitomized their thinking when he said that the measure led "the masses to believe that it is the Government's duty to put them on the pay roll. This idea, carried to its extreme, approximates the doctrine of Communism." He talked of the "exercise of autocratic power" by the President and "wanted nothing to do with any such gigantic legislative mistake." Beedy was strongly supported by the Republican minority leader, Bertrand H. Snell of New York, by Representative John Taber, Republican of New York, and by Representatives Lister Hill of Alabama, and John J. McSwain of South Carolina, both Democrats, all of whom protested the further concentration of power in Presidential hands.[60]

Vociferous as it was, the opposition from both political wings had little substance to it. Some Republicans vigorously favored the bill, others agreed with Representative Thomas G. Cochran of Missouri, who, in a statement indicative of a large segment of Republican thought at this time, said: "I disliked the economy bill, I disliked the farm bill. I do not like to see us go along on a project such as this, but I do like the way the President of the U.S. is trying to meet this emergency, and I have gone along with him. I propose to continue to go along with him."[61] Not entirely happy with Roosevelt's remedies for the economy's ailments, yet having none of their own to offer, many Republicans voted repeatedly with the Democrats in the critical first months of the New Deal. Indeed, the vast body of the House was disposed to

58. *Ibid.*, pp. 957-959.
59. *Ibid.*, pp. 972, 974-975.
60. *Ibid.*, pp. 963-967.
61. *Ibid.*, p. 991. Other Republicans who supported the bill included Reps. George W. Blanchard (Wis.), p. 972, and Clyde Kelly (Pa.), p. 975.

support the bill substantially as it stood, and the call of Representative Robert Ramspeck, Democrat of Georgia, to "stand by our leader in the White House and vote down amendments" was well heeded. Because of Connery's opposition, Ramspeck guided the bill through the House. Like Senator Walsh, he emphasized the emergency nature of the legislation and its relief function, arguing that "the real purpose of the bill is relief and not wages."[62]

Three amendments only were adopted, the most important being that proposed by the sole Negro Congressman, Representative Oscar De Priest, Republican of Illinois, "that no discrimination shall be made on account of race, color, or creed . . . under the provisions of this Act."[63] Added almost as an afterthought, the clause was to have far-reaching consequences.

The Connery Amendment to introduce a $50 monthly wage rate failed by 290 votes to 90, as did a last-ditch struggle by Republicans Taber and Beedy to prolong proceedings on a point of order.[64] The Committee of the Whole reported back to the House, the three amendments were passed, and a further attempt by the indefatigable Connery to recommit the bill with his amendment inserted failed. It was passed by a voice vote. The next day the Senate accepted the House amendments, and the President signed the measure on March 31.[65]

The opposition to the measure in Congress may have had some significance in that the bill represented the Administration's first entry into the field of relief work and social legislation. No doubt certain Republicans who were able to swallow their principles as the President attempted to solve the financial and business problems of the nation through strong Executive action were unable to stomach the entry of the federal government into the field of human welfare: the result was their opposition to the CCC. The Chicago *Tribune*, in commenting on the passage of the "reforestation bill," spoke of the "storm" in the House, and of the "intensive" Republican opposition to the measure. The paper implied that Roosevelt's honeymoon with Congress was

62. *Ibid.*, pp. 980-981.
63. *Ibid.*, p. 983.
64. *Ibid.*, pp. 983-990.
65. *Ibid.*, pp. 1012-1013; see also Harper, p. 19.

ending and that the struggle heralded the return of vigorous Republican opposition to his proposals.[66] But this was wishful thinking; the bill was never in danger of defeat, and the Republican opposition, though vocal, was numerically weak. The CCC began its existence on a broad, bipartisan base of support, something it never really lost.

The leading newspapers supported the measure as a gesture toward relief of unemployment, without attaching too much significance to its passage. The New York *Times* outlined the bill's "double purpose," namely, the "employment of hundreds of thousands, and the regaining of our lost forest lands." The New York *Herald Tribune* doubted if "it would ever justify the expenditure contemplated," but thought that "as a means of reducing as rapidly as possible the army of unattached jobless now roaming the country" the CCC promised well. Other newspapers and periodicals echoed these views.[67]

In a sense the bill creating the Civilian Conservation Corps slipped unobtrusively through the legislative process at a time when the public eye was occupied with bigger events at home and abroad. Its passage, and the events leading up to it, prompted little newspaper correspondence, and not even Green's criticism caused any real public stir. The CCC, moreover, was only the vanguard of a more comprehensive relief proposal. Work in the forest, away from their homes and families, was clearly out of the question for the majority of unemployed Americans. They had to wait for the further unfolding of Roosevelt's relief plans. Administration officials questioned at the hearings had indicated that young, physically fit, unmarried men were thought to be those most likely to enter the Corps, and thus the legislation was probably of immediate interest to them alone.

The new President had received his Civilian Conservation Corps. Though the final shape of the legislation was as much due to congressional circumstance as to presidential desire, and though undoubtedly he was influenced by the prior experience of the Forest Service with work camps and by the advice of men

66. Chicago *Tribune*, March 30, 1933.

67. New York *Times*, March 31, 1933; New York *Herald Tribune*, April 1, 1933; St. Louis *Post-Dispatch*, March 31, 1933; *New Republic*, LXXIX (April 5, 1933), 202; *Literary Digest*, CXV (April 15, 1933), 6.

like Pinchot, much of the responsibility for the bill must lie with Franklin Roosevelt. The idea was in large part his, a product of his long adherence to that great liberal tenet, conservation of the land, and it was given urgency by the unemployment crisis. For him, the signing of the bill must indeed have meant real satisfaction.

The legislation, moreover, had given Roosevelt wider powers than he had sought originally. These now had to be used, with all due speed, to transform the Civilian Conservation Corps from a statutory provision into a working operation.

2. *The CCC Is Mobilized*

If the new Emergency Conservation Work scheme was to be successfully organized, speed, above all, was needed.[1] The accomplishment of the President's plan to have 250,000 men at work in the forests by early summer would require feats of organization, construction, and mobilization never before attempted in the United States during peacetime. As the agency would have to be operating almost immediately, the co-operating departments had begun their planning in anticipation of the legislation's passage. By March 24, though the CCC Bill itself was still in committee, the General Staff had drafted complete regulations governing the Army's role in the establishment and maintenance of the Corps. The regulations included the division of the country into nine Corps areas for administrative purposes and provided cost estimates for such items as clothing, shelter, supervision, welfare, and transportation. Thus, the Army was ready to begin its task as soon as the legislation was passed.[2]

Nor had the Department of Agriculture been idle. Using its recently completed survey of the American forest situation, the Forest Service had quickly drawn up a work schedule, and Major Stuart had also prepared a draft executive order embodying Forest Service suggestions on the relationship between the co-operating agencies; this was widely circulated before the passage of the CCC Act.[3] The secretary of agriculture, too, had called a conference of state authorities for April 6 to discuss the extension of the conservation program to state-owned forest lands.[4]

Similarly, the Departments of Labor and the Interior were ready for immediate action. Officials in the Department of Labor,

1. The official name for the agency created by the act of March 31 was Emergency Conservation Work (ECW). However, the name Civilian Conservation Corps, as used by the President in his message to Congress on March 21, quickly caught on and supplanted the official title. There was no statutory CCC until June 28, 1937, when it was created by act of Congress.

2. Col. Duncan K. Major to Roosevelt, June 30, 1933, Roosevelt Papers, O.F. 268, Box 2. This famous report, which will be referred to often in this chapter, traces the role of the Army in the mobilization of the CCC. It was released to the press on July 3 in modified form.

3. *Unemployment Relief, Joint Hearings,* 1933, p. 4. C.R.M., No. 780, Organization.

4. Wallace to State Governors, March 31, 1933, *ibid.*

charged with the selection of the youths, realized that there was no time to build a nationwide organization of their own. They decided, therefore, to use agencies already in existence. Casting her net wide for a chief of CCC selection, Secretary Perkins remembered W. Frank Persons, a Red Cross adviser and administrator with whom she had worked during the war. She contacted him, convinced him that he should take the job, reconstituted the United States Employment Service with Persons as head, and turned the whole business of CCC selection over to him. It was a happy choice. The able, articulate Persons held the position throughout the Corps' existence and proved a liberal counterweight to Army opinion during the formation of policy. As far as the immediate problems of selection were concerned, Persons resolved to rely on local relief agencies, which were already acquainted with the young men qualified by need to be CCC enrollees; a state director of selection would co-ordinate the agencies' activities.[5] Selection was to be made on a state quota basis in proportion to population. Thus, though Persons was told only on April 3 to start selecting men, he had a going organization ready to meet the challenge by April 6.

Even before the legislation was passed, the Administration began to search for a man to administer the Civilian Conservation Corps. In this search, their choice was somewhat circumscribed; organized labor had been most vociferous in its criticism of the scheme, so it was decided that the director of the new organization should be someone who could mollify labor's protests.[6]

The man eventually appointed was Robert Fechner, a widely respected labor leader. Born in Chattanooga, Tennessee, in 1876 and educated in the public schools of Macon and Griffith, Georgia, he had quit school at sixteen to sell candy and newspapers on Georgia trains. After spending a year at this occupation, he became a machinist's apprentice in the Augusta shops of the old Georgia Central Railroad. He joined the union then,

5. Perkins, pp. 178-179. *Summary Report of the Director of Emergency Conservation Work* (Washington, 1933-1943), 1935, pp. 11-12 (hereinafter cited as *Report of the Director*).

6. Schlesinger, II, 338; Lela Stiles, *The Man Behind Roosevelt* (Cleveland, 1954), p. 267.

but after serving his time he "took to the road" as an itinerant machinist, working principally in Central and South America. Fechner returned to Georgia in the late 1890's and settled in Savannah. He threw himself into union activities, and in 1901 helped lead an unsuccessful strike for a nine-hour day. In 1914 he was elected to the General Executive Board of the International Association of Machinists and became a vice president of the AF of L, positions he still held in 1933.

Fechner was no radical. A "down-the-line" Gompers man in his approach to labor questions, he attained a degree of respectability sufficient to bring him appointments as lecturer in labor relations at Harvard, Brown, and Dartmouth. During World War I, Fechner came to Washington as a special adviser on labor policy, and it was in this capacity that he first met Franklin D. Roosevelt. As assistant secretary of the Navy, Roosevelt had many an opportunity to mark the lean, rawboned machinist's skill and patience as a negotiator. Fechner was particularly instrumental in settling the 1917 strike of the Boston and Maine Railroad. The two men subsequently maintained a tenuous relationship, and Fechner, an active Democrat, worked hard for Roosevelt in 1932, eventually swinging the Machinists Union to him. When Roosevelt was looking for a labor leader to head the CCC, therefore, Fechner's name came readily to mind.

As a New Dealer, Fechner was, as he once wryly observed, "a potato bug amongst dragonflies." Indeed, he was fond of proclaiming that his clerks were all better educated than he. A simple, homely man, who still wore in 1933 the high-topped hooked shoes fashionable around the turn of the century, his idea of a good time was to see a movie and his idea of mental stimulation was to shed his boots and read a magazine, lying on a bed in the modestly priced hotel room he always occupied while in Washington. He had very little in common with the bulk of Roosevelt's advisers and departmental heads.

By and large, Fechner ran the CCC camps well. Hardworking, honest, and affable, he was a favorite both with his office staff and the enrollees. But as the CCC developed, certain limitations in his ability were to become apparent: he lacked sufficient vision ever to see the Corps as possibly having wider functions than the simple provision of relief and performance of useful work, and he was often too ready to defer to Army advice. Moreover, the particular virtues of a conciliator—patience and caution—were not always the qualities required in the director of a large and complex organization, a post which often called for swift decisions and immediate action. Given organized labor's declared opposition to the Corps, however, his selection in 1933 was a wise move.[7]

Fechner chose another machinist to be his assistant director. He was James J. McEntee, a bluff, quick-tempered Irishman from Jersey City. Born in 1884, McEntee served his apprenticeship at the Blair Tool Works in New York. He first met Fechner in 1911 when he became a full-time officer of the International Association of Machinists. In 1917 McEntee was appointed by President Wilson to the New York Arbitration Board and was active in adjusting disputes in munitions plants. In the 1920's he helped to settle several newspaper strikes and was also associated with railway contract negotiations. Fechner and he had been close friends for more than twenty years, and it was at the director's personal request that Roosevelt asked McEntee to come to Washington. These two men ran the Corps until its abolishment.[8]

Co-ordinating both men and organization in the first few days of the CCC's life was, of course, the duty of President Roosevelt. At a White House conference on April 3 which decided finally the position of the co-operating agencies, he personally drew up a chart stating in graphic form the roles of each. Lines drawn from the name Fechner (he misspelled it Fechter)[9] led to boxes

7. New York *Times*, Jan. 1, 1940; Albert B. Rollins, *Roosevelt and Howe* (New York, 1962), p. 403; *Time*, XXVIII (Feb. 6, 1939), 12; see also Fechner to Howe, April 25, 1932, Roosevelt Papers, Private Personal File (P.P.F.) 6386.

8. New York *Times*, Feb. 16, 1940.

9. This misspelling has, on occasion, caused speculation as to whether Roosevelt did know Fechner before his appointment. Herbert Maier, in a letter to Daniel J. Tobin on Jan. 29, 1958, found in Roosevelt papers, O.F. 268, Box 11, claimed that F.D.R. drew the chart without having selected a director. He then asked for the name of a good labor man, and someone suggested Fechner. Not knowing the man, Roosevelt misspelled his name in writing it down. This is unconvincing, as ample evidence exists to indicate that Fechner was known both to Roosevelt and to Howe during the war. Moreover, Horace Albright, director of the National Parks Service, who was present at this meeting on April 3, reported to the secretary of

labeled Labor, Army, Agriculture, and Interior. Within each box, the President outlined the task of that particular department. He also clarified his own function when he wrote underneath the chart: "I want *personally* to check on the location and scope of the camps, assign work to be done, etc."[10] His genuine interest in the Corps cannot be doubted; yet, by insisting that he approve personally every single camp site, the President greatly limited Fechner's authority and geared the pace of the work to his own availability. Busy with a host of other projects, his failure to give prompt attention to camp approvals seriously retarded the CCC's early progress.

Specific functions were assigned at this April 3 meeting: the Department of Labor was directed to select the men for enrolment; the War Department was to enrol the men, feed, clothe, house, and condition them, and transport them to the camps; the Departments of Agriculture and Interior, through their various bureaus, were to select work projects, to supervise the work, and to administer the camps.[11] Apart from the almost immediate extension of the Army's role, these divisions remained relatively stable until the CCC came to an end in 1942.

Several other questions were also decided on April 3. An Advisory Council, consisting of one member from each of the co-operating departments, was authorized to assist the director.[12] Basic policy decisions governing selection were also made. It was decided to limit initial enrolment in the CCC to single men aged eighteen to twenty-five—primarily, but not exclusively, to those whose families were on the public relief rolls, and who were willing to allot $22 to $25 out of their monthly $30 wage check to their dependents. Thus, assumptions about the breadth of the CCC's appeal were shown to be correct. It was to be almost solely concerned with a specific sector of the unemployed, the

---

the interior the same day that Fechner's selection had been officially announced. See Albright to Ickes, April 3, 1933, Records of the Office of the Secretary of the Interior, in National Archives (hereinafter cited as Secretary of Interior, Records).

10. For a photostat of the chart, see Roosevelt Papers, O.F. 268, Box 1. It is reproduced in Nixon, I, 150.

11. *Report of the Director*, 1933, pp. 1-2.

12. C.R.M., Appendix Vol. 1, Document 23. Apart from one meeting on April 13, minutes of Advisory Council meetings were not kept until July, 1933.

young. The vast majority of Americans were placed, by deliberate action, outside its purview. Other solutions would have to be found for their problems. These regulations were forwarded to Corps area commanders and selection agents and announced in the press. Persons was directed to begin selection on April 6. He did so, and the first enrollees were accepted by the Army the next day. The first camp was established at Luray, Virginia, on April 17 and named, appropriately, Camp Roosevelt.[13]

The decisions taken at the important meeting of April 3 were embodied in *Executive Order No. 6101*, issued by the President on April 5, 1933. With it, the Civilian Conservation Corps began its official existence. The order confirmed Fechner's appointment as director of emergency conservation work, at an annual salary of $12,000, and provided that "The Secretary of War, the Secretary of Agriculture, the Secretary of the Interior and the Secretary of Labor, each shall appoint a representative, and said representatives shall constitute an Advisory Council to the Director of Emergency Conservation Work." Funds were provided for the proper performance of the work, and authority was given for the furnishing of supplies and equipment.[14] Just one week after the passage of the act which gave it statutory existence, the Civilian Conservation Corps was now a working agency. It remained to be seen if its makeshift organization was adequate to cope with the mighty tasks of selection and mobilization which lay ahead.

Scarcely had enrolment begun when it became obvious that utter confusion would result unless the Army was given a larger share of responsibility. It had been decided that the strength of each CCC company would be two hundred men, to be organized and transported to camp by the Army.[15] Thus, the Departments

13. *Report of the Director*, 1933, p. 2; 1935, p. 22; see also New York *Times*, April 6 and 7, 1933. One of Fechner's first official acts as director was to announce the selection regulations. They, of course, were soon published by the Department of Labor in an *Official Handbook for Agencies Selecting Men for Emergency Conservation Work* (Washington, 1933). See also Harper, p. 65.

14. For a copy of Exec. Order 6101, see *Report of the Director*, 1933, Appendix B.

15. *War Department Regulations, Relief of Unemployment* (Washington, 1933), p. 12. *Report of the Secretary of War to the President*, 1933 (Washington, 1933), p. 4.

of Agriculture and the Interior had to build, equip, staff, and operate about 1,300 camps by July 1 if the President's plan was to be a success. The chief forester, Stuart, had been quite confident that the Forest Service alone could perform this feat. As Colonel Duncan Major, War Department representative on the Advisory Council, put it: "Major Stuart was very bombastic about his ability to do this, stating on several occasions that he did not need the Army. The fact was that he had no conception of the task involved."[16] However, once operations were under way, the enormity of the job soon dawned on Stuart. He quickly realized that neither the Department of Agriculture nor the Department of the Interior possessed the men, equipment, or experience to administer the camps. In a letter to Colonel Louis Howe, President Roosevelt's secretary and close friend, Stuart urgently insisted that a division of authority between the Army and the technical agencies was the only practical arrangement by which the camps could be run. He was now convinced that the Army alone had the resources to build and operate the camps, and transport, feed, and discipline the men. The technical agencies would be responsible only for the work project and for the men during working hours.[17]

The President, at Howe's urging, saw the wisdom of Stuart's suggestion and therefore made sweeping changes of the original plan. The Army's former role had ended with the transportation of the recruits to camp. It was now greatly extended "to assume under the general supervision of the Director, complete and permanent control of the CCC project."[18] The authority of the project superintendent, the technical service representative, was limited to working hours only. This division of control gave rise, perhaps inevitably, to interdepartmental disputes and rivalries, but given the exigencies of the time, it was the best practical solution. The Army accepted its expanded assignment without

16. Col. Major to Howe, May 8, 1933, Louis McHendry Howe Papers, Box 60, in Franklin D. Roosevelt Library, Hyde Park, N.Y.

17. Stuart to Howe, April 8, 1933, Roosevelt Papers, O.F. 268, Box 1. "Technical Agencies" was a term used repeatedly by CCC officials to differentiate between the Departments of the Interior and of Agriculture, and the Departments of War and of Labor. I have used the term throughout this work, mainly for reasons of brevity.

18. *Report of the Secretary of War*, 1933, p. 4.

great enthusiasm, yet resigned itself to the fact that it was the only agency capable of accomplishing the task ahead.[19]

Other important and basic policy decisions which were made in the first few weeks of the CCC's existence added to the number of men in the camps. On April 14, 1933, for example, it was decided to extend the provisions of the Emergency Conservation Work Act to 14,400 American Indians.[20] Few ECW decisions were more popular. For some years prior to 1933 there had been a most unusual scarcity of rainfall throughout the Plains region and in the Far West where the majority of Indians lived, and erosion had ruined much of their land. The Indians, moreover, as a class had very little capital other than natural resources, and as these "could not be converted into subsistence supplies in a period of economic distress, the native American faced an almost hopeless situation in mid-1933."[21]

The Civilian Conservation Corps program on the reservations attempted to carry out various types of physical improvement and to develop natural resources. Because of the special nature of the Indian work, the rules governing administration were greatly modified when enrolment began on June 23. Practical action was carried on outside the bounds of the CCC organization. The Office of Indian Affairs in the Department of the Interior selected the men and administered the work. The Indians were not subject to the formal regulations of the CCC; few camps were established, because most of the enrollees were married and they were allowed to work from their homes.[22] Furthermore, a unique feature of the Indian program was the participation of the tribal council in its administration. Indians received wide latitude in the selection of work projects and supervisors in an effort to give them experience in the management of their own affairs.[23] Other provisions were similar to the CCC organization proper. The cash allowance of $30 monthly was paid to the Indians, while they also benefited from the education and health schemes.

19. *Ibid.*
20. *Report of the Director*, 1933, p. 3.
21. *Ibid.*, 1935, p. 35.
22. Ickes to Fechner, April 24, 1933, Secretary of Interior, Records.
23. New York *Times*, Aug. 27, 1933; see also Harper, p. 73.

Work on the reservations was one of the most successful aspects of the whole CCC program. It made possible the building up of resources, it provided opportunities for Indian advancement, and it changed Indian attitudes. By July, 1942, 88,349 men participated in the program and were "happy to be able to compete in this work with the white man."[24]

Vital to the initial success of the whole CCC venture was the decision of April 22, 1933, to enroll 24,375 local woodsmen to act as technical assistants to the project supervisors. Usually eight such "local experienced men" (L.E.M.'s as they were known) were assigned to each camp. The reason for this decision to expand the enrolment was twofold. First, the transfer to the nation's forests of 250,000 youths, most of them quite ignorant of "outback life," could have had disastrous consequences without the adequate supervision of men experienced in woodcraft. The Forest Service did not have enough men available for the job; indeed, they were hard-pressed even to find enough qualified men to act as camp project supervisors. Consequently, Stuart wrote to Fechner on April 14, 1933, requesting the hiring of "technicians and other overhead" at Civil Service rates of pay, "in order to meet the President's insistence that all work done under the Conservation work relief program be adequately supervized."[25] He then adumbrated thirty-four types of technician which he believed were needed. Fechner approved his request tentatively on April 17, "subject to change to meet future developments or any existing situation," and subject to Bureau of the Budget acquiescence on the suggested wage scale.[26] Second, this decision enabled the Corps to deal immediately with a particularly urgent local problem. Ever since the passage of the ECW Act on March 31, Stuart had been receiving periodic reports from regional foresters that trouble could be expected from local unemployed woodsmen unless they were incorporated into the scheme of things.[27] These men had lost their jobs for reasons

24. Conrad L. Wirth, *Civilian Conservation Corps Program of the United States Department of the Interior, March 1933 to June 1942* (Chicago, 1944), p. 25; J. B. Nash, director of Indian ECW, to Fechner, June 28, 1933, Secretary of the Interior, Records.

25. Stuart to Fechner, April 14, 1933, C.R.M., No. 780, Organization.

26. Fechner to Stuart, April 17, 1933, *ibid.*

27. Joint memorandum from Regional Foresters to Stuart, April 4, 1933, C.R.M., No. 784, Local Experienced Men.

generally connected with the economic crisis. Some had formerly been employed by private logging interests and, with the reduced demand for timber because of the failing construction industry, they were now unemployable. Others were former state foresters jobless as a result of the general cutback of state employees. Unless they too had a part in the CCC program, they meant to oppose the importation of youths to work in areas the foresters considered their own.

The arguments for employing such men as technicians were summarized in a joint letter to the President from the secretaries of labor, the interior and agriculture, members of the Advisory Council, and Fechner and McEntee. It was stated succinctly that "It is clearly impossible to import into forest regions non-residents even from within the same state, and have peace there unless local unemployed laborers, accustomed to making their living in the woods in that very place are given fair consideration as concerns their own means of livelihood." The signatories believed that if such men were not included in the project it would inevitably cause "antagonism which may result in incendiarism (with great loss of timber by fire) and even in personal tragedies." Accordingly, they recommended that the initial enrolment be increased by 24,375 men, so that such woodsmen could be included. Their request was immediately approved.[28]

There was some objection to the proposed wage scale for these men by the Bureau of the Budget, where the director, Lewis Douglas, stood strong against federal spending. Eventually, however, the representatives of the technical services gained their point: that adequate supervision required adequate remuneration. Selection of the L.E.M.'s proceeded under the Department of Labor until 1935, when the responsibility was delegated to the technical services.[29] This policy avoided the possibility of ugly incidents as the camps were built, incidents which could have done irreparable damage both to the nation's resources and to the image of the CCC. Moreover, experienced supervision on the work project was assured, even down to the "platoon level."

A third special group, veterans of World War I, was soon to

28. Joint letter to Roosevelt, April 22, 1933, *ibid.*
29. *Report of the Director*, 1933, p. 2.

be inducted into the Corps. With an average age of forty in 1933, often impaired in bodily health and mental stability by their war experiences, thousands of former soldiers had endured a long period of privation and hopelessness and were among those hardest hit by the depression. Many, out of despair, had made their way to Washington in the summer of 1932 as members of the "bonus Army" seeking early payment of their wartime service compensation pension, which was not due till 1945. They had been met instead by guns, bayonets, and tear gas.[30] Now, in May 1933, a second "bonus Army" contingent had descended on Washington, hoping that the new President would be more receptive to their petitions.

It was in this context of privation and unrest that General Frank T. Hines, the veterans' administrator, frantically searching for a solution, first saw the CCC as a way in which many of these former soldiers could be aided. Accordingly, he wrote to Roosevelt on May 6, 1933, suggesting that they be selected and put in a special camp.[31] Corps officials were receptive to the idea, and Budget Director Douglas gave it his personal blessing.[32] Thus, *Executive Order No. 6129*, issued on May 11, 1933, authorized the enrolment of 25,000 war veterans into the Corps, with no age or marital limitations imposed.[33] President and Mrs. Roosevelt's treatment of the second "bonus Army" had already won them a favorable reputation among the veterans and prompted the adage, "Hoover sent the Army, Roosevelt sent his wife." Now he offered every marcher the chance of immediate enlistment in the CCC. Though understandably cool to the suggestion at first, most of the men eventually accepted it, and by May 22 all possibility of a crisis was over. Once again the CCC had been used to resolve a troublesome situation.[34]

The veterans were selected on a state quota system by the Veterans Administration and became, in a very real sense, the career men of the CCC. Re-enrolment provisions were always generous, yet during the nine-year period of its existence the

30. Schlesinger, I, 257-265.
31. Hines to Roosevelt, May 6, 1933, Roosevelt Papers, O.F. 268, Box 1.
32. Major to Howe, May 6, 1933, Douglas to Roosevelt, May 8, 1933, *ibid.*
33. *Report of the Director*, 1933, p. 2.
34. Schlesinger, II, 15.

Corps employed more than 225,000 such men. They were housed in separate camps, and performed regular conservation work, modified to suit their age and physical condition. They too benefited from the education and medical programs.[35] To many veterans, the CCC became a rehabilitation center, a place where they could regain health and self-respect. Here they received a second chance, an opportunity to gain the knowledge, skill, or confidence they needed to earn a decent living. For others, it was a permanent home. One such veteran expressed in verse the feeling of hope rekindled, when he wrote in the CCC newspaper:

> . . . while we help grow
> More woods for ages yet to come
> And when the bugle and the drum
> Again calls forth we'll answer, "Here". . .[36]

The CCC was indeed for this man, and for many like him, proof that some people yet remembered their sacrifice in 1917-1918.

The inclusion of these special groups within the Corps framework, while important, was peripheral to the main task of having 250,000 young men in camp on July 1. By early May it had become distressingly obvious that at the current rate of progress, there was very little likelihood of this goal being achieved. On May 10, only 52,000 men had been enrolled and a mere forty-two camps established. Confusion and delay in Washington had resulted in a situation which could well discredit seriously the efficiency of the CCC as a relief organization.[37] It would take a "minor miracle" to have even 100,000 men placed in camp by the July 1 deadline.[38]

The reasons for this major breakdown in mobilization were in large part implicit in the complex organization of the CCC. More specifically, they arose out of differences of opinion and misunderstanding between the co-operating agencies. Most serious were the disputes between the War Department and the Forest Service. These two agencies clashed directly over matters

35. *Report of the Director*, 1942-1943, pp. 61-62.
36. *Happy Days*, June 17, 1933.
37. Major to Fechner, June 30, 1933, Roosevelt Papers, O.F. 268, Box 2.
38. Persons to Secretary of Labor, May 2, 1933, *ibid.*, Box 1.

of fiscal procedure, over methods of camp construction, and in general over their particular areas of responsibility within the CCC organization.[39] An irate Colonel Duncan Major, War Department Advisory Council representative, protested to Howe that he was "constantly haggling with Major Stuart, due to his insistence in letting me know how the Army should perform its mission, even though he himself was unable to do it."[40] While their superiors argued in Washington, men in the field remained idle and camps were unbuilt.

The Forest Service, furthermore, was also embroiled in a dispute with the Bureau of the Budget over the wage schedule for technical service supervisors and local enlisted men. Budget Director Douglas seriously objected both to the number of L.E.M.'s contemplated and their proposed rate of pay.[41] Not until a White House conference of May 9 was the dispute resolved in favor of the technical services, and until then no supervisors could be appointed. Without them, there could be few camps.[42]

Another major source of delay was the limitation placed on Fechner's authority, together with his reluctance to use to the utmost what power he did possess. President Roosevelt virtually insured administrative confusion by insisting that all camp locations and important equipment purchases needed his personal approval. His preoccupation with a myriad of other tasks often meant that important memoranda seeking authorization for new camps or the purchase of equipment lay on his desk for days, as confusion in the Corps areas increased.[43] Moreover, those sites which did pass scrutiny often showed evidence of hasty judgment. Although projects were generously approved in the Rocky Mountain and Western states, few were initially established in the East, where the bulk of the men were enrolled. By

39. Stuart to Fechner, May 4, 1933, C.R.M., No. 782, Hammatt, Source Data. Civilian Conservation Corps: Minutes of Advisory Council, 1933-1942 (hereinafter cited as Advisory Council, Minutes), April 13, 1933.

40. Major to Howe, May 8, 1933, Howe Papers, Box 60.

41. Douglas to Howe, May 8, 1933, *ibid.*

42. File record memorandum of White House Conference, May 9, 1933, C.R.M., No. 780, Organization.

43. Stuart to Wallace, May 19, 1933, Files of the Secretary of Agriculture—Conservation.

May 1 there were 18,700 men out of an enrolment of 35,000 for whom there was no work in their own or nearby states.[44] Obviously, there was need for a greater concentration of authority in the director's office rather than the White House.

Fechner himself was in part to blame for the delays. Unsure in his new job and not yet adjusted to the pace of the undertaking, he insisted on a close personal scrutiny of all contracts for the purchase of equipment, refused to allot funds without detailed estimates and ordered that the provisions of government competitive bidding be rigidly applied in all purchases.[45] His meticulous supervision of contracts and his insistence on repeated conferences before authorizing purchases, admirable in an endeavor of less compelling urgency, threatened to reduce the whole pace of CCC advancement. Reports from the field indicated the demoralizing effect of the delays. Persons warned Fechner that many states, having selected their quotas, had nowhere to send their enrollees, and that there was a real danger of "deep public disapproval of the whole conservation program" because of "disappointed expectations." Letters from camps similarly indicated dissatisfaction with existing conditions.[46]

On the afternoon of May 10, Stuart, Persons, and Horace Albright, director of the National Parks Service, as members of the Advisory Council, met in conference with Fechner. Here they stated that "Emergency Conservation Work had reached a crisis and that nothing short of a definite stand setting up an objective to be attained would be satisfying. . . ."[47] They informed Fechner that they had adopted the President's plan to have 250,000 men in camps by the middle of summer as the basis for their efforts but were sure that "as the project is now going, there seems little probability that any such objective will be at-

44. *Ibid.*; see also Fechner to Roosevelt, April 11, 1933, Roosevelt Papers, O.F. 268, Box 1.

45. Major to Fechner, June 30, 1933, Roosevelt Papers, O.F. 268, Box 2.

46. Persons to Fechner, May 8, 1933, *ibid.*, Box 1; Enrollee Robert A. Taylor to Fechner, April, 1933, Records of the CCC, Correspondence of the Director (hereinafter cited as Director, Correspondence). "[W]e have not got any bath in this camp, and no light. . . . We haf to seat down on the grown to eat."

47. Stuart memorandum for files, C.R.M., No. 782, Hammatt, Source Data.

tained."[48] The need for establishing a definite goal, one agreeable to all concerned, was seen as crucial, "otherwise," as Stuart put it, "there will be continued confusion and misdirected effort."

Fechner reportedly expressed his disappointment at any such prospect, though he must have long suspected its likelihood, and reaffirmed the President's objective. He wanted 250,000 youths, plus 24,375 locally enlisted men, in camp by July, and he turned to the one department capable of resolving the stalemate. On May 10 he contacted Colonel Major, requesting that the War Department present a plan to the Advisory Council on May 12 analyzing the steps required if the President's objective was to be met.[49] At the May 12 meeting Colonel Major announced a bold scheme to end the emergency, a plan which presupposed a radical departure from the existing policy. Specifically, its main provisions called for:

> (*a*) immediate action;
> (*b*) an Executive Order, permitting the waiving of all peace-time restrictions covering bids, contracts, deliveries and open-market purchases and authorizing the exercise of the fullest possible freedom of purchase;
> (*c*) the delegation of wide authority over the movement of men to the War Department;
> (*d*) the maintenance by the Department of Labor of a flow of 8,540 men per day, certified for acceptance to the War Department, completing its selection of the full number by June 7;
> (*e*) wider disciplinary powers over recruits;
> (*f*) the approval of 290 more work projects by June 1.[50]

The plan was unanimously adopted by the Advisory Council. Howe and Douglas secured Roosevelt's approval, and it went into effect the same day. As Colonel Major, in a self-congratulatory mood, wrote later: "It was a momentous day. In a few short hours, more had been accomplished than in the previous

48. *Ibid.*

49. Major to Fechner, June 30, 1933, Roosevelt Papers, O.F. 268, Box 2.

50. *Ibid.* In addition, they asked, if possible, that 5 per cent of the enrollees in each company be designated as leaders at $45 a month, and 8 per cent as assistant leaders at $36 a month. This was done on June 7.

month."[51] The task assumed by the War Department was awesome. It envisaged the establishment of 1,300 camps by July 1, at the rate of twenty-six daily. Moreover, "the rate demanded of 8,540 men received, processed, and equipped per day was greater than the average for the United States during the World War for both Army and Navy combined."[52] As the War Department plan was translated into action in the succeeding weeks, the whole temper of the CCC changed, each agency striving desperately to achieve the July 1 goal. The crucial test was whether the Department of Labor could maintain the vital flow of 8,540 men per day. This it was able to do. Indeed, with the full quota of 274,375 selected by June 7, the President's goal was well in sight.[53]

In addition to the specifics of the plan of May 12, other policies were modified to suit the Army's needs. On May 22, for example, in a move which further decentralized authority, Fechner permitted the movement of camps up to twenty-five miles from the original site without specific approval from Washington. Aimed at lessening the delay caused by faulty camp location, this directive greatly facilitated speedy camp construction and was enthusiastically received by the War Department.[54] A leader and assistant leader system, approved June 7, was set up on June 16. The men to fill these capacities were chosen from the enrollees and were paid a slightly higher wage. Twenty-six were assigned to each camp—eight to the Army, and the other eighteen to the work agency.[55] By June 16 there were 239,444 men either in camp or on the way there. The July 1 goal had every chance of being met, due almost entirely to the successful War Department plan.[56]

Of course, there were still checks and delays in Washington, though these had been greatly reduced. Important authorizations were still held up by the White House, and significant memo-

51. *Ibid.*; see also Fechner to Roosevelt, May 12, 1933, *ibid.*, Box 1.
52. *Ibid.*
53. *Report of the Director*, 1933, p. 3.
54. Fechner to Regional Foresters, May 22, 1933, C.R.M., No. 788(a), Development.
55. Order of Director, June 16, 1933, C.R.M., No. 784(1), Leaders and Assistant Leaders.
56. Major to Howe, June 21, 1933, Roosevelt Papers, O.F. 268, Box 2.

randa had a habit of getting buried among the mounting files on the desks of Roosevelt and Howe. On one such occasion, Stuart was called to Howe's office to locate certain correspondence which needed urgent approval but which had somehow gone astray, an occurrence which led him to be sharply critical of Fechner's filing system because no copies of the missing documents had been kept.[57] Then, too, the Forest Service and the War Department had not yet entirely solved their difference of opinion on fiscal procedure, each wishing to use its own means of disbursement in purchasing equipment, while Fechner still insisted on too many conferences to suit Stuart.[58]

Moreover, a new problem appeared, one which was to be of persistent irritation to the CCC organization. On May 12 Stuart complained to Fechner that the postmaster general, James A. Farley, had been hinting that the jobs of the technical service personnel could be used for patronage purposes. Stuart demanded that Fechner protect them from "political interference which would prevent the selection of wholly competent men."[59] The director, after investigating the charges, expressed his concern over Farley's behavior and agreed that political influences in appointments "would be harmful to the project."[60] As shall be shown later, he was not able to prevent patronage entirely. The political issue, though rarely predominant as with the WPA, was always present and on more than one occasion caused Fechner acute embarrassment.

In the panic and confusion of the CCC's early development, Roosevelt's secretary, Louis Howe, was always a central figure. Indeed, Albert B. Rollins, in his book *Roosevelt and Howe* credits him with the major part in co-ordinating and directing the Corps during its first two years.[61] Too much can be made of Howe's role; the President had the final word on important

57. Stuart to Giles, May 20, 1933, C.R.M., No. 782(2), Hammatt, Source Data.

58. Stuart to Howe, May 26, 1933; Wallace to Secretary of War, May 31, 1933, *ibid.*

59. Assistant Forester C. M. Granger to files, May 15, 1933, *ibid.*

60. Stuart to Howe, May 22, 1933, *ibid.* Report of interview with Fechner.

61. Rollins, pp. 404-405.

policy matters, as much of the initial delay indicates.[62] But in the first three months, at least, Howe's actions as an administrative co-ordinator were crucial. It was Howe who proposed that the function of the Army be enlarged to include camp administration, who settled the dispute between the Forest Service and the Bureau of the Budget, and who helped secure Roosevelt's approval for the plans of May 12.[63] As well as being a conciliator, Howe had power of decision in matters of minor policy. Thus, when Fechner wrote to him on May 24, asking for permission to enrol a limited number of college graduates into the Corps, Howe was able to decide against the proposal without referring it to the President. It was to Howe that Colonel Major sent enrolment details for analysis and comment, while he also did much of the detailed checking into proposed work projects.[64]

It is scarcely surprising that Howe's part should have been a large one. With Roosevelt unable through pressure of business to devote much of his time to the specifics of CCC organization, and with Fechner still coming to grips with his new job and still unsure of himself in Washington and needing guidance, it was obvious that another co-ordinating authority should be required temporarily. There is surely nothing unusual in the fact that it was the President's secretary and friend who undertook the task, attending to much of the minor policy work, helping the director to find himself in his new position. In Howe's correspondence after June, 1933, there are significantly fewer documents dealing with CCC matters,[65] and this could well indicate that his importance diminished after the formative three months. He remained connected with certain aspects of CCC

62. As an example of this, there is in the Howe Papers, Box 59, a memorandum for Fechner from the War Department, dated April 5, giving various cost estimates for food, shelter, etc. Howe had tentatively approved it, yet written in the President's handwriting are the words, "this figure of $1.92 a day, not including transportation or wages, is absurdly high—it must be greatly reduced, F.D.R."

63. Major to Howe, May 8, 1933, *ibid.*, Box 60; see also pp. 32, 40, above.

64. Fechner to Howe, May 24, 1933, Major to Howe, April 25, 1933, Albright to Howe, April 22, 1933, Roosevelt Papers, O.F. 268, Box 1.

65. See Howe Papers, Box 62. During August, 1933, only one item can be found in Howe's correspondence pertaining to CCC matters, yet three months earlier, at least half of the correspondence had done so.

work, particularly the education program, yet once the organization was moving smoothly there was much less for him to do.

Howe was also in part responsible for the first scandal to rock the CCC organization, one which, given less delicate handling, could have had grave consequences for the new Administration. On May 16, 1933, a certain Mr. Bevier appeared at Howe's office, bearing a letter of introduction from Howe's friend, Basil O'Connor, a New York attorney. Bevier had heard that the CCC was contracting for the supply of toilet kits to the enrollees. He offered to save the government money by furnishing them at $1.40 each. Howe, apparently convinced, referred the man to Fechner, with a letter authorizing him to purchase the kits from any source. Fechner, used to receiving Howe's instructions, promptly stopped negotiations on a proposed contract with the War Department for the purchase of the kits, and signed with Bevier.[66] There the matter rested until a Republican senator, Robert Carey of Wyoming, disclosed to a surprised Senate on May 26 that the War Department would have furnished the kits for 32 cents each. Bevier's price of $1.40 was more than four times as much. It looked suspiciously like favoritism in contracts, and the Senate Military Affairs Committee was directed to investigate the transaction.[67]

Both Fechner and Howe testified before the committee. Fechner admitted arranging the contract but insisted that Howe had directed him to do so. Howe flatly denied the charge. All he had done, he insisted, was to place the affair in Fechner's hands. He had assumed that the Bureau of the Budget had investigated the contract prior to its acceptance, and the whole business had caused him great anxiety. The committee eventually found no evidence of corruption, but it considered that both Howe and Fechner had been somewhat negligent in accepting Bevier's credentials so readily.[68] The chairman, Senator Morris Sheppard, Democrat of Texas, later remarked that Howe was "fortunate" to receive so favorable a verdict.[69] Though Howe

66. New York *Times*, June 3 and 7, 1933; see also Rollins, p. 405.
67. New York *Times*, May 27, 1933.
68. *Ibid.*, June 2, 3, 5, and 11, 1933.
69. Sheppard to Howe, June 15, 1933, Roosevelt Papers, O.F. 268, Box 2.

complained that the "Committee has left me in an entirely false light with the public,"[70] he allowed the matter to drop and the "toilet kit incident" was soon forgotten.

In spite of this brief scent of scandal, the organization and mobilization of the CCC continued unhindered throughout June, the President's goal being assured by the success of the War Department's plan. In a report to Roosevelt on July 1, 1933, Colonel Major was able to state that the full quota of 274,375 men was now enrolled and in camp. The President's wishes had been met in full, and with justifiable pride Major disclosed that in so doing "all American war and peacetime records" had been shattered.[71] In the short span of three months the CCC had developed from a statutory authorization to the largest peacetime government labor force the United States had ever known. Colonel Major more than anyone else deserves praise for the CCC's successful mobilization. It was his scheme which made the task feasible, and his close supervision helped to carry it through. Gruff, obdurate, relentless in argument, Major became devoted to the CCC and served the agency admirably. Unlike some of his fellow officers, he was wholehearted in his belief that it was "a most beneficial source of training for those lucky enough to have any part in it."[72]

The mobilization of the CCC had not been without pain. Certain deficiencies of organization had already appeared, cracks which needed immediate attention if the success of the experiment was not to be compromised. Moreover, the director had yet to show that his ability as an administrator matched his undoubted talent as a conciliator. Yet, despite this administrative confusion and structural shortcoming, the success of the War Department's plan cannot be impugned. The Army had successfully undertaken the largest peacetime mobilization of men the United States had ever seen, had built more than 1,300 camps, and had installed recruits in all of them. The CCC was off to a fine start.

70. Howe to Sheppard, June 19, 1933, *ibid.*
71. Major to Roosevelt, July 1, 1933, *ibid.*
72. Major to Chief of Staff, Dec. 14, 1939, C.R.M., Appendix III.

3. *The Policies of Expansion, 1933-1937*

After the hectic activity of May and June, 1933, it is hardly surprising that the succeeding six-month period should be primarily one of consolidation, of building on the framework constructed in the first weeks of the CCC's life. Nevertheless, several policy decisions were made in the latter half of 1933 which were of great significance to the Corps' existence. One of the first of these concerned the establishment of "side camps," small subcamps set apart from the main site. Without such camps, much work, peripheral to the main project but important nevertheless, could not have been undertaken because of the distances involved. The responsibility for administering such camps was a source of dissension between the Army and the work services. The technical agencies wanted to have them placed under their control and, though both the Army and Fechner bitterly opposed the decision, the President acceded to this demand. On July 19 he approved the establishment of side camps, provided that not more than 10 per cent of the company strength was inducted into them, and he freed them from military control.[1] Such small camps were widely used, particularly in forests and state parks, and accomplished much useful work.

Another important decision was taken on August 17, 1933, when Fechner authorized the use of CCC units to fight fires in Craig, Montana, thus beginning a long chronicle of CCC assistance in local and national emergencies. Public authorities and private citizens came to look to the CCC for immediate assistance when disaster struck, and it did not let them down. Other disasters at which the CCC rendered valuable aid were the Winooski, Vermont, and Walkill, New York, floods in 1937, the blizzards of 1936-1937 in Wyoming, Utah, and Nevada, the Florida tornado of 1933, and the New England hurricane in 1938. Such work, besides its immediate humanitarian value, was of tremendous assistance in firmly establishing a favorable public impression of the CCC.[2]

1. Advisory Council, Minutes, July 6 and 19, 1933.
2. A. T. Hibbard to Ickes, Aug. 17, 1933, Secretary of Interior, Records; C.R.M., No. 788(4), CCC in Emergencies.

On August 15, 1933, the President made the first of many tours of inspection when he visited five CCC camps in the Blue Ridge Mountain–Skyline Drive area of Virginia. He received a tremendous reception, and was entirely in his element, laughing and joking with those accompanying him as he dined "on steak, mashed potatoes, green beans and salad, iced tea, and a so-called apple pie."[3] With typical political acumen, Roosevelt had included in his touring party the erstwhile chief critic of the Corps, the president of the AF of L, William Green. Already partially mollified by Fechner's appointment, Green counted the excursion "one of the most pleasing experiences" of his life and admitted that because of the President's deep interest in the Corps he "could not help but view the whole project in a most sympathetic way."[4] Though organized labor and the CCC authorities occasionally had their differences, principally over wage rates for contract work, the unions were never again unreservedly hostile to the whole operation.

The visit to the camps confirmed for the President that the CCC was a success. It came as no surprise, therefore, when on August 18 he extended the Corps at full strength for another six months. This announcement was followed a week later by the decision to permit re-enrolment for a second six-month term, an act which caused great jubilation in the camps.[5] The most important policy decision taken in 1933, however, was to develop an education program. On November 22 the President approved a plan for a nationwide, Washington-directed, CCC education service, supplanting the scheme then existing which left the introduction of educational work entirely to the discretion of the camp commander. Thus began a new phase of CCC expansion.[6]

The credit for first stimulating interest in the possibilities of using the CCC for educational purposes probably belonged to

3. Ickes, *Diary*, I, 78-79; New York *Times*, Aug. 15, 1933.

4. Green to Roosevelt, Sept. 18, 1933, Roosevelt Papers, O.F. 142; Saalberg, p. 45.

5. New York *Times*, Aug. 19, 26, and 27, 1933; see also *Happy Days*, Aug. 26, 1933.

6. Roosevelt to Gen. Douglas MacArthur, No. 22, 1933, C.R.M., No. 790, Training.

the director of selection, W. Frank Persons. As early as May 18, 1933, he had submitted an ambitious plan for a centralized education scheme to Fechner, which broadly suggested the appointment of an educational counselor to each camp and which presupposed close co-operation with university extension services.[7] Persons' plan was circulated widely and was well received by a cross-section of people and professions, including university teachers and trade-union officials.[8] Fechner was not similarly impressed, however, and Persons was forced to report rather ruefully on June 6 that his plan stood "disapproved by the Director of Emergency Conservation Work."[9] Fechner was solidly supported by the Army, whose fear of radical and leftist infiltration of the camps colored its whole attitude to educational work.[10]

Still the pressure was kept up. Fechner was deluged by requests from state selecting agencies for a comprehensive education program,[11] and the new federal commissioner of education, George F. Zook, who was enthusiastic about the educational potential of the Corps, occasionally discussed the question with the President.[12] Roosevelt showed enough interest in the various schemes to keep Colonel Major in a state of "suspended agitation." On August 11, reacting to a rumor that the President had authorized the employment of 10,000 jobless teachers in the camps, the Colonel thundered:

> I have constantly fought the attempts of long-haired men and short-haired women to get in our camps . . . we are going to be hounded to death by all sorts of educators. Instead of teaching the boys how to do an honest day's work we are going to be forced to accede to the wishes of

7. Persons to Fechner, May 18, 1933, *ibid.*

8. George B. Zehner, director, Extension Division, University of Virginia, to Persons, May 6, 1933, Spencer Miller, secretary, Workers' Education Bureau of America, to Persons, June 1, 1933, Records of CCC Selection Division (hereinafter abbreviated S.D.), Education, General Correspondence.

9. Persons to J. Prentice Murphy, June 6, 1933, *ibid.*

10. Persons to R. L. Evans, Aug. 29, 1933, *ibid.*

11. E.g., Allen Johnstone, state director of relief, S.C., to Fechner, June 3, 1933: "It is of the utmost importance that reading, education and cultural programs for these young men should be provided," *ibid.*

12. Holland and Hill, p. 96.

> the long-haired men and short-haired women and spend most of the time on some kind of an educational course.[13]

Major claimed that the youths could not possibly be induced to attend classes after a hard day's work, leaving the teachers with so little to do that he advocated their employment as clerks as well. The Army, in short, stood completely opposed to a centralized educational program for the Corps.

Nevertheless, the idea slowly gained support in Washington, even Fechner himself beginning to recognize the need for a more comprehensive plan, especially as pressure from the field increased. On October 16, 1933, the Association of State Foresters at its annual meeting passed a resolution urging that "this educational opportunity should not be neglected" and supported the idea that planned instruction be given in the camps.[14] University teachers also contributed suggestions,[15] and the President even added a few ideas of his own. He wrote on November 8 that he was "very anxious to try out in one or two places the idea of giving the men in the CCC camps some kind of formal instruction in forestry and the natural history of trees. I am going to ask them to do this in the Virginia camps this winter."[16]

The first really positive move toward the establishment of an educational program in the camps was made on October 25 when Howe sought from Persons "a definite and specific plan for education in the CCC."[17] Zook, too, was consulted, and between them they evolved a comprehensive program which was presented to Fechner on November 2. The plan advocated a director of CCC education working under Fechner, with an office staff and an advisory committee, an education co-ordinator in each Corps Area, and a camp education adviser and two enrollee assistants in each camp.[18] Education in the CCC was becoming a real possibility.

13. Major to Howe, Aug. 11, 1933, S.D., Education, Correspondence.
14. Advisory Council, Minutes, Aug. 17, 1933; Holland and Hill, p. 96; State Foresters to Fechner, Oct. 16, 1933, C.R.M., No. 790, Training.
15. E.g., Prof. E. V. Jolter, University of Michigan, to Fechner, Oct. 11, 1933, S.D., Education, Correspondence.
16. Roosevelt to Maj. William A. Welch, Palisades Interstate Park Commission, N.Y., Nov. 8, 1933, in Nixon, I, 212.
17. Secretary of Labor to Persons, Oct. 19, 1933, S.D., Education, Correspondence.
18. Zook to Fechner, Nov. 2, 1933, *ibid.*

The War Department, too, realizing the inevitability of some type of program being adopted, changed its tactics. It now merely aimed at insuring that whatever the outcome, the Army would retain ultimate control over all camp activities. Accordingly, General MacArthur presented a modification of Zook's program to the President on November 22. Retaining enough of the original features to mollify the Office of Education, it nevertheless firmly established the principle of Army control of education. MacArthur proposed that the program be administered by the Office of Education in the Department of the Interior. It would be headed by a director, aided by an advisory committee, who would communicate directly with the secretary of war on all important matters and would "recommend to the Secretary the outlines of instruction, teaching procedure, and the type of teaching materials for use in the camps."

The responsibility for carrying out the program was vested in the corps area commander, assisted by a corps area educational adviser who was selected by the Officer of Education but was directly responsible to the corps area commander. The procedure was duplicated in each camp, where the camp commanders were to be in charge of all instruction in their respective camps, assisted by one camp educational adviser. It was expected, however, that both the military and technical service people would co-operate with the adviser in giving instruction and settling general camp policy. As there was to be no encroachment upon working hours, education would have to be given at night, and attendance was to be purely voluntary.[19] This modified scheme was immediately approved by the President, and centralized education in the CCC had officially begun.[20]

Though many found the dominant position accorded the Army repugnant, and though, as will be discussed later, the program as approved did contain many unsatisfactory features, it probably represented the best possible compromise between the ambition of education officials and the nervous apprehension of the War Department. Because of the strategic importance of the Army to the CCC organization, it was necessary to gain

19. MacArthur to Roosevelt, Nov. 22, 1933, C.R.M., No. 790, Training.
20. *Ibid.*; see also Holland and Hill, p. 96.

military acceptance of the program if it was to have any success at all. Thus, the vesting of ultimate responsibility with the Department of War was the best practical solution.

Much had to be organized before the program could operate at full strength. A director, staff, and advisers were needed, and curricula had to be prepared. Clarence S. Marsh, dean of the evening session at the University of Buffalo, was appointed director on December 29, 1933, and he immediately proceeded "to marshall a working force and prepare it for its duties," selecting his advisers mainly from the ranks of the unemployed teachers and university graduates.[21] By June, 1934, the program was fully staffed and had begun its operations.[22]

The problems with which education officials and advisers had to contend were urgent and alarming. In the first place, they had to provide instruction for 250,000 youths and men of widely divergent skills and background, whose educational attainments ranged from no formal schooling to university degrees. Within each camp, therefore, a wide variety of courses had to be scheduled, both academic and vocational, in order best to meet the needs of the enrollees. Thus, advisers, even if they were able to secure technical service co-operation or outside teaching assistance, were forced to become instructors in many fields, often well outside their own level of competence, with inevitable deterioration in both preparation and teaching performance.

Second, the material available was often grossly inadequate. The adviser seldom had an office of his own, let alone a classroom, and most of the instruction was done in the mess halls or barracks. Library facilities and classroom equipment were invariably substandard and in insufficient supply. It is scarcely surprising that the turnover of supervisors was always high and that after one year only 50 per cent of original appointees were still in the camps.[23]

21. Frank E. Hill, *The School in the Camps: The Educational Program of the Civilian Conservation Corps* (New York, 1935), p. 10; Zook to Howe, March 14, 1934, Howe Papers, Box 72. Howe took over much of the responsibility for organizing CCC education, passing judgment on the suitability of candidates for advisers' posts, etc. See Zook to Ickes, May 1, 1934, *ibid.*

22. Hill, p. 10.

23. *Ibid.*, pp. 17-21, 56-58.

Third, it is clear that the initial success of the program in the individual camps depended on the attitude of the camp commander. Some co-operated enthusiastically with the adviser, but others were frankly skeptical and uninterested. As one commander bluntly put it: "why pamper [the enrollees] with this hocus-pocus of education. It's a lot of bunk, anyway."[24] Such open contempt could effectively kill the camp program, making it, as one disillusioned adviser complained, "futile and wasteful."[25] Many corps area commanders, too, were most uncertain about the scheme's value. General Fox Connor, commander of the First Corps Area, once issued instructions to abolish forthwith what he termed "cultural courses." As disciplines like history, sociology, foreign languages, and philosophy were deemed to fall within this category, the scope of academic instruction available to the individual adviser was somewhat reduced.[26]

Fourth, Army officers too often tried to discourage discussion of social and political issues. One corps area officer for example, refused to allow any books on sociology to be used in the camps on the grounds that "all writers on sociology were somewhat radical." Unrestrained discussion, he believed, could bring discontent and agitation. The official instructions issued to all education advisers contained detailed advice on "how to avoid dangerous issues" as an added safeguard against controversial debate. Advisers resented this high-handed infringement of the right of free speech and asserted that it hindered their efforts to keep the enrollees well informed on the basic issues of the day.[27]

Finally, most CCC education officials were sure that Fechner did not co-operate fully with them in plans for the advancement of their work, and in this allegation they were undoubtedly correct. Fechner always considered that relief of unemployment and the promotion of useful conservation work were the chief activities of the CCC; education was secondary. His attitude was, in a sense, commensurate with his responsibilities as director of an

24. *Ibid.*, pp. 14-15.

25. See *Literary Digest*, CXIX (May 8, 1935), 360. A letter is printed from a former education adviser, bitterly critical of Army control.

26. Gen. Fox Connor to all officers and education advisers, First Corps Area, July 2, 1936, S.D., Education, Correspondence.

27. Hill, p. 55; see also *New Republic*, LXXVI (Feb. 12, 1936), 6.

organization which he had to justify each year on the basis of work performed, not lessons learned. He was therefore reluctant to spend more money on education because this would simply mean less for the work projects, and work was what the CCC had been created to do. One can understand his reasoning, narrow in vision though it seems, but to Marsh and his associates it smacked of non-co-operation. In fact, Marsh resigned in 1935, frustrated by his inability to develop a coherent program, believing that he was being deprived of finance, time, and encouragement. He was replaced by a former educational adviser to the Liberian government, Howard Oxley, who held the post till the Corp's demise, though he too had a full share of frustrations.[28]

Nevertheless, despite military antagonism, directorial apathy, and confused aims and intentions the CCC education program not only survived its first three years but achieved some measure of success in the process. In remedial education, for example, it performed a great function. By June, 1937, 35,000 illiterates had been taught to read and write, more than a thousand youths had gained high school diplomas, and thirty-nine had received college degrees. To this end, forty universities gave courses to CCC camps by mail and twenty-six had granted scholarships to former enrollees.[29] Here were at least some criteria by which to judge the program's effectiveness.

Within each camp the courses offered were extraordinarily varied and could range from wood chopping to empirical philosophy. More than half were vocational in nature; the rest were academic courses. Of the total number of academic offerings, 16 per cent were on the elementary school level, 27 per cent on the high school level, and 5 per cent were college courses.[30] Much of the best vocational training was given "on the job." Boys who had never swung a pick nor used an ax now learned to run jack-

28. Holland and Hill, p. 97; *New Republic*, LXXXIII (June 12, 1935), 127-129. See Selection Division, Minutes of Advisory Committee on Education (hereinafter, Education, Minutes), June 25, 1935.

29. Report of Director of CCC Camp Education to Commissioner of Education, June 30, 1937; *Report of the Director*, 1936, p. 19; *Happy Days*, Nov. 21, 1935.

30. *Report of the Director*, 1935, p. 28.

hammers and drive trucks. Though the success of more sophisticated vocational courses, such as boilermaking or metal work, was often compromised due to lack of equipment, space, and time, the basic instruction in the use of tools and machinery stood many an enrollee in good stead when he left the Corps and sought employment.[31]

Thus, by 1937, CCC education had survived the controversies of its origin and the vicissitudes of its development to take its place as a legitimate aspect of the Corps' work. Though it was to encounter more hostile criticism in later years, it had achieved enough success to insure its continuance.

The Civilian Conservation Corps entered the new year, 1934, on the crest of a wave. On January 25 the President informed Fechner that he wanted the work continued at least until April, 1935, and that he had sought an appropriation of $275,000,000 to cover the cost. Fechner was authorized to plan ahead on that basis, maintaining enrolment at the present figure of slightly more than 300,000, including veterans and Indians. Re-enrolment was again to be permitted, but no man was to remain in camp for more than a year in an effort to distribute the benefits of CCC life over as wide an area as possible.[32]

On April 7, 1934, the CCC celebrated officially its first anniversary. This was, of course, a time to review the accomplishments of the past year, and they made very impressive reading. By March, 1934, the Corps had improved millions of acres of forest and park land, thousands of miles of telephone lines had been erected, and 420,000 dams had been built to aid in erosion control. Losses from forest fires in national forests had decreased spectacularly over the year to less than 17 per cent of the average annual loss, a splendid tribute to CCC endeavor. The health of enrollees had improved, and on an average each had gained seven and one-quarter pounds. Moreover, about $72,500,000 had been allotted to dependents during the year, lightening local relief burdens and stimulating local business. The satisfaction

31. Hill, pp. 46-53.
32. Nixon, I, 246; Advisory Council, Minutes, March 2, 1934.

felt by officials as they celebrated the anniversary was indeed well justified.[33]

There was still, however, much room for improvement. One particular area of concern was the number of accidents in camp. In October, 1933, Fechner had expressed his anxiety at the number of accidental deaths in the Corps and had stressed the "need for greater vigilance" on the part of the military and technical services. Such appeals had little effect, however, and it seemed that a thoroughgoing safety program was needed.[34]

Such a program was approved on April 9, 1934, in one of the first major policy decisions of that year. Curiously enough, Fechner had opposed the program as presented because of excessive cost, but it was so strongly supported by the War Department and the technical services that he capitulated.[35] Samuel M. Lauderdale, a bluff, experienced Forest Service engineer, was subsequently appointed director of the Civilian Conservation Corps' Safety Division. Working with a council composed of one representative from each of the co-operating agencies, his organization did much good work throughout the CCC's existence.[36] Safety Division representatives visited each camp, demonstrating accident prevention techniques, checking camp equipment for safety hazards, insuring that high sanitation standards prevailed, and giving instruction in work safety measures. By June, 1936, in large part due to their labors, the death rates from disease and injury had been reduced to a point much lower than those of the Regular Army for the same period, and lower also than those prevailing among men of similar age groups throughout the United States.[37]

In mid-1934 came the first significant expansion of CCC enrolment. In the spring and summer of that year drought devastated much of the Midwest, blasting its way as far south as Texas and east to the Alleghenies. Millions of acres of topsoil

33. New York *Times*, April 16, 1934; *Report of the Director*, 1933-1934, pp. 6-10.
34. Fechner to Adjutant General, Oct. 19, 1933, in Director, Correspondence.
35. Advisory Council, Minutes, April 9, 1934.
36. *Ibid.*, May 21, 1934.
37. *Report of the Director*, 1936, p. 13.

were lost, crops withered and died, and cattle languished without water.[38] There was desperate need for immediate government action, both to ameliorate somewhat the physical devastation left by the drought, and to relieve the increased regional unemployment situation which it had caused. Roosevelt decided to use the CCC as one of the agencies to implement drought policy and asked Congress for an additional $50,000,000 for Corps work in the drought areas. He planned to enrol as many men in the drought-affected states as the increased appropriation would allow, form them into regular CCC units, and put them on work projects in the stricken areas, principally to check soil erosion and to develop irrigation schemes.[39] Once Congress had voted the money, the Department of Labor was instructed to select 50,000 additional men, including 5,000 veterans, from cities of more than 2,500 population in the drought-affected areas of twenty-two states, as it was in urban areas where unemployment was most widespread. They began work on July 1, the increased enrolment raising the strength of the Corps to 353,000 including Indians and veterans, and the number of camps to 1,625.[40]

The quality of the work in the drought areas added more kudos to the already favorable public image of the CCC. The New York *Times* commented on the success of the agency, stating that the absence of criticism—"even from Republican quarters"—was a phenomenon "watched with interest by the Administration," while the Detroit *News* admitted that prospective critics of the Corps had been "silenced by the prompt and unmistakable dividends" it had paid.[41] The agency certainly rested firmly on a broad base of support which transcended party and regional lines.

Delighted with its achievements, the President made plans to

38. Schlesinger, II, 69-70.

39. Advisory Council, Minutes, June 9, 1934.

40. Department of Labor to State Directors of Selection, June 21, 1934, C.R.M., Appendix II, Document 180. The states affected were Arizona, Arkansas, California, Colorado, Idaho, Illinois, Indiana, Iowa, Kansas, Minnesota, Missouri, Montana, Nebraska, Nevada, New Mexico, North Dakota, Oklahoma, Oregon, South Dakota, Texas, Utah, and Wisconsin. See New York *Times*, June 28, 1934; Rosenman, ed., *Papers*, III, 424.

41. New York *Times*, Aug. 26, Sept. 12, 1934, reprint of editorial from Detroit *News*.

extend the life of the CCC after the expiration of the existing enabling legislation on April 1, 1935. He wrote to Fechner: "This kind of work must go on. I believe that the Nation feels that the work of these young men is so thoroughly justified, and, in addition the benefits to the men themselves are so clear, that the actual annual cost will be met without much opposition or much complaint."[42] Not only did he seek continuation of the Corps, but he also planned a drastic extension of its size and compass as part of the expanded relief organization which he outlined in his message to Congress on January 4, 1935. Roosevelt proposed a bold new approach to the problem of unemployment. "Continued dependence on relief," he proclaimed, induced "spiritual and moral degradation"; consequently, he sought legislation aimed at putting 3,500,000 people back to work. To this end, he asked for the massive appropriation of more than $4.8 billion in order to create a public works program which would be self-liquidating, non-competitive with private business, and which would pay a "security wage," higher than the dole, but not so high as to become a lucrative alternative to private employment. The President "envisaged the extension and enlargement of the successful work of the CCC" as an integral part of this development.[43]

The decision to enlarge the CCC again caused further paeans of praise to ring out in the nation's press, in contrast with the mixed reception given the work relief scheme in toto. Even the violently anti-New Deal Chicago *Tribune* thought that "The CCC is one of the best projects of the Administration, and the great majority of its recruits, we believe, appreciate its opportunities and are being benefited."[44] Such words from the most bitter of Republican newspapers indicated dramatically how high the Corps stood in popular esteem.

Anticipating the passage of the legislation, the Advisory

42. Rosenman, ed., *Papers*, III, 423.

43. *C.R.*, 74th Cong., 1st Sess., Vol. 79, Pt. 1, pp. 94-97. See also Schlesinger, III, 265-272, for an explanation of the scheme.

44. Chicago *Tribune*, Jan. 16, 1935; see also San Francisco *Examiner*, Jan. 3, 1935, Boston *Evening Transcript*, Jan. 3, 1935, St. Louis *Post-Dispatch*, Jan. 4, 1935. For a less adulatory though still pro-CCC view, see New York *Herald Tribune*, Jan. 10, 1935.

Council drew up a blueprint providing for the mobilization of the CCC to 600,000 men and their full employment in work camps as soon as possible after the appropriation was authorized. This document the President approved on January 17.[45] There were other steps taken to meet the demands of expansion. On April 12 Roosevelt authorized the use of Navy and Marine Reserve officers to augment the six thousand Army Reserve officers already employed in the camps.[46] The expansion program could quickly be implemented as soon as Congress approved the work relief scheme. But this took some time. The plan's very magnitude and philosophy caused much misgiving on Capitol Hill, and weeks passed without action. Though Fechner was concerned at the effect of the delay, mainly because the CCC was running out of funds, the future of the agency was never in serious doubt.[47] The debates on the work relief measure were often most acrimonious, but there was virtually no criticism of the provision extending the CCC. Indeed, the success of the agency was of positive value to the Administration. Supporters of the President's plan were able to remind their opponents that its failure to pass Congress would spell doom for the CCC, a prospect few congressmen relished.[48] The work relief resolution was eventually signed by the President on April 8, after passing the House by 317 votes to 70 and the Senate by 66 to 13.[49] CCC expansion could now begin.

On April 11, 1935, Fechner discussed with the Advisory Council the burden of a recent interview with Roosevelt in which the President had outlined his latest idea for the future organization of the CCC, a plan intimately concerned with his hopes of reducing government expenditure in the election year. The increase to 600,000 enrollees was to be only temporary. Starting on October 1, 1935, Roosevelt wanted the numbers gradually tapered down until only 450,000 remained in camp on

45. Roosevelt to Fechner, Jan. 17, 1935, Roosevelt Papers, O.F. 268, Box 5.

46. Roosevelt to Fechner, April 12, 1935, *ibid.*

47. Fechner to Roosevelt, Feb. 25, 1935, *ibid.*

48. Rep. John H. Hoeppel (Dem., Calif.) made this point forcefully on Jan. 24. See *C.R.*, 74th Cong., 1st Sess., Vol. 79, Pt. 1, p. 296.

49. New York *Times*, April 6 and 9, 1935.

June 1, 1936. Fechner tried to point out that such a scheme was fraught with dangerous possibilities, in that it meant that work projects might have to be left incomplete and men discharged before finishing their full term. Though Roosevelt did not choose to develop the idea further at this stage it was an ominous augury of policies to come, policies which for the first time were to incur a substantial amount of congressional and public criticism for the Corps.[50]

Meanwhile, expansion continued briskly. There were 2,916 camps to be filled, 2,106 under the Department of Agriculture and 690 under the Department of the Interior, and to facilitate full enrolment the upward age limit was increased from twenty-five to twenty-eight years and the maximum time of service from one year to eighteen months. There seemed no reason at this time why the figure of 600,000 could not be easily met.[51]

However, a new and controversial figure began to pose problems for the CCC. This was Harry Hopkins, newly appointed director of the Works Progress Administration and rising star in the hierarchy of presidential advisers. The President had decided that all projects paid for by the $4.8 billion appropriation had to be voted on by a specially constituted Committee on Allotments. The CCC clearly came under this category and Fechner was forced to submit his plans to this committee for approval. The chairman of the committee was Frank Walker, former executive secretary of the Executive Council and Democratic national committeeman, but the dominant member was Hopkins.[52] It was at a meeting of this committee that Roosevelt, influenced by Hopkins, announced a decision which was to have the gravest

50. Advisory Council, Minutes, April 11, 1935.

51. New York *Times*, April 23 and 25, 1935. In September, in a further attempt to boost enrolment, the minimum age limit was reduced to seventeen (*Report of the Director*, 1936, p. 23). The remaining 120 camps were under the control of the Department of War.

52. Schlesinger III, 345-346. Walker was a Montana lawyer who was deeply devoted to Roosevelt. He was noted for his evenness of temper and lack of aggression. Consequently, his services were often required as arbiter between warring factions of Roosevelt's advisers. The Executive Council was a body formed in July, 1933, to attempt to bring some measure of co-ordination to the various endeavors of the multifarious government departments and agencies. It was an experiment which lasted only a few months. See Schlesinger, II, 545-546.

consequences for the CCC's whole expansion program. In future, he ruled, all enrollees and employees had to be taken from public relief rolls, even skilled persons like stenographers and clerks.[53]

Fechner protested that this decision would radically alter the whole basis of selection. While the overwhelming majority of enrollees had always come from the relief rolls, states had been permitted to take other needy youths in order to fulfil their quotas. Boys without dependents, for instance, were often inducted, and made their allotment to some destitute family recommended by the local board, but their selection would in future be impossible under the new ruling.[54] Fechner also wanted to know about the status of specially trained persons, stenographers, technicians, and above all, educational advisers. Many of these people had not come from relief rolls. Would their continued employment be barred?

The answers Hopkins and Roosevelt gave to these concerned inquiries were quite definite. Hopkins insisted that if a given state could not fill its quota from the relief rolls, the remaining enrollees were to be selected from states with overflows of qualified applicants. Thus, he effectively wrecked the quota system of selection. Moreover, Hopkins asserted that he "had five million people on his relief rolls, and among them were people capable of substituting in any position."[55] All future CCC employees were therefore to come from these rolls, a decision the President spelled out in a letter to Fechner in which he confirmed that education advisers certainly were included under such a provision.[56] Fechner's objections had been disregarded. With these rulings the CCC entered a four-month period of drift and indecision as officials attempted to implement the Hopkins-controlled enrolment provisions. As early as June 6 it was apparent that, given strict adherence to the relief clause, the 600,000 enrolment figure was unlikely to be reached. The alternatives, therefore, were either to cut the quota, which was

53. Advisory Council, Minutes, May 10, 1935.

54. Roosevelt to Stephen Early, May 10, 1935, Roosevelt Papers, O.F. 268, Box 5.

55. Advisory Council, Minutes, May 10, 1935.

56. Roosevelt to Fechner, May 14, 1935, Roosevelt Papers, O.F. 268, Box 5.

inadvisable because of camp construction already begun, or to expand the eligibility rules.[57] The problem was emphasized to both Roosevelt and Hopkins on June 18 at a White House conference which, however, produced nothing definite. Neither Hopkins nor the President was willing to withdraw the relief provision, nor would they authorize a specific reduction in the number to be enrolled, though the President hinted that this might be considered at a later date. In the meantime the 600,000 enrolment was still to be the goal.[58]

Faced with ever-increasing evidence from the states that the quotas would not be filled under existing regulations, Fechner implored the President once more a week later for some relaxation of the provision, but again he was brusquely treated.[59] Roosevelt insisted that enrolment and construction be continued on the existing basis, with the goal still to be 600,000 men in 2,916 camps. All state quotas were to be completely disregarded, and all qualified applicants were to be taken.[60] There was little to do but attempt to comply with the ruling and watch as the situation deteriorated.

In a desperate attempt to end the prevailing climate of drift, Fechner proposed a new solution to the President without either of them first consulting Hopkins. On July 24 the director reported to Persons that Roosevelt had verbally authorized the enrolment of single men up to the age of thirty-five in the Corps and that camps would henceforth be divided into two groups, one for ages eighteen through twenty-four, and the other for men twenty-five and over. With this extension, Fechner believed that the quota would be reached. Accordingly he had advised the state directors of the decision but had instructed them to await confirmation from Persons before beginning selection. Persons, therefore, was now instructed to confirm Fechner's prior announcement and order selection of the older men to begin.[61]

But Persons bitterly opposed the extension of the age limit.

57. Major to Fechner, June 6, 1935, *ibid.*
58. Advisory Council, Minutes, June 18, 1935.
59. *Ibid.*, June 25, 1935.
60. Fechner to Persons, July 2, 1935, Director, Correspondence.
61. Fechner to Persons, July 24, 1935, Records of the CCC Selection Division, Discussions of Selection Policy, 1935.

Over the head of the director, he protested to Hopkins against its implementation.[62] Hopkins apparently knew nothing of Fechner's talk with the President and was similarly opposed to extending the upper age limit. The selection of older men would affect his own relief schemes, principally the WPA, and so he instructed Persons, again without Fechner's knowledge, to delay ordering the enrolment of the new group while he attempted to persuade Roosevelt to reverse his decision.[63] He was successful, and the President withdrew his verbal assent to the extension, much to Persons' relief. In thanking Hopkins for his good offices, he said that the proposed relaxation of the age limit would have "affected the CCC and its morale."[64]

Fechner, out of town, was in due course apprised of the decision. He accordingly informed Persons of the change. With some heat he reported that Hopkins had once more interfered in selection policy and had convinced Roosevelt that the extension of the age limit would not be desirable.[65] There is no evidence to indicate that he ever learned of the vital part his own director of selection played in influencing the President's decision. From the point of view of staff relations, his ignorance was no doubt just as well.

It is likely that the raising of the age limit to thirty-five would have created more problems than it could have solved. It would have allowed a complete new age group into the Corps, men who were by no stretch of the imagination the youths for whom projects, education, and remuneration had been designed. State directors were bitterly opposed to selection of older men, and a radical reconsideration of policy would have been necessary.[66] The controversy provided a striking indication of the importance of Harry Hopkins as a controlling factor of CCC policy at this time and shows just how circumscribed was Fechner's position. In an important matter of policy he was unable to claim the loyalty of his own director of selection.

No further attempt was made to adjust policy to meet the

62. Persons to Hopkins, July 24, 1935, *ibid.*
63. Hopkins to Persons, July 24, 1935, *ibid.*
64. Persons to Hopkins, July 26, 1935, *ibid.*
65. Fechner to Persons, Aug. 6, 1935, *ibid.*
66. McEntee to Persons, July 29, 1935, *ibid.*

exigencies of the relief provision. The enrolment period ended in September, 1935, with 502,000 men in 2,514 camps, well short of the original goal. This was due partly to the creation of the National Youth Administration which provided unemployed youths with an alternative to the CCC, but there is no doubt that Hopkins' obstinacy was also a key factor. Moreover, much discontent had been generated in the process. Selection agents found real resentment in local areas at the rigid adherence to the relief provision. Technical service representatives grimly reported that in many communities which had prepared for camps under the expanded plan, and where construction had started only to be abandoned because of the failure to meet the goal, a reservoir of anger had built up against the policies of the Corps. Such hostility was a new experience for Fechner, one that particularly chafed him because he was not responsible for it. The director was apprehensive that the issue could be used against the President in his re-election campaign in 1936.[67]

The September, 1935, figure of more than 500,000 was to be the high point of CCC enrolment, for election apprehension affected the President differently. While Fechner still advocated relaxation of the relief provision as the way to salvage the situation, the President, influenced by the desire of a budget reduction in election year, decided on a policy of extensive camp closings. He envisaged a progressive shutdown with no new enrolments, until by July 1, 1936, the total in camp would be but 300,000 men. He then hoped to make the CCC a permanent federal agency on this diminished scale.[68]

In vain Fechner argued against the wisdom of such a dubious scheme, pointing out the further reductions would serve only to exacerbate the discontent already smouldering in the localities. The President regretted the "embarrassment" which his plan would cause, but nevertheless he insisted on its immediate application, starting with the curtailment of additional expenditure on supplies and equipment.[69] As Roosevelt's reduction plans became more widely known, public protest grew in volume. The

67. Advisory Council, Minutes, Sept. 9, 1935.
68. *Ibid.*, Sept. 24, 1935; see also New York *Times*, Sept. 14, 1935.
69. Advisory Council, Minutes, Sept. 24, 1935.

announcement that 489 camps, existing or approved, were to be closed or canceled by January 1 produced such a vigorous reaction, particularly in the Midwest, that Fechner wrote requesting a "special allotment of $25 million to establish at least 12 camps in areas of tremendous political value."[70] The request was denied.

Congressmen added their substantial support to the protests. Representative Braswell Dean, Democrat of Georgia, in pleading for the re-establishment of a camp in his district, said the reduction policy would have "tragic" consequences for the Administration. Representative John W. McCormack, Democrat of Massachusetts, was similarly pessimistic. Petitions of protest pouring in from all parts of the country gave point to their argument.[71]

Alarmed at the intensity of feeling which had been aroused, other Administration officials joined Fechner in criticizing the reduction policy. Secretary of Agriculture Wallace discerned "grave consequences to the Administration" in the move and protested that "discontinuance of the number of camps necessary to bring Corps strength down to 2,078 camps in January and 1,456 camps in April will make it impossible to carry out agreements entered into in good faith by these local co-operating agencies and will result in widespread charges that the Administration had broken its promises."[72] He advocated continuing all camps till their work projects were played out, then "knocking them off." He also mentioned that he had been inundated with memoranda from state foresters stressing the bad effect the decision had had in local communities.

However, Roosevelt stood adamant in face of the rising tide of criticism both within and without the Administration. He was sure that Fechner was exaggerating the seriousness of the reaction and that the political benefits of budget reduction would

70. Fechner to Roosevelt, Oct. 25, 1935, Roosevelt Papers, O.F. 268, Box 6.

71. Braswell Dean to Fechner, Sept. 17, 1935, Director, Correspondence. See the telegram from the forty-six farmers of the Batesville, Miss., area protesting the closing of a soil erosion camp there. P. Pettit, president, Batesville Chamber of Commerce, to Fechner, Dec. 16, 1935, *ibid.*

72. Wallace to Roosevelt, Dec. 6, 1935, Files of the Secretary of Agriculture—Conservation.

far outweigh the brief spell of tarnished popularity.[73] Accordingly, at a meeting on December 18 attended by the secretaries of labor, agriculture, and the interior, the director of the Bureau of the Budget, the chief forester, Tugwell, Walker, and Fechner, he insisted that the reduction plan was still fully effective and would start on January 1, 1936. By June 30, he declared, he wanted only 300,000 men enrolled in 1,456 camps.[74] Consequently, the Corps entered the new year with considerable trepidation.

The CCC lost 489 camps as of January 1, 1936, an occurrence which pleased few and which prompted a further batch of protest mail.[75] Leading Democratic congressmen made strong personal appeals to the President to stay his hand, but to no avail.[76] Fechner reported to the Advisory Council on February 5 that Roosevelt was pleased with the way the first reduction had been carried out and wanted detailed plans drafted for cutting the number of camps to 1,456 by June 1.[77] On February 13 Fechner himself made a further plea for modification. He asked for funds to operate 1,807 camps till June 30 but again his request was denied. The President was determined to have only 1,703 camps in operation by April 1, which therefore meant the immediate reduction of a further 455 camps.[78] In addition, Roosevelt announced that because the CCC would no longer operate on funds taken from relief appropriations, but would be provided for in the regular War Department appropriations, a substantial reduction in funds was to be expected for the financial year 1936-1937. It seemed as if his determined stand for camp reduction would succeed.[79]

On March 14, 1936, however, a new element entered the situation, one which within ten days had changed it entirely. Congressmen, increasingly concerned as pressure from the grass

73. Frank Walker to Roosevelt, Oct. 30, 1935, Roosevelt Papers, O.F. 265, Box 6.
74. New York *Times*, Dec. 19, 1935.
75. *Ibid.*, March 24, 1936.
76. Rep. T. L. Blanton (Dem., Tex.) to Roosevelt, Jan. 7, 1936, Roosevelt Papers, O.F. 268–Misc., Box 17.
77. Advisory Council, Minutes, Feb. 5, 1936.
78. Fechner to Roosevelt, Feb. 13, 1936, Roosevelt to Fechner, Feb. 17, 1936, Roosevelt Papers, O.F. 268, Box 6.
79. New York *Times*, March 6, 1936.

roots mounted, resolved to take positive action themselves to save what camps they could. On that day, therefore, the speaker of the House, Representative Joseph W. Byrns, and Representative Samuel D. McReynolds, both Tennessee Democrats, called on the President with a petition signed by 233 members of the House, including a substantial number of Republicans, urging Roosevelt to discontinue the wholesale closing of camps.[80] The President considered the plea but rejected it. His intention was definitely to continue the reduction policy. He wanted only 300,000 in the CCC by July 1, he said, and "did not see how it could be maintained in greater strength after July 1 without throwing the Budget further out of balance."[81] The reference to budget balancing is important, for it indicates that this was not merely a convenient catchphrase to the President. He genuinely sought fiscal stability and was willing to sacrifice much of the CCC program to attain it.

Congress, however, was not of a similar mind. Balanced budgets, desirable in principle, could not be allowed to interfere with re-election prospects. On March 18, therefore, a letter signed by Representative Jack Nichols, Democrat, of Oklahoma, was sent to all Democratic congressmen, requesting their attendance at a meeting on the morning of March 20 "to lay plans for a continuous fight to prevent this order going into effect." Congressmen were reminded that "whether you have a CCC camp in your district or not, you are affected, for the threatened reduction in personnel will mean that an average of 300 families in each district would lose their breadwinner."[82] The President would henceforth have to implement his reduction plan in the teeth of serious congressional opposition from his own party.

At a meeting which was attended by more than two hundred House Democrats, strategy was thoroughly deliberated. The plan was to act as a bloc and force the continuation of the CCC at its present strength of 2,158 camps and 400,000 enrollees. Furthermore, as a supplementary appropriation, congressmen decided to fight for the earmarking of part of the President's new $1.5

80. *Ibid.*, March 15, 1936.
81. *Ibid.*, March 18, 1936.
82. Nichols to Congressman, March 18, 1936, Roosevelt Papers, O.F. 268, Box 7.

billion relief bill for CCC purposes. To emphasize their determination, seventy-five representatives signed a petition to force the whole Democratic caucus to discuss the issue. Representative Nichols was delegated to appoint a committee to call on the President and inform him of their intentions.[83]

The revolt of such a substantial section of the House Democratic strength caused Administration leaders to have doubts about the fate of the President's whole legislative program. Pointing out that the insurgents had threatened to block the passage of the relief appropriation until their demands were met, they urged on Roosevelt the necessity of compromise.[84] The President could do little else but capitulate in the face of such strong pressures. Accordingly, he advised Fechner that all existing camps were to be maintained and camps were to be closed only as they completed their work projects. Another $6,800,000 would be allotted to pay for the change in plans.[85]

Thus the congressional revolt was ended. Roosevelt's policy of cutting the CCC in the interest of economy, a plan in which he genuinely believed and which he had advocated consistently for more than six months, had been defeated by his own party, led mainly by rural representatives who in other days and other contexts could usually be counted among those supporting the curtailment of federal expenditure.

The reasons for the revolt were not hard to identify and the newspapers lost no time in exploring them. The New York *Times* correctly concluded that the uprising originated in the country, coming "from the hundreds of communities and hundreds of Congressional districts which would have been affected by the proposed reduction." Representatives and senators from all states had been deluged with mail, telegrams, and calls attesting to the popularity of the CCC camps and seeking immediate reversal of the reduction policy.[86] Faced with such a dramatic manifestation of the extraordinary popularity of the CCC, congressmen saw compliance with the President's plan as political suicide. As

83. New York *Times*, March 21, 1936.
84. *Ibid.*, March 23, 1936.
85. Roosevelt to Fechner, March 23, 1936, Roosevelt Papers, O.F. 268, Box 7.
86. New York *Times*, March 26, 1936.

one representative said: "it would have been tough for me if [the camps] are moved out of my district. I would have hated to face the people in that community if that one had been slashed."[87] Discussing the revolt, Arthur Krock in the New York *Times* made the point that few Republicans had supported retrenchment and that they were just as interested as the Democrats in having camps retained in their particular districts.[88] The attitude of Republican newspapers to the revolt lends credence to this view. The New York *Herald Tribune* called the CCC the "most popular" of all New Deal legislation, and talked both of its success in conserving natural resources and its effectiveness in stimulating local trade in "thousands of small communities."[89] The Des Moines *Register*, generally anti-New Deal in policy, was pleased at the success of the revolt. While it considered retrenchment in federal expenditures to be necessary, it believed that "the CCC should be one of the last of the government agencies to face the axe." The Boston *Evening Transcript* was similarly complimentary.[90] The reaction of the Republican newspapers again indicates the strong bipartisan flavor of CCC support.

Nowhere was this bipartisan trend more in evidence than in the 1936 election. The Republican presidential and vice-presidential candidates both specifically indorsed the CCC, thus effectively removing it from the arena of campaign criticism. Governor Alfred M. Landon had long admired the Corps. In 1934 in a letter to Roosevelt he had termed it "one of the most constructive policies of the Administration."[91] During the campaign he even tried to associate himself specifically with its success. Speaking at Los Angeles, Landon claimed credit for an amendment to the original bill, namely the one permitting work on state lands. He proudly stated that "subsequent experience has shown this has greatly enlarged the value of the Conservation Corps" which had "great opportunities for lasting good." Landon

87. *Ibid.* 88. *Ibid.*, March 24 and 30, 1936.

89. New York *Herald Tribune*, March 25, 1936.

90. Des Moines *Register*, March 26, 1936; Boston *Evening Transcript*, March 28, 1936.

91. Landon to Roosevelt, Jan. 16, 1934, Roosevelt Papers, O.F. 268, Box 3.

promised: "Once I am elected President, I will do everything within my power, not only to continue the CCC, but to improve the organization."[92] Such statements could scarcely be termed partisan criticism. The Republican vice-presidential candidate, Colonel Frank Knox, admitted that "the CCC has been a valuable institution in time of great distress," though its cost had been high. Only the Socialist party proposed its abolishment. The party platform claimed that the CCC "threatened the wage and living standards of organized labor"; the platform also expressed its dislike of the Army's role.[93]

In the first weeks of the campaign the Republican national chairman, John D. M. Hamilton, made sporadic attempts to prove political influence in the CCC organization, an accusation which, as Arthur Knock commented, should surprise no one, patronage "being one of the means by which national political machines are maintained."[94] Few papers took much notice of Hamilton's charges. The New York *Herald Tribune* said that "Farleyization" would "introduce a note of demoralization into an organization that above all New Deal innovations has received almost unanimous approval" and that "the camps . . . deserve a better fate than to be made the tools of cynical place-seekers," but the issue did not catch on.[95] Hamilton soon dropped it, and the Corps survived the rest of the campaign unscathed.

For the Democrats, of course, it was a positive source of gain and a regular ingredient of campaign speeches. The President himself invoked its success from time to time, promising that if re-elected he intended to make it permanent.[96] Moreover, he was able to use the Corps for both practical and political effect in September, once more increasing enrolment in drought areas.[97] Few of Roosevelt's legislative actions during his first term caused him less campaign embarrassment than the CCC. It came as no surprise, therefore, that in his 1936 report to the President, Director Fechner requested "that this program of

92. New York *Times*, Oct. 21, 1936.
93. *Ibid.*, May 27, Aug. 9, 1936.
94. *Ibid.*, July 18 and 21, 1936.
95. New York *Herald Tribune*, July 19, 1936.
96. New York *Times*, Oct. 28, 1936.
97. Advisory Council, Minutes, Sept. 8, 1936.

conservation work, among men and natural resources, be adapted as a part of our permanent national governmental activities, the size and extent of the work to be governed by the dual factors of employment conditions and the urgency of the conservation work to be accomplished."[98] Within three years the CCC had become probably the most highly regarded of all New Deal agencies. Its continuation seemed inevitable.

98. *Report of the Director*, 1936, p. 6.

4. *The Problems of Administration, 1933-1937*

The relationship between the Office of the Director of the CCC and the four co-operating federal departments could in some ways be likened to that between a holding company and its far larger components. Fechner's office was limited in size and in function. The technical services and the War Department were immediately responsible for work and administration; they hired and fired employees, and they implemented camp policy. The director's task, in this respect, was simply to co-ordinate their efforts.[1]

There were, however, certain branches of CCC work directly controlled by Fechner's office, and there were two other assistant directors in addition to McEntee. One was Fechner's legal and administrative adviser, Charles H. Taylor, who also directed the preparation of reports and correspondence. The other was Guy D. McKinney, director of publicity, in charge of press relations and general publicity work. His skilful efforts played an important part in molding a favorable public reaction to the CCC. Other special assistants advised Fechner on procurement and specific legal matters.[2]

Within the central organization there were four separate subagencies, each with its clearly delineated role. They were the Statistical, the Information, the Investigation and Correspondence, and the Safety divisions. The Statistical Division and the Information Division both worked under McKinney's direction. It was the responsibility of the former division to edit and supervise Fechner's reports to the President, while the latter division prepared and distributed information on all CCC activities and helped to co-ordinate the work of the technical agencies. The Investigation and Correspondence Division prepared camp inspection plans, evaluated inspectors' reports, and dealt with general office correspondence. The Safety Division directed the safety program, which was conducted through a committee in each camp. Including clerks, secretaries, and messengers, there

1. Harper, pp. 30-32.
2. *Ibid.*, p. 30; *Report of the Director*, 1935, frontispiece. For an example of McKinney's work, see Guy D. McKinney, "An Army in the Forests," *Natural History*, XXXIV (Feb., 1934), 141-150.

were about fifty people employed in the Washington office of the CCC.[3]

In the field, Fechner's office employed liaison officers, who were hired by the technical services, special investigators, and inspectors. One liaison officer was attached to each of the nine Corps area headquarters, his main duty being to co-ordinate the activities of the participating federal departments. The special investigators were responsible for scrutinizing the administrative conditions in each camp, while the inspectors checked on the work projects to see that they conformed to legal requirements.[4]

Probably more important than the Director's Office as a co-ordinating agency for the whole program was the Advisory Council to the director, authorized on April 5, 1933, by *Executive Order No. 6101.* The intention in creating the council was that it would become a forum for debating policy matters between the director and the four federal departments, a platform where opposing points of view could be heard and reconciled, thus reducing the chance of tension in the field. To this end, each department was originally invited to send one representative to the meetings, but because both McEntee and Fechner wished to attend, the departmental representatives were also allowed to bring an assistant, membership thus rising to ten.

In a comparatively short time, the council grew so large that it was almost unable to function effectively. The Veterans Administration, the Office of Indian Affairs, and the Office of Education all sent representatives to its meetings once they had become connected officially with the CCC. Technical services and War Department membership were therefore increased as a counterweight, until in 1935 twenty-five members were present at one meeting. Attendances of twenty-two were quite common.[5] Though he was a reluctant administrator, Fechner recognized the need for streamlining. On October 9, 1936, therefore, a greatly reduced council met. The number present had been cut back to ten: Fechner, McEntee, and two representatives from each of the four federal departments. Attendance was held at

3. Harper, p. 31.
4. *Ibid.*
5. Advisory Council, Minutes, Oct. 11, Nov. 14, 1935.

this level for the rest of the CCC's existence, though special representatives could be invited to speak if and when the occasion demanded.[6] The council met irregularly, depending on the pressure of business. During the trouble over selection policy in 1935, for example, it met every two or three days,[7] but at other times months would elapse between sessions, often because of Fechner's absences from Washington on visits to camps. Lapses of three to four weeks between meetings were common.[8]

The establishment of the council was a happy decision, for it certainly prevented unnecessary friction in what was already an extremely complex organization. All important policies were thoroughly discussed in advance, points of view expressed, and objections met. The basic decisions concerning selection policy were always propounded at the council meetings, where the War Department's selection and mobilization proposals were closely scrutinized. Departmental suggestions for improving the effectiveness of the work or the camp environment were always given the closest attention.[9]

The council was, as its name implied, purely advisory. None of its decisions was binding on Fechner, and all were subject to veto by the President. Fechner never tried to dominate the council; he used it frequently and respected its advice, though not necessarily agreeing with it.[10] Occasionally, however, Fechner authorized a policy which he personally did not favor, purely because the council had approved it. The safety program was established, for example, in spite of Fechner's strong reservations.[11] Fechner's willingness to use the council helped to maintain the relatively stable relations between the co-operating agencies which were so essential to the success of a complex organization like the CCC. Indeed, one of the reasons for the

6. *Ibid.*, Oct. 9, 1936.

7. *Ibid.*, June 18, 25, and 27, 1935.

8. *Ibid.* For example, the minutes record no meeting between March 23, 1936, and Sept. 8, 1936, a time when Fechner was in the camps. There was no meeting recorded between Dec. 5, 1935, and Feb. 5, 1936, nor between Sept. 8, 1936, and Oct. 9, 1936.

9. *Ibid.*, Feb. 28, 1934, Jan. 17, 1935. Much to the Army's displeasure, the council decided against including rifle shooting as a sport for enrollees for fear of being called a military organization.

10. Wirth, p. 3.

11. Advisory Council, Minutes, April 9, 1934.

increased tension between the director and federal departments in the Corps' last years was Fechner's and McEntee's increasing reluctance to air important policy matters before the council. Meetings were held only rarely, departments were ill-informed on program changes, and the reservoir of good will and co-operation built up earlier began to disintegrate.[12]

Much of the work of the director of the CCC was performed at the direction of the President. Fechner developed in detail policies sketched in outline by Roosevelt; he also issued regulations at the President's behest. In certain fields Fechner had final authority, subject to later presidential review. These principally involved the re-location of work projects and decisions on the type of work to be done on them.[13] Though he sometimes complained about his lack of authority, the director was certainly the most important figure in the CCC organization.[14]

Fechner was painstakingly thorough in his work and devoted to it. At his desk by seven A.M. every working day, he set an example few government officials cared to emulate.[15] Much of his time, however, was spent out of Washington visiting the camps, and it was during these jaunts that he was happiest, returning with long and glowing reports for the President about the success of the work. Indeed, Dean Snyder, assistant to Persons in the Selection Division, thought that Fechner's chief contribution to the CCC organization was in his thorough knowledge of camp conditions, something most Washington officials had little chance to acquire.[16] To the enrollees he was "big boss," and they both respected and loved him. One enrollee expressed his sentiments in the CCC newspaper when he wrote: "The other day, while on his way through Skyland Drive, there was a visitor who stopped to have a talk with us—and a friendly talk it was. As he walked about here and there through the Company Street I was impressed with his kindly attitude toward the men in our

12. Wirth, p. 4.
13. Harper, p. 30. Fechner later received authority over the siting of all work projects.
14. Fechner to Roosevelt, Nov. 2, 1934, Roosevelt Papers, O.F. 268, Box 4.
15. *Literary Digest*, CXXI (April 18, 1936), 48.
16. Nixon, I, 327; interview with Dean Snyder, Dec. 12, 1962.

camp. . . . This man is Mr. Robert Fechner."[17] That was Fechner's way. He loved to visit a camp without ceremony, talk to the boys, commend them, and then move on.

Fechner was no dynamic innovator. He seldom proposed any bold new policies for the Corps himself, and indeed he discouraged others from doing so. This quality of caution, almost certainly a legacy of his long days as a labor conciliator, irritated his younger, university-trained, idealistic colleagues. Snyder thought the director did not sense the possibilities inherent in the CCC. Under Fechner, he was certain that the program suffered "from a lack of co-ordination and integration" in both purpose and organization, and he complained that "Mr. Fechner's office does not seem to tie the program together in an effective way." He thought that Fechner, by being content to coast along instead of grasping the initiative, was "losing an opportunity for constructive action." As an alternative, Snyder looked to the Office of Education to provide some sort of centralizing authority through the education program.[18] Rexford Tugwell also believed Fechner to be unimaginative, and Hopkins claimed he could run the camps for 60 per cent less than Fechner could.[19]

Some of these assertions were doubtless true. Fechner was indeed unimaginative, at least in the sense that he did not share with individuals less close to the Corps their lofty aspirations as to its aims and possibilities. For Fechner, the Corps always had "just two principal objectives—the relief of unemployment, and the accomplishment of useful work." Anything else was "incidental."[20] Furthermore, he had adopted a policy toward Negro enrollees which was not only an unfortunate stain on the CCC's record, but also indicated his imperfect grasp of the possible value of the Corps as a job retraining agency.[21]

It is also true that Fechner seemed inclined to stumble along

17. *Happy Days*, June 17, 1933.
18. Snyder to Persons, April 29, 1936, S.D., Education, Correspondence.
19. Schlesinger, II, 339-340.
20. *To Make the Civilian Corps a Permanent Agency: Hearings Before the Committee on Labor, House of Representatives, 75th Congress, First Session, on H.R. 6180, April 14 and 15, 1937* (Washington, 1937), p. 98-99 (hereinafter cited as *Permanency Hearings*, 1937).
21. See chap. v, below.

administratively, making little attempt to strengthen his own position relative to the co-operating departments, nor to co-ordinate work more effectively. Although he occasionally demanded "more definite authority over the co-operating Federal Departments," there is little evidence to suggest that his situation worried him greatly during the first four years of the CCC.[22] In fact, the only administrative proposal which he pressed with any degree of consistency was his unsuccessful demand that the Civil Service provisions be extended to cover Corps employees and that all future employees first take a non-competitive examination.[23]

Fechner cannot be described as a New Dealer in the same sense as Harry Hopkins, Donald Richberg, or Aubrey Williams, head of the CCC's sister organization, the National Youth Administration.[24] He was never a member of the "inner circle"; his Southern, unionist background stood in stark contrast to those of the Northern, city-bred, Harvard-educated young lawyers who swarmed to Washington in early 1933 and who stayed to administer the New Deal agencies. Unlike them, Fechner had not been trained to innovate, but to conciliate; not to lead, but to suggest. Fechner's background, however, may explain in part why the CCC escaped with so little congressional criticism. Often an agency was branded because of its head. Many congressmen from the South or rural areas distrusted the "new men" who directed most of the New Deal projects. Fechner, by having an environmental rapport with critics of Administration programs, may perhaps have disarmed them and drawn criticism away from the CCC.

22. Fechner to Roosevelt, Nov. 2, 1934, Roosevelt Papers, O.F. 268, Box 4.

23. Fechner to McIntyre, May 4, 1936, *ibid.*, Box 7.

24. The National Youth Administration, like the CCC, was created to help destitute young people, but its original aim was to help them to complete their high school or college education. To this end, students were given part-time work, often related directly to their particular fields of academic interest. The NYA did, however, aid 2.6 million young men and women who had left school by providing them with full-time work. It was a far broader institution than the CCC, broader in the total numbers employed of both sexes, and broader in the type of tasks undertaken. Moreover, the approach was vastly different. The NYA built few camps, concentrating rather on helping young people within their home environment. See William E. Leuchtenburg, *Franklin D. Roosevelt and the New Deal* (New York, 1963), p. 129.

Moreover, Fechner must not be accounted a complete administrative failure. In fact, by refusing to stretch his authority, he probably acted more wisely than he knew. His position was circumscribed, not only by presidential policies, but also by the very size and tradition of the four government departments which co-operated in the CCC enterprise. By attempting to strengthen the Corps' central organization and arrogate more power to himself, he might have created such tensions between the federal departments and the Director's Office that the whole enterprise would have suffered acutely. For the most part, his union experience led him to let sleeping dogs lie, to patch up holes in the organization as they appeared, but not to attempt to change its structure. The Corps functioned reasonably well because of the administrative efficiency and experience of the federal departments. Generally, Fechner was content merely to perpetuate this arrangement, imperfect though it was in some respects. He saw that changes, apparently beneficial, could have unanticipated results—results harmful to the CCC and director-department relations. It is worth noting that when Fechner and his successor, McEntee, attempted some consolidation in the agency's final years, they only succeeded in disrupting existing relationships entirely, to the great detriment of the CCC.[25] Moreover, Fechner had to maintain a working relationship, not only with the co-operating departments, but also with a whole host of government officials, presidential advisers, and, of course, the President himself. In all such dealings he conducted himself with the best interests of the Corps as his guide.

Fechner and Roosevelt had a relatively harmonious relationship. The President sketched broad policy lines, and Fechner translated them into administrative detail. There was a strong common bond between them, in that they were both delighted at the success of the Corps and committed to its progress. Roosevelt always took great encouragement from Fechner's lengthy reports about camp conditions; he enjoyed discussing the progress of the work with him, and Fechner, for his part, found him a good listener.[26] Both Fechner and the President held similar views

25. Wirth, pp. 3-4.
26. Rosenman, ed., *Papers*, III, 423; Nixon, I, 239.

concerning the aims of the CCC. Roosevelt, too, believed that conservation work and unemployment relief were its principal objectives; thus, he implicitly rejected many of the more sophisticated roles suggested from time to time by other Administration officials. For example, he sometimes expressed dissatisfaction with the education program, thinking it to be "too costly and complicated" and likely to interfere with the more important aspects of Corps life. He would never permit working hours to be shortened to allow more teaching. Thus, he usually supported Fechner against any attempt to complicate Corps life or to increase the scope of its endeavor.[27]

It is a commonplace now to assert that the invariably amicable treatment which Roosevelt accorded his officials did not necessarily indicate the depth of his feeling toward them, yet it is probable that his regard for Fechner was indeed genuine. After Fechner's death the President called him a "faithful friend," a man who "did a difficult job admirably."[28] Indeed, in 1939 when Fechner resigned his position because of Roosevelt's administrative reorganization plan which placed the CCC under the Federal Security Agency, the President refused to accept it. He suggested that the director "take an extended leave and rest up, and enjoy it, and then come back," advice which Fechner eventually followed.[29] The regard the two men had for each other was based on mutual respect, mutual love of the land, and mutual participation in the success of the CCC.

Nevertheless, Fechner found the President extremely difficult to work with at times. His bland disregard for rules he himself had made and his penchant for proposing often conflicting policies without considering their implications and impediments greatly irritated Fechner.[30] Thus, though Roosevelt insisted that

27. E.g., Advisory Council, Minutes, March 2, 1934; Nixon, I, 325, 351. Roosevelt turned down a proposal by Ickes to increase the scope of National Park work because Fechner had so recommended.

28. Roosevelt to Gov. Henry Horner, Ill., Jan. 2, 1940, Roosevelt Papers, P.P.F. 6386.

29. Advisory Council, Minutes, May 26, 1939.

30. Fechner, of course, was not alone in becoming exasperated at Roosevelt's disregard of established administrative practices when it suited him. Most New Deal officials who had any contact with the President complained of the same "occupational hazard." See Schlesinger, II, 533-552.

costs be kept as low as possible, he still arranged with the commander of the Salvation Army to have wood delivered from the camps to the nearest city free of charge, at a cost to the Corps which, Fechner wrote in anguish, "would be prohibitive." Fortunately, in this instance, Harry Hopkins agreed with him, and the operation was restricted to Washington, D.C.[31] The President's frequent requests that Fechner provide camps to suit deserving congressmen were other irritants. In October, 1933, for example, he asked Fechner to "get one or two camps for Congressman Algood's district" and blithely disregarded Fechner's plea that to do so would upset arrangements on camp distribution which Roosevelt had originally approved.[32] In time Fechner came to view these requests as an "occupational hazard," yet he never failed to be angered by them.

More important, however, were Roosevelt's ventures into the broad field of expansion policy, actions which have already been considered and which showed clearly the President's preference for the grand design and his lack of appreciation of the full consequences of his proposals. Fechner argued in vain that only unfortunate effects would come of the decision in 1935 to reduce enrolment from 500,000 to 300,000 by July 1, 1936. The President stood firm beside his plan, and Fechner, despite his objections, had to work out the details. Indeed, it took the congressional revolt of 1936 to change the President's mind. Still, in spite of occasional friction, Fechner and Roosevelt maintained a good working relationship. In his dealings with some of the President's advisers, the director was perhaps less fortunate.

With the departure of Louis Howe from the center of the Administration because of illness, and especially after the passage of the $4.8 billion relief measure, the man with most influence on CCC policy was Harry Hopkins, director of the WPA. His attempt to control enrolment in 1935 was thought by Fechner to be only the most blatant example of Hopkins' un-

31. McIntyre to Fechner and Hopkins, Nov. 13, 1933, McIntyre to Early, Nov. 20, 1933, Hopkins to Howe, Nov. 2, 1933, Roosevelt Papers, O.F. 268, Box 3.

32. Roosevelt to Fechner, Oct. 11, 1933, Fechner to Roosevelt, Feb. 19, 1934, *ibid.* This was Rep. Miles C. Algood (Dem., Ala.).

warranted interference into CCC affairs.[33] Their rivalry had begun in 1934, when they had disagreed over drought relief policy. Hopkins at this time had told Fechner that the cost structure of camp operation was too high and boasted that he could run the camps for one-third less.[34] Direct contact between the two men was less frequent after July, 1936, when the CCC was no longer provided for out of the multipurpose relief appropriation, but there is no evidence to suggest that they ever became friends. Though engaged in similar work, their differences in character, outlook, and abilities were too great to admit of any sustained personal contact.

Similarly, Fechner had his troubles with the Bureau of the Budget. Here the problem was not so much one of a personality clash as of the complete antipathy of the budget director, Lewis Douglas, to New Deal fiscal policies. Douglas opposed spending and public works; he therefore opposed the CCC and often entreated the President to dissolve the organization. "History demonstrates," he once wrote, the futility of attempting to beat depression by "huge government expenditures," and the CCC fell "naturally within the category of those things which we might like to do, but which in the public interest we cannot and should not do."[35] Because of his attitude, any scheme for the CCC which involved spending was bound to be vehemently opposed. Douglas deplored the purchase of land for reforestation purposes, for instance, and disapproved of extending the work to Alaska. To Fechner, his resignation in August, 1934, must have brought great relief; under his successor, Daniel Bell, the Bureau of the Budget proved much more co-operative.[36]

Fechner also had difficulties within the CCC organization proper, especially with those officials connected with the education program who were bitterly critical of his casual attitude

33. Advisory Council, Minutes, Oct. 11, 1935; see also chaps. ii and iii, above.

34. *Ibid.*, June 9, 1934. Hopkins' causticity, candor, and shrewdness irritated many others besides Fechner. See Schlesinger, III, 351-361. Hopkins' various claims regarding the CCC were not always consistent. See above, p. 75.

35. Douglas to Roosevelt, Dec. 30, 1933, Roosevelt Papers, O.F. 268, Box 1; see also Douglas to Roosevelt, Jan. 24, 1934, *ibid.*, Box 3.

36. Nixon, I, 160, 208; Douglas to Roosevelt, Sept. 26, 1933, Roosevelt Papers, O.F. 268, Box 2; Schlesinger, II, 289-292.

toward the development of camp educational work. Matters came to a head when Fechner barred a booklet, *You and Machines*, published by the Office of Education, from use in the camps. The work, written by William G. Ogburn of the University of Chicago, purported to stress to the enrollees the need for them to adjust to the machine age or "machines will enslave government, family and church."[37] To Fechner, the whole message of the pamphlet was "too gloomy." It would "inculcate a philosophy of despair, not a healthy questioning attitude"; consequently he ordered its removal from all camps.[38] This action brought the wrath of such groups as the National Education Association and the American Association of University Professors upon his head, but he refused to rescind the order.[39] The booklet remained banned, and another link was forged in the chain of animosity between Fechner and the Office of Education.

Fechner's relations with the War Department and the technical services were remarkably good during the first few years of the CCC's existence, because he made no attempt to direct too closely their operations in the camps but merely kept a supervisory eye on the whole enterprise. From time to time, of course, dissension arose, most of which was settled at the Advisory Council level without causing the CCC much pain. The War Department, always jealous of its authority, seriously objected to Fechner's position on enrollee discipline. At one time Fechner had reinstated about 50 per cent of the enrollees dropped by the Army for breaches of regulations, and this action was considered so damaging to military authority that the War Department's Advisory Council representative, Colonel Major, threatened that "it will be brought to the attention of the President." The matter was settled by compromise, and a possible disruption of relations was averted.[40] Later the Army would occasionally insist that some policy considered detrimental to military interests be modified, but in general the War Department restricted its role to administering policy, not formulating or criticizing it.[41]

37. New York *Times*, Nov. 16, 1934.
38. Fechner to Adjutant General, Nov. 2, 1934, C.R.M., Appendix III.
39. New York *Times*, Nov. 25, Dec. 2, 1934.
40. Advisory Council, Minutes, Sept. 21, 1933, Feb. 5 and 24, 1934.
41. *Ibid.*, Nov. 21, 1934. Col. Major objected violently to the seating

Fechner's relations with the secretary of agriculture and his field representatives were similarly harmonious. The Department of Agriculture had the lion's share of the camps, and the secretary, Henry Wallace, enthusiastically supported CCC work, backing Fechner completely in his protests against camp closings in 1935.[42] As long as Fechner refrained from attempting to direct specific work policy too closely, the Department of Agriculture was well satisfied.

It was with the Department of the Interior and its irascible secretary, Harold L. Ickes, that Fechner experienced the most trouble. Ickes and the director were not personally compatible; Ickes rarely found Fechner "co-operative."[43] More important, the secretary was most dissatisfied with the Corps' organization, and particularly with the subsidiary role of his department in relation to that of the Department of Agriculture. Ickes, who had himself wanted to head a Department of Conservation, was convinced that the number of camps allotted to the Department of the Interior (for instance, 497 out of a proposed 1,456 in 1936-1937) was always far too meager,[44] and he frequently badgered Fechner for more. The director usually ignored Ickes' complaints, and as Fechner had the firm backing of the President, the secretary could do little about it.[45] Ickes always regarded the Director's Office with acute disfavor, and in later years he was to advocate its abolition.[46] Other officials of the Department of the Interior were less antagonistic. For example, Conrad Wirth, Advisory Council representative, thought the "CCC was well-organized, and that the co-operation of all participating agencies and officials was excellent" because of "Director Fechner's ability and leadership."[47]

Apart from a disagreement on Negro selection policy,[48]

---

of project assistants on boards of discipline because he considered this would undermine military authority.

42. Wallace to Roosevelt, Dec. 6, 1935, Files of the Secretary of Agriculture—Conservation.

43. Ickes, *Diary*, II, *The Inside Struggle, 1936-1939* (New York, 1954), 375. Ickes, of course, rarely found anyone to be "co-operative." See Schlesinger, II, 282-283.

44. Ickes, *Diary*, II, 8, 23; Ickes to Fechner, Dec. 2, 1935, Secretary of Interior, Records; Nixon, I, 351.

45. Nixon, I, 474.

46. *Ibid.*, II, 416.

47. Wirth, p. 3.

48. See chap. v, below.

Fechner had few differences with the Department of Labor, which acted as the chief agent for CCC selection. Though Persons, the director of CCC selection, did oppose Fechner's plan in 1935 to extend the age limit to thirty-five, most of the difficulties which the Selection Division had to surmount were encountered at the state and local level.[49] There the job was to convince local agents that the CCC was not to be regarded as a dumping ground for delinquency cases, parollees, or youths who were obviously under seventeen years. This task was attempted mainly by moral suasion. Letters were sent frequently to all agents stressing the need to select the "best available young men," and explaining that "the selection of those likely to be unadaptable to camp life and who would quickly eliminate themselves from the Corps is to be avoided as both unsuitable to such young men and as a loss to the government and the community."[50] Such warnings were usually effective enough, but in the last resort quotas could be withheld pending compliance with regulations.[51]

There were, of course, certain tensions—not of Fechner's making—between the federal departments. The troubles arose out of a long history of interdepartmental rivalry transferred to the context of the CCC. Most had to do with the overlapping of functions between the Department of Agriculture and the Department of the Interior. Probably the most significant, as it affected the CCC, was the dispute over soil erosion work. By 1935 it was apparent that there was considerable duplication of function between erosion camps working under the Forest Service and those of the Soil Conservation Service in the Department of the Interior.[52] The matter was brought to the conference table, where representatives of both departments recognized the division of responsibility but could not agree on a solution. The President intervened, strongly backed by Fechner, and the result was the transfer of the Soil Conservation Service to the Department of

49. Fechner to Persons, July 24, 1934, S.D., Correspondence, Discussion of Selection Policy, 1935.

50. E.g., Persons to State Directors, Dec. 19, 1936, March 11, 1937, S.D. Correspondence, Selection Policy, 1937.

51. Interview with Dean Snyder, Dec. 12, 1962.

52. Hugh H. Bennett, director, Soil Conservation Service, to Ickes, Feb. 3, 1935, in Nixon, I, 357.

Agriculture, an administrative move which did nothing to improve relations between the secretary of the interior and the director of the CCC.[53] There were other minor disputes, especially the frequent complaint of the Forest Service that the Army was usurping its prerogative in the field, but such squabbles were to be expected in such an organizational amalgam.[54]

By far the biggest task in the CCC program, that of administering the camps, was, of course, the War Department's responsibility. For this purpose the country was divided into nine Corps areas, each one usually commanded by a major general or brigadier general. The Corps areas were in turn divided into districts (comprising one or more states), whose commanding officers were stationed at designated Army posts. Their chief function was to interpret the voluminous messages from Corps area headquarters to the individual camps. At each district headquarters there was usually an executive officer, an adjutant, a chaplain, and a medical officer.[55]

The final administrative unit was the camp. Here the commanding officer was most often a captain or first lieutenant in the Regular Army or Army Reserve, assisted by one or more younger officers and a varying number of enrollee leaders. The

53. Roosevelt to Wallace, March 27, 1935, C.R.M., No. 783, Soil Erosion.

54. E.g., Stuart to Wallace, July 17, 1933, *ibid.*, No. 782(2), Hammatt, Source Data.

55. Harper, pp. 39-41. The number of camps in each state varied according to the total number of camps in existence at any particular time, but the proportions remained similar throughout the CCC's life span. On June 30, 1935, when there were 2,110 camps in all, the number of camps in each state was as follows (see *Report of the Director*, 1935, Appendix D):

California	155	Ohio	40	Oklahoma	23
Pennsylvania	113	Kansas	39	South Carolina	23
Michigan	103	North Carolina	38	Arizona	22
Wisconsin	103	Vermont	37	Connecticut	21
Illinois	88	Kentucky	34	Wyoming	20
Missouri	88	Mississippi	34	Maine	19
Idaho	82	Georgia	33	North Dakota	19
Oregon	75	Montana	32	Utah	19
Minnesota	74	Colorado	31	New Mexico	17
New York	69	South Dakota	31	West Virginia	17
Washington	69	Indiana	29	Maryland	15
Virginia	63	Nebraska	27	Nevada	14
Massachusetts	58	New Jersey	26	Rhode Island	7
Tennessee	57	Louisiana	25	Delaware	3
Texas	55	Alabama	24	Dist. Columbia	2
Arkansas	50	Florida	23		
Iowa	41	New Hampshire	23		

officer's tour of duty was supposedly six months, but it was almost always extended indefinitely. The commanding officer's functions included the complete charge of the camp, the personnel administration, and the welfare of the men. He was responsible for all matters of discipline and was authorized to implement a range of punishments from simple admonition for minor offenses to dishonorable discharge for more serious misdemeanors such as refusal to work, desertion, or unwillingness to abide by camp rules.[56] The second in command had a variety of duties to perform, frequently combining the functions of finance officer, motor transport officer, quartermaster, and, before the educational advisers were appointed, welfare officer. There was also a medical officer, again usually taken from the Regular Army or the Army Reserve, for every two or more camps; he was assisted by two first-aid men selected from the enrollees.[57]

Initially, the Army had undertaken its CCC role with undisguised reluctance, and most top officers never regarded the Corps with complete favor. Nevertheless, by 1937 most of them were willing to concede that the connection had its good points. The CCC proved to be a valuable training ground in command techniques for both regulars and reservists. In fact, the secretary of war thought it the most valuable experience the Army had ever had.[58] In addition, most War Department officials were realistic enough to recognize that there was simply no other agency capable of administering a project as huge and complex as the CCC and that their continued association with it was inevitable.

For many liberal Americans the Army connection was something to be regarded with the gravest suspicion, and for some it was sufficient to render the CCC completely unacceptable. There were, of course, unpleasant sides to the Army's control of the camps. Interference with education programs, suppression of radical ideas, ambivalence on the question of Negro enrollment—all these charges can validly be laid at the military's door. In addition, some of the Corps area commanders were too fond of treating the CCC as a reservoir for the Regular Army. Major

56. Harper, pp. 45-46.
57. *Ibid.*, pp. 47-49.
58. Perkins, p. 179.

General George Van Horn Moseley, for example, commander of the Fourth Corps Area, who was strongly dissatisfied with the existing non-military arrangement, consistently advocated complete militarization of the Corps.[59]

Neither the excoriations of Moseley nor the equivocation of other high-ranking Army officers, however, represented adequately the scope of military attitudes toward the CCC. Effective contact was made principally at the camp level, and here the Army's role was much more positive. By 1936 only 3 per cent of the camp commanders were Regulars; the rest were from the Reserves. The majority of these had been through civilian colleges and were often non-military in their points of view. Not a few had themselves been unemployed, and their sympathies often lay more with the enrollees than with their superior officers. As camp commanders they effectively muted the harsher aspects of Army discipline and control.[60]

The attitude of the military is one of the reasons why close comparisons cannot be drawn between the CCC and the German Labor Service as it was modified under Hitler. By 1935 enrolment in the German agency was compulsory for all young men between the ages of eighteen and twenty-six, regardless of their economic situation. Its function had also broadened. No longer simply involved with relief and conservation, it was now concerned with the molding of character along Nazi lines through massive indoctrination and with preliminary military instruction. The martial caste of Hitler's camps was frankly admitted and thoroughly emphasized.[61] The CCC did not develop similar characteristics; to have done so would have meant opposing the whole course of American history. The Corps always remained a voluntary organization concerned primarily with relief and conservation, with its wider functions never clarified. Despite close military participation in its organization, it was essentially non-military in concept when it began, and, in keeping with the basic

59. See chaps. v, vi, below; Rawick, pp. 132-136. Moseley, who revealed himself in his unpublished autobiography to be a man of decidedly fascist sympathies, also believed in the basic inferiority of Negroes and in the sterilization of all Jews "and their eventual elimination from the human family." In order to save the United States, he thought a five-year plan should be implemented, civil liberties should be suspended, and the country placed under the control of General MacArthur.

60. Saalberg, pp. 52-53.

61. Roberts, pp. 211-218.

beliefs of the Army officers themselves, it always remained so.

The organization of the camp field staff of the Department of Agriculture and the Department of the Interior closely paralleled that of the War Department, though differing in its regional characteristics according to the branch or service involved. There was a project superintendent in each camp, assisted by eight to ten foremen. He was responsible for developing the work project, drawing up instructions to aid his foremen, and organizing the enrollees into small work groups.[62] The actual organization varied, depending again on the particular service. The Forest Service usually divided its camp complement into two platoons of ninety-five or ninety-six men, which were in turn divided into three sections each under a section foreman. The sections were further divided into subsections with an enrollee in charge of each, and the subsections were broken up into squads of six or seven men.[63]

The field organization of the National Parks Service was slightly different. Each camp had attached to it an experienced engineer, a technical forester, trained landscape men, and history and wildlife technicians, all of whom worked under the direction of the project supervisor. The company was divided into sections and subsections, each led by one of these men, and performing its own particular function.[64] Other services had similar organization policies. The Department of Labor had no such field service, apart from employing a selection agent in each state to coordinate local efforts. The bulk of the work was performed by local bodies, county and city relief and welfare agencies, whose services were unpaid.[65]

Obviously the success of such a complex field structure depended in large part on individual camp conditions. Where project superintendent and camp commander were able to cooperate, good work was done; where there was antagonism, the result was less satisfactory. Friction was no doubt often latent for reasons as numerous as there were camps, but the outstanding work record of the CCC would indicate that harmony between the Army and the technical service was probably the norm.

62. Harper, p. 65.
63. *Ibid.*, p. 43.
64. *Ibid.*, pp. 65-66.
65. *Ibid.*, p. 35.

5. *The Selection of Negroes, 1933-1937*

The act of March 31, 1933, which gave the CCC legal existence, contained the clause: "That in employing citizens for the purpose of this Act, no discrimination shall be made on account of race, color, and creed."[1] The intention was clearly to protect the rights of Negro citizens within the CCC organization, but these mere words did not insure them full benefits from the newly created agency.

Certainly the plight of the American Negroes was desperate. The depression had added further misery to their normal condition of chronic poverty. In 1933 Negro unemployment rates were double the national average, and more than two million Negroes were on relief, twice as many as there should have been in terms of national population figures. In Northern states Negro laborers found that the adage "first fired, last hired" rang bitterly true, while in the South the depression had erased even the structure of traditionally "Negro" jobs. White men now cleaned the streets in Atlanta or collected garbage in Memphis, and Negro deprivation was compounded. Federal relief schemes like the CCC were almost all that was left for them.[2]

Scarcely had selection begun, however, when reports from the South indicated that in that desperately poor region local selection agents were deliberately excluding Negroes from all CCC activities. Particularly deplorable were events in Georgia, which had a Negro population of 1,071,125 in 1930, or 36 per cent of the total state population.[3] On May 2, 1933, an Atlanta resident, W. H. Harris, protested to the secretary of labor that in Clarke County, Georgia, with a 60 per cent Negro population, no non-whites had yet been selected for CCC work.[4] Persons, director of CCC selection, immediately demanded an explanation from the Georgia state director of selection, John de la Perriere. The Georgia director blandly replied that all applications

1. *Report of the Director*, 1933, Appendix A.

2. Dixon Wechter, *The Age of the Great Depression 1929-41* (New York, 1948), p. 162; Schlesinger, III, 425-438; Searle F. Charles, *Minister of Relief: Harry Hopkins and the Depression* (Syracuse, 1963), pp. 26-27.

3. Will Alexander to Persons, June 12, 1933, S.D., Correspondence, Negro Selection.

4. W. H. Harris to Secretary of Labor, May 2, 1933, *ibid.*

for CCC enrolment in Clarke County were "classed A, B and C. All colored applications fell into the classes B and C. The A class being the most needy, the selections were made from same."[5] Persons continued to insist that selections be made regardless of race, but reports trickling in from other Georgia counties indicated that de la Perriere was ignoring his orders. Jessie O. Thomas, secretary of the Atlanta branch of the National Urban League, complained on May 9 that in Washington County, Georgia, no Negroes were included in the first fifty men selected, although in that county too the population was more than 60 per cent Negro.[6] Persons was reluctant to take stronger measures at this time, however, stressing to Fechner the importance to the success of the CCC in the South of adjusting the matter locally "without any apparent intervention from Washington."[7] The extent of his action, then, was merely to write to de la Perriere and other Georgia officials demanding that they treat Negro applicants fairly.

On May 19 a long telegram from the widely respected Southern liberal, Will Alexander, director of the Committee on Interracial Co-operation in Atlanta and later head of the Farm Security Administration, spurred Persons into a more positive approach. Alexander claimed that local committees in Georgia were not registering Negroes, nor did they believe that the federal government was serious in directing them to do so. He contended that the men in charge of Georgia's relief measures were "rural politicians," devout adherents to the dogma of white supremacy, and as a result of their discrimination the Communists had been given a strong opportunity "for further agitation" in their drive for Negro support. Alexander pleaded for more decisive federal action.[8]

Upon receipt of the telegram, Persons immediately telephoned de la Perriere, who admitted that Negroes were not being selected, but denied that this was due to racial discrimination. Rather, he insisted that "at this time of the farming period

5. De la Perriere to Persons, May 5, 1933, *ibid.*
6. Jessie O. Thomas to Secretary of Labor, May 9, 1933, *ibid.*
7. Persons to Fechner, May 5, 1933, *ibid.*
8. Alexander to Persons, May 19, 1933, *ibid.* The Farm Security Administration was a New Deal agency created in 1937 to deal specifically with the economic problems of the tenant farmer.

in the State, it is vitally important that negroes remain in the counties for chopping cotton and for planting other produce. The negroes in this way are able to obtain work on the farms throughout the state."[9] Since this optimistic picture of full Negro employment did not coincide with figures on the state of Negro joblessness in Georgia, Persons asked de la Perriere for a definite commitment to increasing Negro enrolment. When this was not forthcoming, he called Governor Eugene Talmadge. At first Talmadge showed few signs of co-operating, but when Persons threatened to withhold Georgia quotas entirely unless Negroes were selected, the governor reluctantly agreed to "instruct Mr. de la Perriere" to proceed with their enrolment.[10]

The Selection Division had won its first battle, though not without further tribulations. Indeed, de la Perriere protested to Persons on June 1 that county committees believed that "there are few negro families who . . . need an income as great as $25 a month in cash,"[11] hence their reluctance to enrol them. Nevertheless, Fechner was able to report to the President that Negroes were at last being enrolled in Georgia, though "not as many as the Department of Labor would like."[12] Persons, however, realized the basic weakness of his position. He knew that the attitudes of local communities in Georgia could not be revolutionized "by means of our own transitory contacts with the race problem in that state," and he was satisfied with what small gains he had made.[13]

Georgia was not the only Southern state to balk at the selection of Negroes on the same basis as white enrollees. The state director of Florida, John C. Huskisson, reported: "on the basis of merit, no negroes have yet been selected for the CCC." After Persons had applied pressure, Huskisson agreed to "lower his standards" enough to accommodate two hundred Negroes, though he refused to select them at the same depots as whites.[14]

9. Persons to de la Perriere (telephone conversation report), May 19, 1933, *ibid.*

10. Persons to Talmadge (telephone conversation report), May 19, 1933, *ibid.* Talmadge later became a violent critic of CCC work.

11. Persons to Secretary of Labor, June 1, 1933, *ibid.*

12. Fechner to Roosevelt, June 1, 1933, *ibid.*

13. Persons to Secretary of Labor, June 1, 1933, *ibid.*

14. Persons' memorandum for files, May 19, 1933, *ibid.*

Similarly, after investigating an NAACP complaint of discrimination in Arkansas, Persons again threatened to withhold quotas. The state's indignant relief director, William A. Rooksbery, unequivocally denied the charge that no Negroes had been selected. No less than three had in fact been enrolled, he protested, but Persons was unimpressed, and told him so. The chastened state official promised to induct more within the following few weeks.[15] In Alabama, on the other hand, Persons won the cooperation of the state director of relief, Thad Holt, who was willing to select Negroes but found that some local councils were "trying to force" them not to enrol. Persons once more threatened to withhold quotas pending compliance with the law.[16]

Gradually, therefore, by combining pressure and persuasion, Persons was able to insist that Southern state directors enrol at least a token number of Negroes in their CCC quotas. By June 12, Georgia had selected 178 and Alabama 776. Mississippi, with a Negro population of more than 50 per cent, had the poorest record with forty-six, or only 1.7 per cent of the total enrolment; South Carolina, also with a Negro population of more than 50 per cent, had the best record of Negro enrolment with 36 per cent of the state's total.[17] The effort expended in effecting these modest returns, however, was an ominous preview of what was to follow throughout the country as the CCC tried to place its Negro enrollees in work camps.

It was never the policy of CCC officials to attempt to create a nationwide system of integrated camps. Given the custom of the era, to do so would have invited trouble. From the first, the mixing of the races was usually permitted only in those regions where Negro enrolment was so slight that no Negro company could be formed. Elsewhere, Negroes were usually assigned to all-Negro camps.

It was soon obvious that the success of Negro camps was conditional on winning the acquiescence of the local communities in their establishment. This was no easy task. No sooner had such

15. W. A. Rooksbery, director of relief, Ark., to Persons, June 2, 1933, *ibid.*

16. Thad Holt to Persons (telephone conversation report), May 20, 1933, *ibid.*

17. Will Alexander to Persons, June 12, 1933, *ibid.*

camps been occupied than angry complaints began to flood Fechner's office insisting that they be filled with white enrollees or be removed.[18] In an effort to relieve local tension, Fechner quickly ruled that no Negro was to be transported outside his own state, and that all Negro campsites were to be selected by the state's governor, but even these moves had little effect in quelling local apprehension.[19]

The South was not alone in such agitation; rather, as Fechner once bitterly attested, "there was far less protest" on this matter from Southern communities than from other regions.[20] The director complained that "there is hardly a locality in this country that looks favorably, or even with indifference, on the location of a Negro CCC camp in their vicinity."[21] The reasons for the disinclination to accept Negro camps varied in detail from locality to locality but were similar in general trend. Residents feared the effect of a large body of Negroes on the social stability of their community. They anticipated great increases in drunkenness and other social vices, and, in particular, they feared for the safety of white women and children. The citizens of Thornhurst, in Lackawanna County, Pennsylvania, for example, hearing a rumor that a Negro CCC camp would be established in their area, petitioned Fechner "righteously and vigorously" for its removal. While "truly disavowing any prejudice against those people on account of race and color," the petition drew attention to the social danger of "isolating so great a number of unattached Negro males" in an area occupied "permanently and exclusively by white people." The petition added:

> Many of these, especially unescorted women of various ages, are obliged . . . to travel by the site of these camps and along the highways thereabouts at all hours of the day and night. Among the families who live . . . at Thornhurst . . . are to be found scores of boys and girls just attaining youth and early womanhood who should not be exposed to dangers that are possible, if not indeed, probable.[22]

18. Advisory Council, Minutes, June 26, 1933.
19. Fechner to Rep. J. G. Polk (Dem., O.), Oct. 20, 1934, to Gov. Herbert Lehman, N.Y., April 3, 1937, in Director, Correspondence.
20. Fechner to W. G. Still, Morton, Miss., Sept. 16, 1935, *ibid.*
21. Fechner to Polk, Oct. 30, 1934, *ibid.*
22. H. S. Sage, chairman, Citizens and Residents of Thornhurst, Pa., to Fechner, Aug. 1, 1935, *ibid.*

Similar protests came from most parts of the country. Residents of Washington, D.C., protested the establishment of a Negro camp near a residential area where "women are left alone."[23] In Ligonia, Indiana, according to a petitioner, "women were afraid to venture on the streets after nightfall," so frightened were they of the enrollees from a nearby Negro camp. These youths, he alleged, periodically "go on a rampage and they do not appear to be responsible to any of the officers of the camp on such occasions."[24] Citizens of Contra Costa County, California, noted that members of a Negro company there were frequently "in an intoxicated condition" and that the camp was "a menace to the peace and quiet of the community."[25] Fechner vainly insisted that there had not been "one single case where the conduct of Negro enrollees in the CCC camps had disturbed the peace and quiet of any community."[26] Negro camps were simply not welcome in most localities.

Almost all of the glimpses of moderation on the issue came, perhaps paradoxically, from some Southern communities, particularly in Alabama, where a well-rounded Negro CCC program developed by Governor Bibb Graves performed much useful work.[27] Arkansas citizens, too, accepted with equanimity many Negro camps. Residents of Laurens County, Georgia, considering themselves "above prejudice" in racial matters, successfully petitioned Fechner for the establishment of a Negro soil erosion camp in their vicinity. White citizens of Morton, Mississippi, declared that they had had no trouble with the two Negro camps in their district and predicted that if only the protesting communities could see the high standard of the work accomplished, they "would be glad to get them instead of some white camps."[28] But such isolated gestures could not balance the widespread hostility to Negro camps. Fechner himself never attempted to

23. Petition to Fechner, Oct. 26, 1934, *ibid.*
24. Ira G. Shobe, Ligonia, Ind., to Fechner, Oct. 3, 1934, *ibid.*
25. Sen. W. G. McAdoo (Dem., Calif.), to Fechner, Aug. 30, 1935, *ibid.*
26. Fechner to H. S. Sage, Aug. 5, 1935, *ibid.*
27. Fechner to Persons, April 18, 1935, S.D., Correspondence, Negro Selection.
28. Sen. Joseph Robinson to Fechner, June 6, 1935, Laurens County Chamber of Commerce to Fechner, Aug. 14, 1935, W. G. Still to Fechner, Sept. 14, 1935, in Director, Correspondence.

force communities to accept them. If protests showed no signs of abating, he usually removed the camps and either cancelled them or placed them on an Army reservation. He was "a Southerner by birth and raising," he said frequently, and "clearly understood the Negro problem."[29] He was reluctant, therefore, to force the issue.

At the same time that Fechner was being petitioned to remove Negro camps, other sources pressed for expanded Negro participation. The NAACP and similar Negro action groups were constantly complaining about discrimination in CCC selection, and, although not all their assertions were well founded, it was clear that Persons had not convinced most selection agents that Negroes should be given an equal chance to enrol.[30] Some appealed directly to the President. Alton Wright, superintendent of the Colored Rescue Mission, Inc., of Kansas City, protested to Roosevelt that "Negroes can't get into the CCC" and that "no-one seems to care."[31] In Delaware, where the state's potential Negro enrolment was insufficient to justify a separate Negro company, yet where racial feeling did not permit of integrated camps, no Negroes at all could be enrolled. When that state's outraged relief director sought redress, Fechner told her that the nonexistence of CCC opportunity for Delaware's Negroes was a fact "she would have to accept."[32] "Just a Colored Mother" wondered "if war was declared, would they pick all the white boys first and leave the negro boys as the last called for service? This is what they do in the CCC."[33] An investigation by the Julius Rosenwald Fund brought the whole question of discrimination squarely to the director's attention. The fund found that "Negroes have not been placed in CCC jobs at anything like their proportion of the population, to say nothing of their greater need of employment as indicated by relief statistics." The fund's report asked Persons if he "could select 863 white juniors in the

29. Fechner to Sen. Robinson, April 22, 1935, *ibid.*

30. Roy Wilkins, assistant secretary, NAACP, to Fechner, Nov. 8, 1933, June 7, 1934, July 31, 1934, *ibid.*

31. Alton Wright to Roosevelt, Nov. 2, 1934, *ibid.*

32. Fechner to Miss Ethelda Mullen, director, Delaware Emergency Relief Assn., Oct. 13, 1934, *ibid.*

33. "Just a Colored Mother" to Roosevelt, June 16, 1935, S.D., Correspondence, Negro Selection.

State of Florida, and only 18 Negro juniors without discrimination against Negroes."[34]

Negro complaints were not confined solely to matters of enrolment policy. The Administration had decided that Negroes would not be widely employed in Negro camps in any position of authority other than that of educational adviser,[35] a ruling predictably opposed by the leading Negro spokesmen. Fechner justified the policy on the grounds that the only way to get communities to accept Negro companies "was on the assurance that white supervisors would be in charge of the camps. Because of the practical difficulties of the situation it had not been felt desirable to extend the appointment of Negroes to include any large responsibilities."[36] Negro pressure groups carried their protests to the President, who decided in 1936 that a few Negro officers and supervisory personnel should be used in the camps. Some white groups, of course, bitterly opposed the extension of any responsibility in the camps to Negroes as "detrimental to the best interests" of the Corps and the country.[37]

In 1934 Fechner, in an attempt to unravel the tangled threads of the Negro problem, asked the War Department to undertake a full investigation of Negro enrolment and placement. The Army reported varying practices in each Corps area. In the New England states, for example, there were about 250 Negroes assigned to sixty-eight mainly white companies, and similar conditions prevailed in most other areas. Strict segregation was maintained in the South, but in all other regions, though segregated camps predominated, Negroes were attached to many white companies. Some had even been sent out of their home state, strictly contrary to Fechner's ruling. The Army realized that such a situa-

34. Garth H. Akridge, field agent, Julius Rosenwald Fund, to Persons, March 10, 1935, *ibid.* "Junior" was the term used to describe enrollees between eighteen and twenty-five years of age, as distinct from veterans, Indians, and other special enrollees.

35. Fechner to Howe, April 4, 1934, Director, Correspondence.

36. Fechner to Rep. Thomas C. Hennings (Dem., Mo.), Sept. 3, 1935, Roosevelt Papers, O.F. 268, Box 6.

37. Stephen Early to Fechner, Nov. 13, 1936, *ibid.*, O.F. 268–Misc., Box 18; Judge R. T. Sessions, Ashdown, Ark., to Robinson, Sept. 23, 1935, and Sen. J. H. Overton (Dem., La.) to Fechner, Dec. 7, 1936, in Director, Correspondence. For a fuller discussion of this particular aspect of the Negro question, see chap. xi, below.

tion was not satisfactory, but recommended against change because the maintenance of strictly segregated camps in all Corps areas would only increase the number of Negro units and compound the problem of their placement.[38]

Fechner's response, however, was unequivocal. He ordered that all Negroes in camps outside their home states were to be repatriated as soon as possible, that they be replaced by white enrollees, and that strict segregation was to be maintained in all Corps areas. There was to be absolutely no latitude allowed. He claimed that only by maintaining rigid segregation would he check racial violence within the camps. Such violence, however, had been a negligible factor in the context of the whole problem.[39] What Fechner had done, in fact, was to exacerbate greatly his own difficulties by increasing the need for Negro campsites without doing anything to lessen the prejudice in local areas against their establishment. His policy on placement would therefore have to be firmer or else Negro enrolment would surely have to be curtailed. It is hard to understand why he made this decision, so contrary to Army advice, unless he was strongly influenced by personal beliefs and prejudices. A Southerner himself, his absorption of the social mores of that region may have been so complete that he preferred not to act as head of an organization which permitted even the smallest amount of racial intermingling.

The Army report also confirmed what reports from the field had long indicated: in defiance of the provisions of the CCC Act and Persons' repeated instructions, local authorities were using a definite quota system in the selection of Negro enrollees. Negroes were chosen in most areas only as vacancies occurred in Negro camps. Furthermore, this quota system had been established with the direct cognizance and encouragement of area and district military authorities. Several state selection agents reported to Persons that Army authorities had refused to accept Negro selectees because they had "no vacancies for colored

38. Maj. C. P. Gross to Fechner, Aug. 27, 1934, *ibid.*

39. Fechner to Gross, Sept 10, 1934, *ibid.* Often those few Negroes who were placed in predominantly white camps were among the most popular enrollees there. See Holland and Hill, p. 112.

men,"[40] and actually had notified selection agents how many, if any, Negro enrollees were required from each particular district.[41]

To Persons, such policies blatantly contravened both the spirit and letter of the CCC legislation. He strongly emphasized to the Advisory Council that "the Department of Labor is responsible for the enforcement and observance of the law. The law definitely states that there must be no discrimination, and it [the Department] cannot be put in the position of discriminating against the negro race. We have been placed in an intolerable position."[42] In his dealings with state directors, Persons was insistent that they adhere rigidly to the Labor Department's position. To the Missouri state director, Wallace Crossley, he wrote: "Arbitrary colored quotas are not to be established by the selecting agencies, nor are limitations amounting to discrimination to be placed in the way of qualified applicants voluntarily desiring the privilege of enrollment."[43] To a New Jersey official, he demanded that all Negro eligibles be accommodated, even if it meant camp reorganization.[44]

The basic fault lay not entirely in the local area, however, as the Missouri selection director recognized when he retorted to Persons that he would enrol more Negroes when his state got more Negro camps.[45] By insisting on the dual policy of rigid segregation and confinement to the home state, Fechner had closed the two safety valves selection agents could use, while his reluctance to override local protests in placing Negro camps put definite limits on their expansion. Given these restrictions, state directors were forced to use a quota system, in spite of Persons' strong protests. Fechner himself was leaning more and more toward authorizing a definite restriction of Negro enrolment as the easiest solution to the problem. He told the Advisory Council: "I think we can easily defend and justify a policy of

40. See J. Fred Kurtz to Persons, March 19, 1935, S.D., Correspondence, Negro Selection.
41. Persons to Major, Nov. 2, 1933, *ibid.*
42. Advisory Council, Minutes, Nov. 1, 1934.
43. Persons to Crossley, Aug. 10, 1935, S.D., Correspondence, Negro Selection.
44. Persons to Chester Barnard, director, ERA, N.J., June 28, 1935, *ibid.*
45. Crossley to Persons, July 26, 1935, *ibid.*

making replacements in accordance with the color of the vacancy existing. The practical thing is to maintain the organization we've got. Every time we make a change, it constantly brings up more friction."[46] Against such a tendency, Persons' fight to uphold the intent of the original act was of little consequence. Fechner now needed only an incident of sufficient importance to enable him to establish his policy of curtailing Negro enrolment on a national basis.

The chance came in July, 1935, when there was serious unrest among white communities in California, Arkansas, and especially Texas at the proposed establishment of new Negro camps as part of the general plan of CCC expansion. To Senator Joseph Robinson, Fechner admitted that he was "completely at a loss to know what I can do in handling these protests. The local welfare boards select the Negroes, and under the law we are compelled to take them. Something should be done to regulate the number of Negroes who are selected."[47] "Something should be done," he had written, and immediately he resolved to do it. He accordingly instructed Persons to stop all colored enrolment in Texas on the grounds that there were no more camps for Negroes there. Incensed, Persons refused to do so. He considered the director's request to be "a direct violation of the law," especially because

> the CCC has never adequately fulfilled its opportunities for the selection of colored enrollees. For us now to expressly deny the right of selection to such men when there are eligible and qualified applications available and when state quotas cannot be filled would be an indefensible procedure.[48]

Fechner was not at all swayed by these protests. After Persons' refusal to order the curtailment of Negro enrolment, he put the whole position before the President. Roosevelt termed the situation "political dynamite" and decided to approve Fechner's policy, though he asked that his name "be not drawn into the dis-

46. Advisory Council, Minutes, Nov. 1, 1934.
47. Fechner to Robinson, July 19, 1935, to Adjutant General, July 16, 1935, in Director, Correspondence.
48. Persons to Secretary of Labor, July 19, 1935, S.D., Correspondence, Negro Selection.

cussion."[49] Since Persons still refused to issue the required instructions, however, Fechner was forced to do so himself.[50] In his announcement that henceforth Negroes would be selected only as vacancies became available in already established Negro companies, he indicated that the policy had the President's approval. The order applied not only to Texas but to the entire country.[51]

The Selection Division, though objecting bitterly, was forced to acquiesce in the new policy. Dean Snyder angrily reminded the Advisory Council that the decision was clearly "a violation of the basic Act," but the council, unmoved, upheld the director.[52] Persons made no further attempt to investigate alleged instances of racial discrimination. He had lost his fight, and he now turned all such matters over to Fechner rather than deal with them himself according to a policy personally repugnant to him. Fechner, courteous but definite, had no interest in reopening the question. He insisted that he was sorry that he could not "accept every person who wanted to enroll in a CCC camp," but, he added, this was not possible.[53] That the "degree of impossibility" varied according to the color of the applicant's skin was conveniently overlooked. Though the problem of the Negro enrollee had not been solved and was to return sharply into focus when increasing white reemployment made the arbitrary racial distinction even more inequitable, Fechner had at least secured some respite from the constant irritation of locating Negro camps and dealing with white protests. That, perhaps, he had also shrugged off some of his responsibilities as director seemed to him only a minor quibble.

The outcome of the controversy over Negro enrolment is an obvious blot on the record of the CCC. The Negro never gained the measure of relief from the agency's activities to which his economic privation entitled him. The clause in the basic act prohibiting discrimination was honored far more in the breach than in the observance. Much of the blame for the curtailment of

49. Fechner to Persons, July 14, Aug. 1, 1935, Hopkins to Persons, Aug. 6, 1935, *ibid.*

50. Persons to Fechner, July 25, 1935, *ibid.*

51. Fechner to Major, July 24, 1935, Director, Correspondence.

52. Advisory Council, Minutes, Sept. 24, 1935.

53. Fechner to Persons, May 15, 1936, S.D., Correspondence, Negro Selection.

Negro enrolment must, of course, lie firmly with the director. His Southern attitudes influenced his approach to Negro policy. Unwilling to permit integrated camps or to allow the Negro the latitude of interstate travel permitted to white enrollees, and only too ready to heed the demands for removing Negro camps, he made little attempt to extend to Negroes the fullest benefits of CCC life. Further, the ambivalence of the War Department on the issue and the willingness of Army authorities to go along with local protests in order to preserve an organizational equilibrium helped to prompt Fechner into making his decision. Though no one expected the Army to be an active agent in promoting social revolution, its equivocation is nevertheless an additional factor in explaining the shabby side of the CCC's treatment of Negroes. Moreover, to place a quasi-fascist like General Moseley in command of the Fourth Corps Area, which included most of the South, indicated at best a lack of tact, at worst a contempt for Negro sensitivities and aspirations.

Neither Fechner nor the War Department, however, can be held entirely culpable. President Roosevelt himself made no attempt to insure fairer treatment for Negroes, and he acquiesced in the restriction of their enrolment. Much of the responsibility must also lie with the local communities, Northern and Southern, which refused to accept Negro CCC camps. Without community good will, some curtailment of Negro selection was probably inevitable, even if Fechner and the Army had adopted a stronger line. Negroes could be enrolled only to the extent that there were camps in which to place them; therefore, in a sense, by restricting their selection, Fechner was merely reflecting a strong section of prevailing white opinion.

It is true, too, that the director was not running the camps to further the cause of American race relations, but to reduce unemployment and accomplish useful conservation work. However desirable, the fullest employment of Negroes was only a matter of subsidiary concern to him and not worth constant irritation and worry. It should be remembered that only 10 per cent of the United States population was Negro, and though their economic state was indeed parlous, there were plenty of white youths whose position was little better. Fechner owed an obligation to them as well; his main concern was to run the CCC as smoothly as possible. A public outcry every time he tried to place a Negro camp was hardly good for public relations, nor did constant bickering with selection agents make for efficient selection policies. Viewed in this light, his decision appears perhaps more easily understood.

Besides, the CCC in its nine-year life span enrolled about 2,500,000 men. Almost 200,000 of these were Negroes.[54] Though their economic state certainly warranted better treatment, the Corps did provide relief for a considerable number. In so doing, it fed many of them better than ever before, provided them with living conditions far superior to their home environments, and gave them valuable academic and vocational training. About 87 per cent of all Negro enrollees participated in the education program, learning a variety of skills particularly suited to their own job opportunities. Some left the Corps to become gardeners, poultry farmers, or cooks; more were placed by Corps officials as janitors, table waiters, or chauffeurs. "Negro jobs" they may have been, but in an era when any employment was prized, training for such fields represented the best practical approach to the problem.[55]

To look at the place of the Negro in the CCC purely from the viewpoint of opportunities missed, or ideals compromised, is to neglect much of the positive achievement. The CCC opened up new vistas for most Negro enrollees. Certainly, they remained in the Corps far longer than white youths.[56] As one Negro wrote: "as a job and an experience for a man who has no work, I can heartily recommend it."[57] In short, the CCC, despite its obvious failures, did fulfil at least some of its obligations toward unemployed American Negro youth.

54. Schlesinger, III, 433-434.

55. Oxley to Fechner, June 30, 1938, Director, Correspondence.

56. Fechner to Sen. Joseph Guffey (Dem., Pa.), March 17, 1939, *ibid.* White enrollees remained in camp about ten months, on the average. Negroes stayed in almost five months longer.

57. Luther C. Wandall, "A Negro in the CCC," *Crisis*, XLII (Aug., 1935), 244-253.

6. *The Popular CCC*

Despite the problems of Negro enrolment and the occasional administrative mistake, the Civilian Conservation Corps in the words of Rexford Tugwell, "quickly became too popular for criticism."[1] He was indeed stating a truism. One of the significant features of the CCC, in contrast to other New Deal agencies, was its enthusiastic acceptance by most segments of the community. The *Literary Digest* did not exaggerate when it claimed that "attacks on the New Deal, no matter how sweeping, rarely or never extend to the CCC."[2] What were the roots of its popularity, among politicians, the press, and the public?

For congressmen, the CCC could be a positive aid to political advancement and a ready means of increasing their prestige among constitutents. The securing of one or more camps for his particular district or state usually redounded to the legislator's political benefit. Consequently, congressmen spent much time flooding CCC mailboxes with requests for camps. Most wrote to Fechner, though Ickes and Wallace also had to deal with such correspondence, and some congressmen even sought favors directly from the President. Roosevelt often acted positively on such demands, much to Fechner's annoyance.[3]

Appeals from congressmen took several forms, the most common being a straight request, usually accompanied by a petition from local residents stressing their desire for a camp and their economic need for one. Thus, when Senator Robert R. Reynolds sought the establishment of a camp in Avery County, North Carolina, he inclosed a letter from J. P. Grindstaff of that county, which discussed in detail the unhappy plight of the area's unemployed and explained how beneficial a camp would be.[4] Often the congressmen would preface his request by referring to

1. Rexford Guy Tugwell, *The Democratic Roosevelt* (New York, 1957), p. 331. In a similar vein, Searle F. Charles has written: "Programs such as NYA and the Civilian Conservation Corps, dealing with youth, seemed to consistently have a popularity not always enjoyed by FERA, WPA and PWA." See Charles, p. 153.

2. *Literary Digest*, CXVIII (Aug. 18, 1934), 8.

3. Roosevelt to Fechner, Oct. 11, 1933, Roosevelt Papers, O.F. 268, Box 3.

4. Sen. Robert R. Reynolds to Fechner, Aug. 14, 1936, Director, Correspondence.

previous camps in the area, noting their popularity and fine work record. He would then press his claim for one or two more.[5] Some Democrats would hint at possible re-election trouble if more camps were not established. For example, in 1935 Senator Joseph Guffey of Pennsylvania, one of the very first examples of a new political phenomenon—the liberal "political boss"—claimed that Republicans were making political capital out of the fact that the state had comparatively few camps and "if carried through, serious affects [*sic*] will be felt in the election."[6]

The quest for camps was by no means a Democratic party prerogative, however, and Republicans took full advantage of the chance to benefit their home districts and states. Representative R. F. Rich of Pennsylvania carried out a constant, and eventually successful, campaign for more camps within his own district.[7] Senators Arthur Capper of Kansas and Gerald P. Nye of North Dakota were a Republican duo whose deep interest in the benefits of CCC work to their states often led them to request more camps. Nye even took the issue to the President, stressing the "dire need of steps in this direction being taken."[8] This should scarcely be surprising. The CCC's appeal was far wider than the Democratic party alone. Much of its best work was, in fact, done in the Midwest or in New England, in rural areas where local Republicanism was strong. In 1936, not only did the Republican presidential candidate warmly support CCC work, but an estimated 67 per cent of all registered Republicans favored its continuation,[9] and in pressing for camps Republican congressmen were merely reflecting grass-roots opinion. As one

5. See Rep. Edgar Howard (Dem., Neb.) to Fechner, June 20, 1934, *ibid.*

6. Sen. Joseph Guffey to Fechner, April 30, 1935, *ibid.* See also the heart-rending plea from Rep. Braswell Dean (Dem., Ga.), who appealed to Fechner by telegram in 1935 "with all sincerity and anxiety give me camp my home county. . . . Will be tragic if unsuccessful. . . . Please help me and the admin. on this point." Dean to Fechner, Sept. 17, 1935, *ibid.*

7. Rep. Robert F. Rich (Rep., Pa.) to Fechner, Aug. 17, Sept. 28, 1934, May 1, 1935, *ibid.*

8. Sen. Arthur Capper (Rep., Kan.) to Secretary of Agriculture, June 28, 1934, Files of the Secretary of Agriculture—Conservation; Sen. Gerald P. Nye to McIntyre, July 16, 1936, Roosevelt Papers, O.F. 268, Box 7.

9. See chap. iii, above. *C.R.*, 75th Cong., 1st Sess., Vol. 81, Pt. 4, p. 4364, May 11, 1937. Rep. Jennings Randolph (Dem., W. Va.) quoted an American Institute of Public Opinion poll to this effect.

such Republican, Charles L. Gifford of Massachusetts, said, "It has been a good thing . . . Republicans and Democrats favor it."[10]

Fechner received complaints as well as praise about the CCC, however, and the agency could hurt as well as help congressmen. The location of Negro camps was always a dominant local issue, and pressure from the constituency often forced harrassed congressmen to demand their withdrawal.[11] Usually, however, congressmen abhorred the removal of a camp from their districts. The resulting loss of local income caused real antagonism, and the local representative often became a scapegoat for an official act originating in Washington. Representative Lyndon B. Johnson, Democrat of Texas, wrote plaintively to Ickes in 1937 that, in the period following his oath of office, four CCC projects had been closed in his district and as a result he was coming in for some serious criticism.[12] Representative Wesley E. Disney, Democrat of Oklahoma, said the removal of a camp in the environs of Tulsa had hurt the Democratic party there. The successful congressional revolt of 1936 against the President's plan to curtail camps was a dramatic manifestation of the importance of this issue locally.[13] Congressmen had received more than enough telegrams and letters from their home communities, from businessmen, storekeepers, contractors, and farmers to convince them that to close more camps could be political suicide.

Democratic congressmen were quick to exploit another source of political gain. A substantial section of the array of jobs created by the establishment of the CCC was available as political largesse. The CCC was never riddled with politics, but the original intention to remove it entirely from such a plane was soon subverted. Congressional Democrats were irate over the possibility that no spoils would be forthcoming; to placate them, an order was issued in July, 1933, requiring that certain supervisory positions not demanding any special skill "shall be

10. *Ibid.*, p. 4365.

11. Rep. J. G. Polk (Dem., O.) to Fechner, Oct. 29, 1934, Director, Correspondence. See chap. v, above.

12. Rep. Lyndon B. Johnson (Dem., Tex.) to Ickes, Nov. 22, 1937, Secretary of Interior, Records.

13. Rep. Wesley E. Disney (Dem., Okla.) to Roosevelt, June 26, 1936, Roosevelt Papers, O.F. 268, Box 7. See chap. iii, above.

filled from lists submitted by Congressmen."[14] Politics thus entered the Corps organization, yet its effect was mild. In fact, many Democrats complained that they did not have enough influence and that too many CCC jobs were held by Republicans.[15] CCC officials usually held firm against the demands by Postmaster General James A. Farley and others that Republican project supervisors be dismissed,[16] even though the President occasionally overruled them in order "to preserve the interests of the Party."[17] Both Republican and Democratic congressmen were also able to use the Corps as a placement bureau for protégés,[18] yet an investigation in 1936 of charges that it was corrupted by politics revealed that out of 18,000 employees who could conceivably owe their jobs to political pressures, only about 3,600 had actually been chosen from congressmen's lists.[19] Moreover, many of these were eminently well qualified for the positions they held. Given the importance of patronage in the American political system, the Corps' record is an unusual one in this respect.

To professional foresters, however, any political influence was to be deplored. Proclaiming that "efficiency in conservation work demands absolute freedom from political dictation," they agitated constantly for the extension of Civil Service provisions to cover all categories of CCC jobs.[20] In this campaign they had the firm support of Fechner, whose concern for an honest and efficient Corps was always emphatic. Fechner often broached the questions of Civil Service extension to the President,[21] who realized the worth of the proposal but was also cognizant of its political

14. Wallace to W. F. Lodge, Central States' Forestry Congress, Monticello, Ill., Oct. 19, 1933, Files of the Secretary of Agriculture–Conservation. See chap. ii, above.

15. Rep. Thomas Blanton (Dem., Tex.) to Ickes, Jan. 9, 1935, C. M. Brown to Daniel C. Roper, May 2, 1933, Sen. J. J. O'Mahoney (Dem., Wyo.) to Ickes, Sept. 5, 1934, in Secretary of Interior, Records.

16. Ickes to Farley, July 12, 1935, *ibid.*

17. Roosevelt to Dr. Charles E. Vercoe, secretary, Wayne County Democratic Organization, Ill., Aug. 30, 1935, Roosevelt Papers, O.F. 268, Box 6.

18. See Sen. Edwin C. Johnson (Dem., Colo.) to Fechner, April 5, 1937, Director, Correspondence.

19. New York *Times*, July 21, 1936. See chap. iii, above.

20. H. J. MacAloney to Roosevelt, Feb. 24, 1934, Roosevelt Papers, O.F. 268, Box 4; Holland and Hill, p. 118.

21. Fechner to McIntyre, March 11, 1935, May 4, 1936, Roosevelt Papers, O.F. 268, Boxes 5, 7.

implications. In 1935 he decided against its implementation because "it would mean throwing out a lot of patronage."[22] Instead, he added a few more jobs to those already available for patronage purposes, much to the satisfaction of the legislators, though not to Corps officials.[23]

The fact that the CCC had become a source of electoral gain for politicians explains in part the overwhelming support for it in Congress. To emphasize this too much, however, obscures the larger issue. Most congressmen were solid in their support of the agency, not solely for what they could get out of it personally, but mainly because its real benefits were increasingly clear. Since it was a service of positive gain to both community and country which was easily perceivable, strongly bipartisan trends of support were only to be expected.

From its inception, the CCC received an overwhelmingly sympathetic press. Newspapers supporting the Administration quickly pronounced it a success, and less partisan papers soon followed suit.[24] The San Francisco *Chronicle* asserted that the "CCC has won golden opinion. There has been in it not more than one-tenth of 1% of politics, which is neutralized by the Army and Forest Service." The *Chronicle* was by no means undiscriminating in its support of New Deal ventures. The same editorial contrasted the CCC with the Civil Works Administration, another public relief scheme, which it brusquely dismissed as a "scandal."[25] The Detroit *News* considered by September, 1934, that "no activity of the entire alphabetical array of New Deal projects has met with an approval so universal as has been accorded the aptly named Civilian Conservation Corps."[26]

The extent of popular approval is reflected in the attitude of the avowedly Republican papers to the Corps. No newspaper was more bitter in its hatred of Roosevelt and New Dealism than the Chicago *Tribune*, as even a cursory glance at its editorial

22. Roosevelt to Fechner, July 12, 1935, *ibid.*, Box 6.

23. Society of American Foresters to Ickes, March, 1936, Secretary of Interior, Records.

24. New York *Times*, Aug. 14, 1933; St. Louis *Post-Dispatch*, Dec. 24, 1933.

25. New York *Times*, Feb. 18, 1934, reprint from San Francisco *Chronicle.*

26. *Ibid.*, Sept. 30, 1934, reprint from Detroit *News.*

pages will show. Administration measures were colorfully described by such epithets as "false and poisonous fare, dictatorship in essence," or "gangsterism."[27] The one great exception was the Civilian Conservation Corps. To be sure, the *Tribune* did not lavish praise on the agency; in fact, it rarely mentioned it editorially. Even those omissions are significant. During the election campaign of 1936, the Chicago *Tribune* did not comment on the charge of "politics in the CCC," even though it descended with unholy glee on even the whisper of jobbery in other New Deal agencies, notably the WPA. Indeed, on rare occasions the *Tribune* specifically singled out the Corps for favorable comment. "The CCC is one of the best projects of the Administration," a leading article in 1935 admitted, "and the great majority of its recruits, we believe, appreciate its opportunities and are being benefited."[28] Whether the *Tribune* genuinely supported the CCC or merely realized the futility of criticism is immaterial. What is important is that there can be few more graphic examples of the CCC's popularity than that newspaper's muted tones when discussing it.

Other Republican newspapers were more positive in their praise. The Boston *Evening Transcript* commented: "in the main, from the start, this army of conservation has shown itself to be well disciplined and efficient in its work, and it has apparently maintained a commendable standard of conduct in its leisure hours."[29] The *Transcript* often voiced what became a common argument in favor of the CCC as expressed by groups normally hostile to the New Deal. To such individuals and organizations, the benefits of the CCC, unlike most New Deal measures, were tangible, immediate, and obvious. Furthermore, it was not a dole to keep city-bred youths from starving. The boys had to work, and work hard. In toiling with their hands in the wilderness, they recaptured for many people the spirit of a unique age now past whose memory was still all-pervasive. As the McKeesport *News* put it in a moment of semi-nostalgia, "theirs is the American way."[30]

27. Chicago *Tribune*, May, 8, 11, 1935, Nov. 2, 1936.
28. *Ibid.*, Jan. 16, 1935.
29. Boston *Evening Transcript*, Jan. 3, 1935, March 28, 1936.
30. McKeesport, Pa., *News*, Nov. 8, 1937.

The expression of such sentiments clearly illustrates one of the sources of the CCC's strength—the romance of its appeal to what Richard Hofstadter has called "the agrarian myth." The pervasive belief that life "lived in close communion with beneficent nature" had by very definition "a wholesomeness and integrity impossible for the depraved populations of cities" had long been part of American folklore, and the CCC "captured the popular imagination" partly because of its "immediate and obvious appeal" to it. To many, the CCC undoubtedly recalled visions of the frontier, of a pristine, open land quite different from the dirt and teeming life of contemporary urban society.[31]

Not all newspapers were unqualified in their praise of the Corps. The Republican New York *Herald Tribune* supported CCC work "because of the excellent effects of the camps on the morale of thousands of youngsters who have attended them,"[32] but at the same time it raised an important point which other papers often overlooked: that the camps were "one of the most costly forms of relief." Though "excellent schools of character" whose abolishment was out of the question, they would, in time, have to be "tapered down."[33] The *Herald Tribune* was also concerned about undue political influence in the Corps. It wanted all political interference stopped, lest the public "feel about the CCC as it does about other agencies," even though the Corps had been of far more value than any other New Deal creation.[34] No major newspaper had seriously proposed abolition of the Corps at this time. Most, in fact, demanded its extension.

After the election campaign of 1936, when the issue of a permanent Corps was becoming more prominent, newspaper comment throughout the country increased. The Director's Office kept a close check on editorials as a gauge to public feeling, periodically reporting its findings to the President. The press was obviously strong on the side of permanency. A survey of sixty editorials, taken in equal proportion from Democratic, Republican, and independent newspapers in twenty-six states, revealed

31. Richard Hofstadter, *The Age of Reform* (New York, 1955), pp. 23-50; Rawick, pp. 381-382.
32. New York *Herald Tribune*, Jan. 10, 1935.
33. *Ibid.*
34. *Ibid.*, July 17, 1936. See chap. iii, above.

that forty-three supported permanency, ten wanted the CCC continued temporarily until business stability resumed, and five wanted it reduced in size, then continued until employment improved. Only two papers opposed continuation: a left-leaning Brooklyn weekly objected to the Corps' similarity to "Fascist work camps," and a daily in Jacksonville, Florida, could see no earthly value in conservation work. But the great majority of the editorials were "eloquent in their praise of the benefits to the young men and their families."[35] A similar survey, carried out in April, 1937, showed that out of 145 editorials, 122 favored a permanent CCC immediately, and twenty-three, while favorable to continuance, urged a further wait before permanence. Not one of the papers supported abolition.[36] As the Houston *Post*, itself a conservative paper, remarked: "Of all the New Deal agencies, the CCC probably has attracted the most unanimous public approval. Democrats and Republicans, Socialists and Share-the-Wealthers, have joined in praising its objectives and accomplishments."[37] The breadth of press favor for the CCC was indeed one of the outstanding features of its first four years.

The heart of support for the Corps was found at the local level, in the communities where camps were established and in the big cities or small towns from which the enrollees came. That camps were popular with the local citizenry is indicated by the hundreds of testimonials sent to Fechner attesting to their worth, and by the anguished petitions of protest whenever a camp was withdrawn. The president of the Chamber of Commerce in Attwood, Kansas, spoke for thousands of rural towns when he wrote Fechner in 1935 to commend

> the officers, men and attached technical personnel of CCC company 731, who have been stationed in Attwood since May 1934. Not only has this organization benefited the community in a material way by its progress on the work project, but all mentioned have shown by their good conduct and personality that they merit the highest praise as men and public-minded citizens.

35. Fechner to Roosevelt, Jan. 6, 1937, Roosevelt Papers, O.F. 268, Box 7.
36. McKinney to Fechner, April 26, 1937, Director, Correspondence.
37. *Happy Days*, Dec. 26, 1936, reprint of editorial from Houston *Post*.

> We know that there is a place in this community for the organization as long as the Government will permit it to remain.[38]

Counties without camps pressed for them. It was usual for Fechner and his staff to receive petitions such as the one from Bamberg County, South Carolina, signed by 102 residents, including local merchants, a judge, a newspaper editor, a druggist, a Presbyterian minister, a schoolmaster, and a dentist.[39] Even more common, and certainly more difficult for the director to deal with, was the flood of telegrams and other messages whenever a camp was due to be removed. The signatures on these telegrams, letters, and petitions, whether of protest, commendation, or supplication, indicated the basic reasons for the CCC's popularity. Businessmen were responsible for much of the heavy response. The decision to close a camp at Iron River, Michigan, prompted the sending of twenty-nine separate telegrams of protest from businessmen alone, as well as a joint resolution from the farming community.[40] On May 10, 1935, Ickes received twenty-six telegrams from businessmen of Greeley, Colorado, protesting the removal of a National Parks camp there, even though the work project was finished.[41] Conversely, it was most often the president of the local Chamber of Commerce who sent the memorial praising the work of the camp in his particular area and recounting its benefit to all sections of the community.

For such local communities, leaving aside all consideration of the work project's success, the very presence of a CCC camp was

38. Wayne H. Egelston, president, Attwood, Kan., Chamber of Commerce, to Fechner, Feb. 20, 1935, Director, Correspondence.

39. Rep. H. P. Fulmer (Dem., S.C.) to Fechner, June 14, 1935, *ibid.* The petition thanked Roosevelt "for relieving distress and giving work to the unemployed, opening up channels of trade and putting the wheels of industry in motion, safeguarding banking institutions and restoring confidence among our people, giving value to and stabilizing prices of farm products, thus making it possible to own our homes and educate our children if these policies are continued, and believing the reforestation program outlined and inaugurated by him to be one of the most progressive of all these measures and one particularly adapted to Bamberg County as a place suited to demonstrate its real value as an economic measure" therefore called for a camp. See also Oral G. Williams, president, Bartlesville, Okla., Chamber of Commerce, to Fechner, March 17, 1935.

40. Communications from Iron River, Mich., to Ickes, Sept. 7 and 9, 1937, Secretary of Interior, Records.

41. Communications from Greeley, Colo., to Ickes, May, 1935, *ibid.*

an economic stimulant to local business. Food purchases alone for the 300,000 men in camp throughout the nation amounted to more than $3 million monthly, and about half of this amount was expended in local areas. It was estimated that nearly $5,000 was spent monthly by each camp in the local market, and, in addition, camp construction provided work for local labor.[42] Sometimes, as in Plaine, Montana, this contribution was enough to remove the city entirely from depression standards.[43] In all cases, it was of the greatest assistance in moving toward that goal. As the Baltimore *Sun* aptly stated in explaining the congressional revolt in 1936: "these local businessmen find it profitable to expand in one way or another to cater for the relief trade. Thus, something in the nature of a vested interest develops . . . curtailment endangers vested interests."[44] The CCC was a most significant experiment in community co-operation.

The economic benefit of CCC work reached far wider than the camp locality. For the fiscal year 1935-1936 alone, almost $123 million was formally allotted by enrollees to their families. Fechner's correspondence files adequately testified to its effect on family income. One mother spoke of the vital difference the extra money had made to her whole family. She thanked God for both the CCC and the President, and pledged: "from now there will be nobody to tell me how to vote. I'll know. And there will be two more votes in this family by that time."[45] The Indiana and Ohio state relief offices indicated that the $25 check had been vital in maintaining relief loads and that most committees were decidedly in favor of the camps. A spokesman for the larger cities concluded that "they have helped to get rid of the gang on the corner" and that employers had indicated preferences for young men with CCC experience.[46]

Equal testimony to the success of the CCC as a relief measure were the letters pleading either for a chance to join the Corps or

42. Harper, p. 104.
43. *Happy Days*, Aug. 5, 1933.
44. Baltimore *Sun*, March 23, 1936.
45. Mrs. Frank E. Kelsey to Roosevelt, May 18, 1933, Roosevelt Papers, P.P.F. 522.
46. Office of State Relief, Ohio, to Persons, July 20, 1934, W. H. Hook, director of Commission on Unemployment, Ind., to Persons, Sept. 14, 1934, in Records of the CCC, Public Relations File, Benefit Letters.

trying to prevent an impending discharge. One mother told Mrs. Roosevelt that "we are so dependent on the money John sends home that I don't know what we are going to do without it."[47] An unemployed twenty year old's plaintive plea to the President graphically revealed the anguish of many of his generation. He wrote: "I have been out of hight school for years and have not been able to get any kind of work. I could not get in the CCC and I need work. If I do not get work I will be turn out when I am 21 which will be in June. Please help me."[48] Ineligible youths and their families had seen the difference camp life had made to friends and wanted a chance to share in its benefits, to provide, as one underage youth put it, "something to live on" for his family.[49]

The economic aid was by no means the only benefit recognized. A woman told Fechner that what she liked about the CCC was that: "the boys are safe there. They are young and inexperienced and need someone reliable to teach them and I think the discipline and strictness are what they need now in their teen age."[50] Judge M. Broude of Chicago estimated that the CCC was largely responsible for the 50 per cent reduction in crime in that city, because it took boys off the streets and inculcated in them a sense of values. The New York commissioner of correction attributed a similar decrease in juvenile crime to the beneficent effect of the Corps.[51] Groups as divergent politically as the Virginia Federation of Labor and the United States Junior Chamber of Commerce were united in recognizing the Corps' social effect. The Junior Chamber members actually acted as godfathers to the boys while they were in camp.[52] Even the Soviet Embassy in Washington commended the CCC and requested detailed information on its operation.[53]

47. Mrs. Susie Strickler, Pittsburg, Kan., to Mrs. Roosevelt, March 6, 1937, Director, Correspondence.

48. Harvey Shaw, Johnston, R.I., to Roosevelt, undated, *ibid.*

49. James Vassellee to Roosevelt, March 21, 1937; see also Mrs. Mary Wilson, Atlanta, Ga., to Hopkins, July 25, 1935, *ibid.*

50. Mrs. Thomas Williams, Russell Springs, Kan., to Fechner, May 20, 1936, Roosevelt Papers, O.F. 268, Box 7.

51. New York *Times*, Oct. 2, 1936, Jan. 17, 1937.

52. Virginia Federation of Labor to Ickes, June 6, 1935, Secretary of Interior, Records; New York *Times*, Oct. 13, 1935.

53. Tugwell to Cordell Hull, Aug. 5, 1935, Files of the Secretary of Agriculture—Conservation.

An extensive survey of the depth of public esteem for the Corps took place in California in 1936. Four thousand people, including businessmen, educators, farmers, bankers, clergymen, editors, doctors, clerks, and laborers, were asked to give their opinion on its record so far and their feelings on its permanent establishment. Of those who replied, nearly 95 per cent approved of both the record of the Corps and its becoming a permanent agency of the federal government. Less than 1 per cent thought the work a complete waste of time. The remainder considered that though it had accomplished much, the time was not yet ripe for a permanent organization.[54] The survey probably underestimated the strength of the opposition to the CCC, but it indisputably indicated the strength of its appeal. Its place in popular esteem was secure.

However, not everyone loved the CCC, and some were quite vocal in their objections to it. A few lovers of nature protested that the Corps was ruining the national forests and reserves with "bungling" conservation practices and was also creating fire risks.[55] A clergyman or two, perhaps misguidedly, protested against its contribution to the increase in the moral delinquency of young people.[56] More significantly, some farmers opposed it because of the poor quality of work done on their land, or because a camp was abandoned without completing its assignment. In Pawnee County, Nebraska, for example, three different soil erosion control companies had been sent there, only to move on after a few weeks of inefficient endeavor. The farmers, "disgusted with having their farms torn up," wanted nothing more to do with the CCC,[57] but such reactions, usually due to some purely local circumstance, were rare. Some right-wing political groups opposed the Corps. The American Liberty League, for example, considered it a scheme to mold youth "into the raw manpower for a colored shirt Fascist army of Roosevelt the Dictator." Yet even the league's criticism was relatively muted.

54. C.R.M., No. 787, Public Opinion.

55. Nixon, II, 66, 166; see also B. C. Billins to Sen. Hattie M. Carraway (Dem., Ark.), Oct. 31, 1935, Director, Correspondence.

56. See the Rev. Mr. Van Dyke, Berlin, N.H., to Roosevelt, undated, *ibid.*

57. Pawnee, Neb., Public Service Club to Roosevelt, March 21, 1936, *ibid.*

Violent attacks would have been a political blunder in view of the Corps' tremendous popularity.[58]

Despite their general commitment to the philosophies and methods of the New Deal, and while applauding the basic human motives which had prompted the CCC's creation, some liberals were sincerely troubled by particular aspects of its structure. They distrusted the intentions of the Army, and even conceding that the boys had worked wonders with the land, they were less convinced that the experience had any permanent value for the youths themselves. These liberals were dissatisfied with the educational program and correctly claimed that there was little use in rehabilitating a boy permanently, even giving him new skills, if all that could be done in the end was to return him to the environment from which he came. Here was where the problems of these youths had to be solved, in the squalid urban slums, in the dying Southern towns, not in forests or parks perhaps half a continent away. These were valid shafts, not so much aimed at the Corps itself, but at what they considered to be an administrative mindlessness which tended to see in this essentially temporary, specialized creation a permanent solution to all the problems plaguing young America. "Let us not deny the real benefits of CCC life," such critics pleaded, "but let us not forget that it functions within clearly defined limits."[59]

By far the most virulent criticism of the CCC came from the leftist political parties and pressure groups. Norman Thomas described it as a system of forced labor, and the Socialist party platform in 1936 proposed its abolition.[60] Carl Minkley, state secretary of the Wisconsin Socialist party, warned that it was "a breeding spot for militarism or Fascism."[61] In the first years of the New Deal, until American Communists adopted a policy of ostensibly supporting Administration measures, Communist Front organizations were bitter in their criticism of the CCC.[62] Most

58. George Wolfskill, *The Revolt of the Conservatives: A History of the American Liberty League, 1934-1940* (Boston, 1962), pp. 132, 165.

59. A good expression of this point of view can be found in George R. Leighton and Richard Hilman, "Half Slave Half Free: Unemployment, the Depression and American Young People," *Harper's*, CXXIII (Aug., 1935), 342-353. See also chap. iv, above.

60. Burns, p. 242; New York *Times*, May 27, 1936.

61. Madison, Wis., *Times*, May 1, 1937.

62. Schlesinger, III, 190, 199, 566-567. For an example of the changed

vociferous was the American League Against War and Fascism, under the leadership of veteran Communists J. B. Matthews and Earl Browder. The league sent delegations to Fechner protesting against Fascism and "military management," attacked the Corps by resolution, and denigrated it in debate.[63]

The CCC was always remarkably free from radical or Communist influence. Fechner made no attempt to prevent Communists from visiting camps and allowed them to distribute their literature.[64] On only one occasion did he specifically bar a left-wing publication from camp libraries, when in April, 1937, he stopped the distribution of a radical periodical, *Champion of Youth*, because it had advocated the organization of enrollees into cells on the Soviet model. Fechner's action drew protests from several Front organizations, including the American League Against War and Fascism and the American Student Union.[65] Probably because of Fechner's liberal policies, carried out in the face of nervous Army protests, Communist infiltration of camps was quite insignificant. Their propaganda had little appeal for young men who were now on the way back from their nadir of despair, and to whom the camps, and the men responsible for them, signified a new hope for the future. For many, the CCC was a place for sloughing off radical ideas, not assimilating them.[66]

Another Front critic of the Corps was the Illinois Workers Alliance, whose branches in March, 1935, sent nearly twenty identical resolutions to Fechner objecting to the trend of CCC organization. The form and content of this resolution was typical of the type of communication expected and received from such

---

attitude due to the Popular Front, see Max Mitchen, secretary of the Workers' Alliance of New York, to Fechner, Feb. 3, 1939, Director, Correspondence: "The Workers' Alliance stands 100% in favor of the New Deal, and seeks material on the benefits of the Youth Program of the Roosevelt Administration."

63. Frances A. Henson, secretary, American League Against War and Fascism, to Fechner, Jan. 25, 1934, Jack Melso to Fechner, Feb. 27, 1935, *ibid.*

64. *Permanency Hearings*, 1937, p. 37.

65. *Ibid.*, pp. 37, 107-114; A. S. Link, *American Epoch* (New York, 1955), p. 444.

66. Schlesinger, III, 93; Holland and Hill, p. 69; M. H. Mulock, Iowa State Emergency Relief Committee, to Persons, June 2, 1934, S.D., Benefit Letters.

groups. The preamble spoke of the "convulsions" within the economic system and of the "unification of the working class taking place as a desperate means for the right to live as human beings." The alliance asserted: "With our economic problems growing worse, the workers are faced with a new problem because of the semi-military training of hundreds of thousands of youngsters in the CCC. If this act is to be continued we can see nothing but a clear trend toward a peculiar American brand of Fascism." The resolution went on to accuse American capitalists of fomenting want and starvation, and described the CCC as a conscious instrument in the policy. The alliance demanded the discontinuance of this "semi-military agency."[67]

Communists and radicals continually played on the theme of militarism in the CCC. They, of course, genuinely feared Fascism, but, more important, by using this issue they were able to make common cause with thousands of non-Communists, people who supported the idea of the CCC but yet distrusted its military connection. This uniting of such diverse groups was one reason why the controversial question of possible military training for enrollees was always of cardinal importance.

The intensity of opposition to the Army's role in the CCC organization, manifested during the legislative hearings of March, 1933, indicated strongly that the success of the Corps depended in large measure on public reassurance concerning Army control.[68] Army authorities, Fechner, and the President explicitly disavowed any intention of training enrollees for combat duty, yet throughout 1933 intermittent protests from individuals, peace groups, and radical organizations showed that some suspicion still existed. Fechner answered such communications by giving an assurance that no military training whatsoever was intended in the camps and that "the only thing expected of the men is that they will behave themselves."[69]

67. Charles Rossio, Unit 39, Illinois Workers' Alliance, to Fechner, Feb. 28, 1935, *ibid.*

68. See chap. i, above.

69. Mrs. Bessie Lowry to Fechner, April 17, 1933, Mrs. Martha Elliott, president, Massachusetts branch of Womens' International League for Peace and Freedom, to Fechner, June 29, 1933, F. Starkins, Rochester, N.Y., to Fechner, undated, S. A. Shaw to Roosevelt, Nov., 1933, Fechner to Starkins, June 13, 1933, all in Director, Correspondence.

In January, 1934, the assistant secretary of war, Harry H. Woodring, provoked the first sustained public opposition to the prospect of military instruction in the CCC. In an article for *Liberty Magazine*, Woodring hailed the camps as "the forerunners of the great civilian labor armies of the future" and strongly suggested that they be put under full Army control. He called the CCC boys "economic storm troops." As Arthur Schlesinger has pointed out, this was "a singularly unfortunate phrase for a nation which was just beginning to dislike Hitler" and which was hypersensitive in its desire to prevent similar developments at home.[70]

Public reaction was immediate and violent to Woodring's implication that the CCC camps were militaristic. Many demanded his resignation and the prompt removal of the CCC camps from the clutches of the War Department.[71] The White House, dismayed at both the article and the outcry, issued a statement which repudiated the offending views most emphatically; and, at Roosevelt's insistence, Woodring himself made a public apology. His argument had been misconstrued, he alleged. He had used the offensive phrase purely as a figure of speech, and he was in fact "fully in accord with the views of the President that there should be no militarizing of the CCC."[72] Nevertheless, pacifist apprehensions had been thoroughly aroused, and groups continued to press charges that the enrollees had had rifles and other equipment issued to them. Though, as Fechner angrily said, there was "not one scintilla of truth" in such rumors,[73] the depth of public feeling insured that the Administration and Army officials would rigidly suppress any development which could possibly be construed as lending them substance. Shooting, for instance, was banned as a camp sport for fear of the passions it might inflame.[74]

70. Schlesinger, II, 339.

71. Early to Woodring, Feb. 5, 1934, Woodring to Howe, Feb. 24, 1934, Roosevelt Papers, O.F. 25, Box 2, 1934.

72. *Ibid.*; see also New York *Times*, Feb. 8, 1934. There was a similar reaction when Maj. Gen. Johnson Haygood, commander of the Eighth Corps Area, wrote of the Corpsmen as having "the makings of 300,000 soldiers." See Saalberg, p. 60.

73. Fechner to Frederick J. Libby, executive secretary, National Council for Prevention of War, Jan. 30, 1934, Director, Correspondence.

74. New York *Daily News*, Dec. 15, 1934.

A few people, on the other hand, were becoming increasingly interested in the possibilities of the CCC as a reservoir of military strength. In February, 1935, General MacArthur proposed to the House Appropriations Committee that enrollees be given the chance to enlist for military training after completing their period of service in the work camps. Ultimately they would be mobilized as an enlisted reserve force.[75] The suggestion found support among veterans' associations and in Congress.[76] Excited by it, Representative J. J. McSwain, Democrat of South Carolina and chairman of the House Military Affairs Committee, introduced H.R. 5592, which sought to add two months to CCC enrolment for the military training of the young men, and their enlistment in an auxiliary reserve.[77] The depth of public reaction against such proposals, however, was impressive. A Committee on Militarism in Education, set up at Yale University and including such august personages as John Dewey, Shailer Matthews, Reinhold Niebuhr, Charles A. Ellwood, and William Allen White, angrily denounced the proposal, demanding the "termination of all War Department participation in the CCC."[78] The Union of Private School Teachers asked that unemployed teachers replace Army officers in controlling the camps.[79] The Anti-War Committee of Union Theological Seminary opposed "Army proposals for the militarization of the CCC."[80] The American League Against War and Fascism climbed noisily on the bandwagon, and hundreds of ordinary citizens added their private protests in letters to representatives, to senators, to Fechner, and to the President himself.[81]

The director and his staff bitterly opposed the measure. Fechner told the Committee on Militarism in Education that there

75. New York *Times*, Feb. 20, 1935.

76. Henry Neuman, national commander, Veterans Association, to Fechner, March 3, 1935, Director, Correspondence.

77. New York *Times*, March 13, 1935.

78. Committee on Militarism in Education to Roosevelt, March 12, 1935, Director, Correspondence.

79. Frank Kaplan, for Union of Private School Teachers, to Fechner, April 1, 1935, *ibid.*

80. Robert G. Andrus to Roosevelt, April 12, 1935, *ibid.*

81. Claremont Branch, American League against War and Fascism, to Fechner, April 11, 1935, Miss Mary Winson, Haverford, Pa., to Fechner, May 22, 1935, *ibid.*

was "no connection" between his office and McSwain's bill.[82] Persons considered that public opinion was so violently antagonistic to military training in the CCC that the passage of the bill would seriously affect selection.[83] McSwain doubted this statement, but because of public reaction and Administration hostility, he decided against further action and the bill died in committee.[84]

The proponents of military training in the CCC were not to be silenced, however, and continued to express their views in the press and on the public platform. An Army officer, writing in *Happy Days*, advocated two hours drill per day, believing that "you could not find one boy in 50 who would not be delighted with such an arrangement." He was contemptuous of "morbid pacifists" who argued otherwise. The American Legion strongly favored the suggestion, and the governor of Massachusetts, James M. Curley, a candidate for the United States Senate in 1936, said that one of his first acts, if elected, would be to introduce a bill making training for one hour a day mandatory in all CCC camps. Major General George Van Horn Moseley, commander of the Fourth Corps Area, advocated military training for all enrollees as a means of strengthening the Army.[85]

All of these suggestions were met with distrust and hostility. A Kansas editor described Moseley's idea as "conscription," a cross "between Hitler's compulsory labor camps and the universal draft features of European military service laws."[86] The Communists screamed "Fascism" and warned of Army plots to gain complete control of the CCC. The American Youth Congress proclaimed that "youth opposes any such program." Nevertheless, the idea of at least a modicum of military training for enrollees slowly gained support. It had friends in Congress, where Representative Jack Nichols, Democrat of Oklahoma, led a group of veterans who strongly favored the scheme, and the correspon-

82. Fechner to Committee on Militarism in Education, March 18, 1935, *ibid.*

83. Persons to Secretary of Labor, March 18, 1935, to McSwain, April 12, 1935, S.D., Correspondence, Military Aspects.

84. McSwain to Persons, April 17, 1935, *ibid.*

85. *Happy Days*, Aug. 31, 1935; Washington *Post*, Aug. 27, 1936; Boston *Herald*, Aug. 7, 1936; New York *Times*, Sept. 15, 1936.

86. Topeka, Kan., *Capital*, Oct. 11, 1936.

dence columns of the newspapers indicated its growing popularity.[87] It is probable that public opinion in 1936 still stood opposed to military training in the camps, and for the moment the issue became submerged in the larger one of the move for permanency. However, it was to be revived with a greater sense of urgency than before as world tensions increased and Europe moved inexorably toward war.

87. New York *Herald Tribune*, Oct. 4, 1936, letter from Harold Partch, American League Against War and Fascism; see also Washington *Herald*, Jan. 2, 1937; New York *Times*, Aug. 16, Sept. 17, 18, 19, and 21, 1936.

7. *The Success of the Experiment*

A popular nickname for the CCC was "Roosevelt's Tree Army," and its activities were often regarded as being primarily concerned with the planting of trees.[1] Tree planting was always an important aspect of the work; in fact, as W. E. Leuchtenburg has pointed out, "of all the forest planting . . . in the history of the nation, more than half was done by the C.C.C."[2] Yet this was but one of the host of tasks performed by the enrollees. To emphasize it unduly is to get a completely false impression of the variety and usefulness of CCC work. Roughly 75 per cent of all CCC camps worked on projects administered by the Department of Agriculture, and of these, more than half were employed in national, state, or private forests, under the direction of the United States Forest Service.[3] Their work can be divided into two broad categories: forest protection and forest improvement.

The most spectacular protective function was undoubtedly the fighting or prevention of forest fires. By 1942 the CCC had spent nearly 6.5 million days fighting fires, a period equivalent to the constant efforts of more than 16,000 men, working for a whole year on the basis of an eight-hour day. Forty-seven enrollees lost their lives in the various blazes. During this time, the acreage lost by fire in the United States reached its lowest point ever, though a record number of fires were reported.[4]

In fighting fires, CCC enrollees used techniques developed over long years of experience. Some served as members of permanent forest fire patrols, covering forest routes by truck, on foot, by canoe, or as members of airplane crews. For most, however, fire-fighting was something outside the work project, and the CCC's unique contribution was its ability to become a readily available, easily mobilized reservoir of assistance. When fire broke out, enrollees were willing and able to use grub hoe, ax, saw, pump, and bulldozer, as well as sheer numbers, against the

1. "Roosevelt's Tree Army," *New Republic*, LXXXIII (June 12, 1935), 127-129.
2. Leuchtenburg, p. 174.
3. New York *Times*, April 16, 1935.
4. *Forests Protected by the CCC* (Washington, 1938), pp. 1-3; C.R.M., No. 788, CCC in Emergencies.

blaze. In 1934, for example, 1,400 men were dispatched to a fire near Los Angeles with such speed that a potential holocaust was controlled before doing much damage to the timber stand or the nearby urban area.[5] Tangible accomplishments of the Corps in the field of fire prevention were the construction of roads, trails, telephone lines, and lookout towers which facilitated communication between fire-fighting units and enabled men, supplies, and equipment to be transported faster. In 1936, a typical year, enrollees laid 44,750 miles of telephone lines and cleared 11,402 miles of truck trails. They maintained 62,920 miles of trail and built 611 lookout towers.[6] CCC workers covered thousands of acres of forest land, removing dead trees and other inflammable material, and constructing fire breaks by clearing woodland strips, including the Ponderosa Way in California, which was six hundred miles long. This giant firebreak separated the brush-covered foothills, where fires often start, from the valuable timber higher up on the slopes of the north-south chain of forested mountains. It was one of the CCC's most important achievements in the field of timber protection. Other important contributions to fire prevention included the construction of water storage basins and ponds in New England, and the manning of motorized well-digging units in Michigan, Minnesota, and Wisconsin forest areas. These insured a ready supply of water for fire-fighting tanks and pumps.[7]

Less dramatic perhaps than the fight against fire but equally necessary was the protection of the forests against disease and insects. By 1933 every major white pine region in the country had been severely affected by blister rust, an alien tree disease whose depredations threatened to eradicate white pine completely from the nation's forests. With the aid of CCC labor, foresters were able to throw heavier control forces against the scourge, usually by the painstaking method of scouring the woods and pulling out by hand currants, gooseberry bushes, and other plants, the "alternate hosts" by which the disease spread from tree to tree. By 1942 its march had been almost completely

5. *Forests Protected by the CCC*, p. 4.
6. *Report of the Director*, 1936, p. 29.
7. *Forests Protected by the CCC*, pp. 7-8.

checked in some areas of the country and brought under a measure of control elsewhere.[8] Insects, too, were silently sapping the life of thousands of healthy trees. The most serious of these was the bark beetle, which laid eggs in tree bark. The larvae then tunneled deep into the wood, cutting off the sap supply and eventually killing the tree. This pest destroyed more than five billion feet of standing timber annually. CCC enrollees, instructed by Forest Service technicians, engaged successfully in a campaign against the pest, mainly by cutting down infected trees; by 1938, forestry losses due to its ravages were on the decline.[9] Other control projects were directed against the gypsy moth—checked by maintaining a barrier zone to prevent the spread of the pest and by destroying egg clusters—the grasshopper, various species of weevil, and Dutch elm disease.[10]

Forest protection was but a section of the work carried out by enrollees working with the Forestry Service. The Corps also devoted much of its time to forest improvement. Workers constructed roads and trails which opened up large areas to greater timber utilization. Structural additions in the forms of warehouses, garages, overnight cabins, shelters, toolhouses, and storage boxes contributed to greater efficiency in forest management.[11] Hundreds of new camping grounds, made more beautiful by building small dams to convert streams into lakes, were developed in public forests. CCC dams ranged in size from small stone, earth, or brush "gully stoppers," used to combat soil erosion, to large earth and concrete edifices involving months of labor; most dams were of the small variety. Stream improvements, too, entailing the building of deflectors, dams, and riffles, aided fishing conditions, while the construction of winter sports facilities, especially ski jumps and runs, met an increasing public demand.[12]

The most important aspect of the CCC's forestry improvement work, however, was simply reforestation. By June, 1936, nearly 570 million young trees had been planted on national forest lands alone. In addition, overcrowded timber stands were

8. *Ibid.*, pp. 8-9.
9. *Ibid.*, p. 10. 10. *Ibid.*, pp. 11-12.
11. *Forest Improvements by the CCC* (Washington, 1938), pp. 3-4.
12. *Ibid.*, pp. 6-9.

thinned and experimental forest plots assiduously tended—valuable assets in the constant search for new techniques. Perhaps it was for its work in reforestation that the Corps was best known. Certainly its record in this field was a fine one.[13]

Other tasks performed under Forestry Service auspices included the improvement of the grazing land situation on national forests in Western states. The Corps re-grassed thousands of acres, dug new water holes and improved existing ones, built storage dams for stock water, killed uncounted millions of prairie dogs, pocket gophers, and jackrabbits, and constructed fences and bridges.[14] Intensive rodent control schemes were also put into operation.[15] Despite occasional complaints that CCC labor was "ruining the forests,"[16] there is ample evidence to indicate that most foresters thoroughly approved of its use. This approbation was reflected in both the public statements and private correspondence of state and regional forest officials, most of whom were ardent proponents of a permanent Corps, with even greater emphasis laid on conservation. In the words of one of their number, "the proven worth of the camps clearly suggests that they continue. . . . By unifying the conservation feature of the CCC on an equal basis with the unemployment relief and rehabilitation features, the whole concept of the Corps will be materially clarified and strengthened."[17]

Next to the Forest Service, the Soil Conservation Service was the Department of Agriculture agency with the most camps under its direction. By 1938 the service had developed more than five hundred project areas in forty-four states, employing about 60,000 youths annually.[18] Their work fell into three categories: the demonstration of practical methods of soil conservation to farmers, actual work upon private land in co-operation with landowners, and the development and improvement of erosion control techniques through research.[19] Most of this work was

13. *Report of the Director*, 1935, p. 41, No. 6, p. 29.
14. *Forest Improvements by the CCC*, p. 5; *Time*, XXXIII (Feb. 6, 1939), 11.
15. *Report of the Director*, 1936, p. 30.
16. New York *Times*, Nov. 20, 1934.
17. Bernard Frank, acting chief forester, TVA, to Morrell, Feb. 28, 1938; C.R.M., No. 793, Appreciation; see also New York *Times*, Feb. 11, 1934.
18. *Hands to Save the Soil* (Washington, 1939).
19. *Report of the Director*, 1936, p. 31.

done in Southern and Western states, where ignorance, improper land use, and climate had wrought havoc with the soil. Techniques included the checking and healing of gullied areas, fence construction, and contour tree planting. By 1938, CCC enrollees had planted more than 200 million trees on soil conservation projects alone. One of the most effective methods of preventing water erosion on steeper slopes was the construction of broad-based terraces. These emptied excess water into designed outlets where it did no harm, while their broad bases and gentle slopes offered little problem to the farmer in planting, working, and reaping his crops. Engineering and surveying were important aspects of terrace construction. Enrollees with special aptitudes were given instruction in these fields, then placed in charge of a terracing project under the general supervision of the camp engineer. This experience often pointed the way to future employment.[20]

One of the more publicized activities of the Corps was its role in the conservation of wildlife, under the direction of the Bureau of Biological Survey in the Department of Agriculture. The coming of the European settlers to the American continent had begun a process of wildlife destruction which continued thereafter virtually unhampered by legal or moral restraint. In 1934 the President's Committee on Wildlife Restoration, appointed in January of that year, revealed a gloomy story of depredation and waste. At the committee's insistence on action, a wildlife restoration program was devised and the CCC was widely used in its implementation.[21] Enrollees developed submarginal land as wildlife refuges, built fish-rearing ponds and animal shelters, developed springs, and planted food for animals and birds. Nesting areas were constructed or improved, streams, dams and rivers were stocked with fish, and sick or injured creatures were collected, treated, and released on federal refuges.[22] One of the wildlife camps occasioned national interest. This was the "Arkansas floating camp," whose enrollees lived on a fleet of houseboats while developing waterfowl refuges in streams,

20. *Hands to Save the Soil.*
21. *The CCC and Wildlife* (Washington, 1939), pp. 4-5.
22. *Ibid.*, pp. 6-13.

swamps, and bayous. They were given "shore leave" on weekends.[23] Wildlife also benefited incidentally from most other Department of Agriculture activities, particularly from forest fire prevention and dam building. By 1938 the most serious aspects of wildlife wastage had been ameliorated, and expenditures on wildlife administration had increased by 450 per cent since 1933. The Forest Service claimed that the largest share of the credit for improved conditions was due to the CCC.[24]

Other camps under the general auspices of the Department of Agriculture included those working on drainage problems. They were directed by the Bureau of Agricultural Engineering, their main function being to assist public drainage organizations in performing neglected maintenance work and in making improvements. The Department of Agriculture also supervised the work of about thirty CCC camps employed on various projects directed by the Tennessee Valley Authority. Most TVA camps were engaged in reforestation, and by June 1942, they had planted 44 million trees. They also performed important work in erosion control, as well as suppressing 114 forest fires within TVA boundaries.[25]

The majority of the CCC camps controlled by the Department of the Interior were employed by the National Parks Service on tasks directly related to the improvement and protection of national parks. In so doing, they performed many functions similar to forestry camps. National Parks Service camps built bridges, installed telephone lines, constructed stoves, fireplaces, and picnic tables, and made dams, lakes, and swimming pools. They opened up many park areas to the public through the construction of roads and trails. Land was purchased and turned into new parks entirely by CCC labor. The largest of these, Big Bend National Park in Texas, was more than six hundred acres.[26]

National Parks Service companies worked extensively, too, on the preservation and restoration of historical sites and monuments. CCC labor, for example, restored Fort Necessity, Pennsylvania, where George Washington in 1754 engaged a force under

23. *Happy Days*, Nov. 21, 1936.
24. *The CCC and Wildlife*, p. 11.
25. *Report of the Director*, 1936, pp. 30, 34; 1943, p. 52.
26. *Ibid.*, 1936, pp. 37-38.

General Coulon de Villiers to start the French and Indian War. The painstaking re-creation of La Purisma Mission in California drew wide acclaim from historians and archeologists. The carving of Mount Theater, at Mount Tamalpois State Park, California, from the solid rock of the mountainside was a lasting tribute to the constructive ability, engineering skill, and creativity of the Corps' labor.[27]

The CCC co-operated with the Bureau of Reclamation, Department of the Interior, on irrigation projects, particularly the building of dams and canals.[28] Several camps were also attached to the Division of Grazing. Again, most of them worked on water development tasks—the drilling of wells, the piping of springs—in drought areas. Grazing camps were also engaged in rodent and insect control, and by 1937 more than 2,590,000 acres had been treated. It was estimated that CCC work advanced range rehabilitation work by ten to twenty years.[29]

One of the most interesting aspects of work done with CCC labor by the Department of the Interior concerned the fighting of subterranean coal fires in Gillette, Wyoming. Seventeen camps were established in the Gillette area at specific fire points, working under the auspices of the General Land Office. Until their advent, no attempt had been made to extinguish the seventeen fires, but the CCC had successfully put out seven of them by 1937 and had the remainder well under control. The method of attack was either to dig out all burning material, then cover the exposed coal bed with several feet of sand and shale, or to smother larger fires by sealing.[30]

Two of the largest, most important, and most publicized of all CCC projects were carried out under the guidance of the Corps of Engineers of the United States Army. These were the flood control schemes on the Winooski River, Vermont, and the Walkill River, New York. The Winooski project, the largest construction project in the country using CCC labor, aimed at reducing flood damage to areas along the Winooski River, a tributary of Lake Champlain. It involved the construction of three

27. *Ibid.*, p. 39, No. 7, p. 48.
28. *Ibid.*, No. 6, p. 40.
29. *Ibid.*, pp. 42-43.
30. *Ibid.*, p. 42.

major dams. Two of these, Wrightsville and East Barre, were completed in 1935. Wrightsville, 1,200 feet long and seventy feet high, controlled the flow from seventy-one square miles of watershed; East Barre, which was slightly smaller, controlled the flow from thirty-eight square miles of watershed. The third dam, the Waterbury dam, completed later, was bigger than Wrightsville and East Barre combined, controlling the run-off from 109 square miles of watershed. Flood control of the Winooski River, whose waters had killed 120 persons in 1927, was one of the most enduring of all CCC achievements.[31]

The Walkill River project, which employed about 2,500 enrollees annually, involved channeling rather than dam construction, though about four miles of levees were also built. Enrollees excavated a channel 4.5 miles long and twenty feet deep, with a seventy-foot bottom width. The channel drew off flood waters, preventing the destruction of crops in the highly fertile farming sections along the Walkill River of upstate New York. This particular job was finished in 1937.[32]

The vast range of CCC work was not performed without considerable expense. One of the charges most often leveled against the Corps was that its cost was excessive for a relief agency.[33] If the agency's function was considered purely one of relief—distributing aid to the unemployed, but receiving little in return—then such charges can be partially substantiated. The annual cost per enrollee was $1,004, which compared unfavorably with that of the Works Progress Administration of $770 to $800, and the National Youth Administration of $400 to $700.[34]

However, to consider the Corps solely as a relief agency is to neglect the whole question of the benefits accruing to the United States as a result of its work. In other words, what was the financial return on every dollar expended on CCC activity? To

31. *Ibid.*, p. 16; *Literary Digest*, CXX (Dec. 21, 1935), 39.

32. *Report of the Director*, 1936, p. 16; New York *Times*, April 9, 1937.

33. New York *Herald Tribune*, Jan. 10, 1935; New York *Times*, Aug. 9, 1936.

34. *Reduction of Nonessential Federal Expenditures: Hearings Before the Joint Committee on the Reduction of Nonessential Federal Expenditures, Congress of the United States, 77th Congress, First Session, Pursuant to Section 601 of the Revenue Act of 1941*, Pts. 1-4, Nov. 28, Dec. 1, 2, and 4, 1941 (Washington, 1942). Hereinafter cited as *Nonessential Federal Expenditures, Hearings*, 1941.

estimate the value to the country of the Corps' work is impossible. McEntee considered in 1941 that the immediate physical value alone of the work done so far was at the very least $664 per enrollee, and this figure could not take into account its future value.[35] There was no way of calculating how much money had been saved because of fire prevention, or by how much the grazing program and erosion control schemes had increased land value and produced better crops and stock, or what the billions of trees planted would be worth in thirty years. Such achievements could not be measured in economic terms; suffice it to say that if this were possible, if the monetary value of all the present and future benefits of CCC work could be added together, then divided by the total number of enrollees, the per capita value thus obtained would far outweigh the per capita cost of $1,004. In terms of value obtained, the CCC surely showed a handsome profit.

Moreover, even this latter figure would not have considered one of the vital aspects of the CCC work. The role of the CCC as a conservor of human beings can in no way be measured economically, yet its importance in this field was seminal. The efficiency of the CCC as a rehabilitation agency can be studied in two ways: through looking at charts, facts, and figures, or by reviewing the testimonies of the enrollees and their families. The figures are impressive. The men gained from eight to fourteen pounds in weight and about one-half inch in height as a result of good food, regular hours, and hard work. The disease rate was low, in most cases lower than the national average for men of the enrollee's age group. The same was true for the mortality rate.[36] The educational program provided measurably useful instruction for many, and job opportunities for some. The Corps' success could often be represented by diagrams, such as graphs indicating weight gains, or similar sets of figures.[37]

35. *Ibid.*, p. 279.

36. *Report of the Director*, 1936, p. 12; 1939, pp. 29, 34; 1940, pp. 24-32. Enrollees received adequate leave time, though no standard leave system was adopted. Conditions and time allowed were rather fluid, depending on how far the enrollee was from his home town, how far the camp was situated from public transport, etc. In general, the enrollee could hope for a home visit at least twice during his enrolment period, as well as enjoying frequent weekend liberties. See chap. viii.

37. *Ibid.*, 1936, pp. 18-19.

No charts could indicate the effect of the CCC experience on the whole outlook of most enrollees. Figures cannot tell of hope regained or horizons broadened, yet such changes were a reality in the camps of the CCC. The words of the enrollees best tell the story. Life in the camp was a completely new experience for the enrollees, often their first taste of country living. For many of them the journey to camp was their first venture outside the home environment, and most found it salutary. A lad from Milroy, Pennsylvania, wrote: "I live in a little town which is smokey all the time and their is no fresh air, whatsoever like there is on the mountains, good fresh air and good eats, better than what over half the fellows are getting at home."[38] A former college student described rather strikingly the effect of camp life on him personally. "The mornings of sunlight," he wrote, "the evening dusk, and shaded sun when the stars are so close to the earth one could almost reach out and touch them, these are glorious days that shall never be forgotten. Each night I face the setting sun that floods the peaks of the distant mountains with crimson grandeur, and with me is the song of the hills, and the strength to face tomorrow's dawn."[39]

Three youths from New York City, who were sent to camp in Iowa, said "they saw a nation's vast resources" while making the journey across the country.[40] The Louisiana state director of relief reported that "boys who had never been away from the small rural community in which they grew up, came home on leave improved in knowledge with an interest in national problems."[41] Enrollee James W. Danner spoke articulately of the broadening effects of CCC life when he asserted that "as an Americanizing influence, the CCC is perhaps without equal." It blended people of different home and racial environments, "getting immigrants' sons away from the old world settlements in our big cities."[42] Few enrollees could have returned from camp

38. Gilbert Varner to Fechner, undated, S.D., Benefit Letters.
39. Karl Kidd, Azusa, Calif., to Fechner, undated, *ibid.*
40. Anon. to Roosevelt, July, 1936, Roosevelt Papers, O.F. 268–Misc., Box 18.
41. Mrs. Maude Barrett, Louisiana state director of relief, to Persons, Jan. 19, 1934, S.D., Benefit Letters.
42. James W. Danner, Cleveland, O., to Roosevelt, Sept. 21, 1936, Roosevelt Papers, O.F. 268–Misc., Box 18.

without having gained in understanding of their country and its people.

For some enrollees, CCC training opened up whole new vistas for future employment. One youth, whose series of articles for his camp newspaper came to the attention of the Metro-Goldwyn-Mayer motion picture studio, was given a position as a scenario writer there.[43] Another found a good job with a billing firm, purely because of the training in typing which he had received in camp. Others received scholarships to colleges and universities.[44] Not all enrollees succeeded in obtaining jobs upon their discharge, but their chances increased as employers became increasingly aware of the beneficial effects of camp life on the youths.[45]

Many enrollees found the chance to do something for their families the most satisfactory aspect of camp life. Enrollee John Ross, of Norwood, Colorado, told of receiving a letter from his mother, who was "proud of me for what I am able to do for her with the money that I am sending home. Her health has been poor for some time and I am helping to pay the necessary bills. This is in itself a great satisfaction to me."[46] Another boy, one of a family of seventeen with an unemployed father, spoke of the great assistance his monthly check had been to his family and to his own self-respect. The feeling of doing something for his people had inspired him to continue his interrupted education while in camp, and he had recently graduated from high school.[47]

In almost all the letters relating the specific benefits of CCC life, there was one common denominator, something at once intangible and very real. For most enrollees, enlistment in the CCC had been the final act, the culmination of a long period of despair and helplessness. It proved also to be a turning point.

43. Vernon D. Northrop, Calif., to Persons, undated, S.D., Benefit Letters.

44. *Happy Days*, Dec. 26, 1936, Jan. 2, 1937.

45. Holland and Hill, pp. 24-31; see also McEntee to Roosevelt, Aug. 10, 1934, O.F. 268, Box 4. McEntee found that 58 per cent of the youths leaving camp during the second six-month work period were idle, compared with 77 per cent of those leaving in the first period. The President was "delighted" with the report.

46. John Ross to Fechner, undated, S.D., Benefit Letters.

47. Boyd Hostetler to Fechner, undated, *ibid.*

The Corps rekindled hope for the future and faith in America and its way of life. Some expressed this experience articulately. Enrollee Karl Kidd said: "the greatest fact which the CCC has given me, as well as thousands of other young men, is the building of a strong and more enduring faith. Not one which is so frequently synonymous with ignorance or credulity, but a faith that restores belief in one's physical, mental and spiritual self, in his associates, and in the future."[48] Joseph E. Bush spoke of his "renewed ambitions and hope."[49] An enrollee who had lived in a transient camp before joining the Corps identified "a new-born fighting spirit within me," and emphatically declared that his CCC experience had made him a far better American.[50] Others, less introspective perhaps, were equally sincere. To enrollee Ray Johnson the CCC was the work of the Almighty. "God created this universe," he declared; "he gave us spring, with its beauty of flowers, and birds and trees. Now he has given us the CCC and this man Roosevelt. For that, I praise God."[51]

Of course, these written testimonies of faith renewed, hope rekindled, and horizons broadened have a somewhat limited value when one is estimating the effect of the CCC experience on the outlook of the enrollees. After all, it was not the typical youth who put his half-formed thoughts to paper, and any opinion on the question must inevitably be largely impressionistic. Certainly, for many enrollees the CCC probably meant three square meals a day, a bed at night, and little else. Nevertheless, and unless the collective testimony of parents, relief directors, camp officers, and the enrollees themselves is to be completely discarded, the camp experience brought benefits which were profoundly more than physical. In January, 1937, when the President accepted an award from the Foresters of America Association "for the greatest individual contribution to conservation in the United States in 1936" because of his "sponsorship" of the CCC, he would have been justified in pointing with pride to the Corps' achievement in the conservation of youth as well as of natural resources.[52]

48. Karl Kidd to Fechner, undated, *ibid.*
49. Joseph E. Bush, Cobalt, Conn., to Fechner, undated, *ibid.*
50. John E. Hussey, Johnstown, Pa., to Fechner, undated, *ibid.*
51. Ray Johnson, Cass, W. Va., to Fechner, undated, *ibid.*
52. Nixon, II, 8.

Not everyone who enrolled during the first four years of the CCC's existence benefited from the experience, however, nor were all enrollees satisfied with the conditions. Small-scale mutinies erupted, most of them due to conditions peculiar to the particular camp involved. Enrollees in camp at Battiest, Oklahoma, for example, once revolted because of the poor quality of the food there.[53] In New York, at the South Mountain reservation, some enrollees would not accept an 11 P.M. curfew, refusing to work until it had been lifted.[54] This type of rebellion involved only a minority of the company and was quelled without trouble, usually by the dismissal of the ringleaders. During the first four years, there was only one mutiny of significant proportions, when members of a camp at Maine refused en bloc to accept a transfer to Maryland, assaulting their officers when they attempted to enforce the ruling. This, too, was ended by dismissing the ringleaders.[55] A few such flurries were doubtless inevitable, and mutiny was never a serious problem in the early years of the Corps. Most enrollees were probably too cognizant of the relief the CCC offered them and were not willing to give it up easily.

Of greater concern was the desertion rate. By February, 1937, 11.6 per cent of all enrollees leaving the Corps were discharged for desertion, and the rate was increasing sharply. Almost all who deserted did so in their first few days in camp because of homesickness, and much was probably unavoidable. Nevertheless, the desertion problem was one which Corps officials had made little attempt to investigate, even after four years of experience, apart from trying to place as many enrollees as possible in camps some distance from their homes.[56] It is probable that a well-planned orientation scheme would have prevented at least some homesick enrollees from leaving camp, but the swift transition from the familiar home atmosphere to the rugged rural environment and the modified Army discipline still would have

53. Col. Major to Fechner, Jan. 24, 1934, Director, Correspondence.
54. New York *Times*, Jan. 9, 1935.
55. *Ibid.*, Nov. 7, 1934.
56. Advisory Council, Minutes, April 20, 1937. Some enrollees reacted violently against the discipline of the Army authorities without necessarily deserting. See Lawrence Bye to Roosevelt, Sept. 19, 1934, Director, Correspondence: "the captain of our camp is trying to enforce military displine on the member of our camp."

been too much for many to take. The problem was more wisely approached in the last few years of the Corps' existence when rapidly rising desertion rates had assumed serious proportions.[57]

Many enrollees, having had their self-respect somewhat restored by their camp experience, left the Corps as possessors of new hope and skills, only to have their optimism destroyed by continued failure to find employment. Often they reverted to their earlier patterns of bleak existence, lacking in morale, confidence, and hope.[58] From 1933 through 1937 the unemployment situation probably made this inevitable. There were simply not enough jobs for all former enrollees, and the fact that the CCC experience did help so many of them to secure employment is a signal argument in its favor. Nevertheless, the CCC organization was tardy in developing any sort of co-ordinated employment agency. Virtually nothing had been done by 1937, and returning enrollees still had to seek out jobs themselves. Individual camp advisers and local relief directors occasionally interested themselves in the problem of placing the returning enrollee, and employers with a vacancy frequently approached camp commanders looking for a suitable man. But it was not until the last four years of the Corps' existence that a serious attempt was made to develop any national job-finding agency, and by this time rising white re-employment rates had made its need less urgent.[59]

57. The desertion problem is discussed in chap. xi, below.
58. Press Release, Sept., 1934, in S.D., Benefit Letters.
59. *Ibid.*; see also Holland and Hill, pp. 242-243; Hill, pp. 51-53.

8. *A Day in the CCC*

For the typical CCC enrollee, actual arrival at camp was the culmination of a fairly lengthy selection process. Some months earlier he had taken the initial step toward entrance by applying to his local selection agency for consideration as an enrollee.[1] He then waited patiently for a period of up to two months until his application had been processed. If accepted, he was sent to a conditioning camp, usually at an Army post, where he was physically examined, vaccinated, clothed, and studied in his reactions to Army discipline and hard labor. If the youth measured up to the somewhat rigorous standards demanded there, he was formally enrolled, took an oath of obedience, and was sent to an ordinary work camp.[2]

CCC publications used to claim that the average enrollee was twenty years old when he entered camp, and came from a family of six children. His father was unemployed, and he himself had not worked for at least nine months. He had completed the eighth grade. He weighed 147 pounds and was 5 feet 8¼ inches tall; thus, he was underweight and below average in height.[3] This is a rather rigid picture and obviously could not have fitted exactly the description of the vast majority of enrollees, yet it is probable that many of them shared at least some of these characteristics.

The spectacle which greeted the new enrollee, the type of camp which was to be his home for at least six months, varied both from region to region and according to when the enrollee entered the CCC. The first camps were often simply tents which, though lined in neat rows, had all the disadvantages attendant to life under canvas.[4] In the early days of the CCC, existence could indeed be most uncomfortable, particularly in the mountains when the spring thaw started. Such conditions, however, were neither widespread nor permanent. From the very start

1. See U. S. Department of Labor, *Handbook for Agencies Selecting Men for Emergency Conservation Work* (Washington, 1933), pp. 2-5.
2. Harper, pp. 35-37.
3. *Report of the Director*, 1937, p. 5; Holland and Hill, pp. 58-61.
4. Dorothy E. Bromley, "The Forest Army that Lives By Work," New York *Times*, July 23, 1933, sec. viii, p. 2.

many enrollees lived in wooden barracks, and these quickly became general. Each camp consisted of four or five barrack buildings, one hundred feet long by twenty feet wide, together with a mess hall, a recreation hall, administration buildings, officers' quarters, a hospital, a garage, and often a schoolhouse. The buildings usually lay in a rough "U" shape around an open space which was either planted to grass or cleared for sports purposes. Sometimes the structures were painted brown or green, but more often than not they were simply creosoted or covered with tar paper. Though usually wired for electric light, they were frequently inadequately illuminated.[5]

The buildings were solidly constructed, usually of cedar, and could not easily be dismantled once the camp had finished its work project. Sometimes they were turned over to a nearby community for its own particular purposes, but more often than not they were left boarded up and desolate, a waste of time, effort, and money. In 1936, therefore, Fechner took a radical step in camp planning, deciding that all future CCC camps were to be of a pre-cut portable variety, of standard design, easily dismantled at the end of a work project, ready to be transported wherever a new camp was authorized, and there set up, waiting for new occupants.[6] This was a far-reaching change, and one which was generally welcomed by Corps officials. Camps were now standardized, each having four barracks buildings, one mess hall, one schoolhouse, bath houses, one latrine block, and twelve officers' and service buildings.[7]

Though the camp buildings henceforth conformed to a standard plan, the way they were situated depended on the type of country in which the camp was located. There were about fifty ways that the basic functional plan could be altered, depending on the particular contours of the terrain. Thus, the camps did not all seem to be dreary replicas of the same model. Some, it is true, were constructed and appointed with a startling lack of originality, but others were designed and finished with pride

5. Holland and Hill, pp. 36-37; Hill, p. 57.
6. U. S. Department of Agriculture, Forest Service, Region 8, Handbook of the Civilian Conservation Corps, 1938 (typescript in Duke University Library), p. 114.
7. *Ibid.*

and imagination. The enrollees labored long hours to lay gravel paths between the barracks. They built rustic gates and railings, planted trees, and added swimming pools, outdoor amphitheaters, fishponds, or flower gardens. Within the buildings, they built fireplaces of brick and stone, painted or polished the walls to bring out the natural wood grain, adding charm in many different ways to the basic camp plan.[8] At its best, the CCC camp was a construction of real beauty. Frank Hill has described a number of startlingly attractive camps he had visited throughout the land; a camp on the Yosemite Valley floor in winter, surrounded by snow-laden pines, another perched high on a crag above Los Angeles, one in New York situated beside twin lakes, a soil erosion camp in Texas standing uncompromisingly strong—"the gaunt wastes of plain around it."[9] Such camps as these, he said, either contrasted starkly with the barrenness of their surroundings or enhanced the natural beauty of the sites. Not all camps maintained the same high standards, but there were few which did not try to capture something of the unique, almost pioneer, flavor of the whole CCC enterprise.

Whether the camp was in Alaska or Oklahoma, Florida or Puerto Rico, the daily routine was carried out according to the same broad program. Reveille was at 6 A.M., and enrollees could not afford to dally in bed because they had to be washed and dressed in their work clothes by 6:30 A.M., ready for physical training.[10] Upon arrival at camp, enrollees were usually given two sets of clothing, a blue denim work or fatigue suit and a renovated Army olive drab uniform for dress purposes. In 1938, however, Roosevelt ordered that a special, spruce-green dress uniform be issued to all enrollees. The President, while visiting a camp at Warm Springs, had been disagreeably surprised by the

8. Hill, p. 2.

9. *Ibid.*, pp. 2-4. Each camp had a letter of designation which identified both the type of work on which it was engaged and the agency which was controlling it. Thus, camps operating in national forests under the direction of the Forest Service were identified by the letter "F" before their numbers, those in state forests by the letter "S." Other common letters of designation were "A" (Bureau of Agricultural Research), "D" (Drainage, Bureau of Agricultural Engineering), "SCS" (Soil Conservation Service), "BR" (Bureau of Reclamation), "NPS" (National Parks Service), and "GLO" (General Land Office).

10. *Report of the Director*, 1937, p. 3.

poor quality of the dress uniforms. Shoddy clothing, he believed, weakened morale, and he immediately asked the Department of the Navy to design him a special CCC uniform.[11] These were in widespread use by 1939.

After physical training, the enrollees trooped off to breakfast, a noisy but satisfying meal eaten at long tables, at each of which six to twelve men could be seated. CCC food was plain, nourishing, and served in large quantities. A typical breakfast could consist of stewed prunes, cereal, ham and eggs, coffee, and milk.[12] Fechner once described camp food as "wholesome, palatable and of the variety that sticks to the ribs," and the monthly camp food order would seem to bear this out. Typical commodities purchased included bacon, beans, beef, butter, cheese, chicken, eggs, flour, lard, milk, onions, pork, potatoes, rice, sugar, syrup, apples, baking powder, cinnamon, cocoa, coffee, flavoring extract, corn, macaroni, peaches, peas, pepper, pickles, pineapple, prunes, rolled oats, salt, tea, tomatoes, and vinegar.[13] CCC food was not perhaps prepared according to the best French cuisine, but it was usually well-balanced and nourishing.

After breakfast, the enrollees usually policed the grounds, tidied their huts, and then, in one of the few concessions made to military practice, formed up in rough platoons for roll call and inspection before departing for work about 7:45 A.M.[14] Enrollees walked or rode to work, depending on how far the work project was from the camp. The jobs on which the enrollees were engaged were as various as the types of camps authorized. Enrollees in a forestry camp might find themselves working in small groups under an enrollee leader, clearing dead wood, planting trees, digging out rocks, or building trails.[15] Some might be clearing strips for firebreaks, others building lookout towers, telephone lines, small dams, or bridges.[16] Those working on erosion control projects might be planting kudzu grass as cover, building

11. C.R.M., No. 781, Special Enrollee Uniforms.
12. Holland and Hill, p. 38.
13. *Report of the Director*, 1938, pp. 8-9.
14. Holland and Hill, p. 38; Frank Ernest Hill, "The CCC Marches Towards a New Destiny," New York *Times*, Feb. 21, 1937, sec. vii, pp. 10-11.
15. Bromley, "The Forest Army that Lives by Work."
16. *Forest Improvement by the CCC*, pp. 2-9.

small check dams on the edge of a hillside, or marking a terrace prior to turning it into contour patterns.[17] Bureau of Reclamation camps were usually engaged in the construction of small storage dams, frequently made of earth, while those under National Parks Service control were engaged in a whole host of functions, ranging from the planting and thinning of trees to the building of simple picnic spots complete with rustic furniture.[18]

Work continued till about noon and then ceased for lunch, which was usually brought to the work project. Again it was substantial fare, sometimes a full-scale hot meal, but more often sandwiches, pie, and coffee.[19] Lunch break lasted for an hour and then work was resumed, continuing until 4:00 P.M. when enrollees returned to camp.

The evening meal was usually not held before 5:30 P.M., and the time between the return to camp and dinner belonged to the enrollees. They used it in various ways. Most camps had sports fields adjacent to them, and many youths enjoyed taking part in football, baseball, or basketball, depending on the season. Sometimes the sports were quite highly competitive, with representative teams being chosen for contests against nearby camps or neighborhood community teams.[20] Indeed, some CCC athletes won football scholarships to major colleges, and a score of baseball players were signed by major league scouts traveling the CCC circuit.[21] More often than not, though, sports activities were loosely organized, with the emphasis on participation rather than excellence. For those less energetically inclined, there were pool and table tennis facilities, as well as the camp library. Libraries were arranged on a mobile basis. In a given area, the books available were divided into nine groups, and each group was rotated among nine camps. The type of book available in a typical library was roughly as follows: adventure and mystery, seventeen volumes; miscellaneous fiction, twenty-nine; westerns, twelve; travel, twenty; history and biography, twelve; science fiction, twenty-nine; athletics, five; and religion, three. Popular

17. Holland and Hill, p. 113.
18. *Report of the Director*, 1938, pp. 45-46.
19. Holland and Hill, p. 38.
20. Harper, p. 52; *Happy Days*, June 24, 1933.
21. *Happy Days*, Jan. 2, 1937.

authors were Rex Beach, Sax Rohmer, Rafael Sabatini, and Edgar Wallace.[22] Each library also contained forty-five periodicals, usually including *Life, Time, Newsweek, The Saturday Evening Post, Radio News,* and the Sears-Roebuck catalogue. *The New Republic* and *Nation* were banned, because in the eyes of many CCC officers they bordered on the subversive.[23] No doubt the camp libraries provided enjoyable reading for many enrollees, and instruction for a few, but they were often subject to criticism. Sometimes the books were locked away, the enrollee could not "browse around," but had to ask for a specific book, scarcely encouraging for those wanting to read but whose knowledge of books and authors was severely limited. More substantial was criticism of the types of books available. It was asserted that CCC officials had catered too much to popular literary tastes, had been unimaginative in their selection of books, and had made little attempt to insure that enrollees came in contact either with literary masterpieces or radical points of view on major issues.[24] These judgments were just. Certainly the youths could not be forced to read, and most did so only cursorily and purely for recreation. Nevertheless, a library which seeks only to amuse and not to challenge or to inform is failing in its duty. CCC librarians, without stacking their shelves solely with cheap copies of classics or with political tracts, could surely have provided better fare for the enrollees than the pap which they were satisfied to dispense.

After the recreation period, dinner was served, enrollees wearing their dress uniforms to this meal. Again the food was substantial, with plenty of meat and fresh vegetables, invariably followed by fruit and dessert.[25] After the meal, most of the youths attended classes as part of the camp education program, but study was not the only evening activity planned. Table tennis and pool tables were very popular, and for those enrollees with time on their hands there was always the chance of a ride to the nearest town, there to see a movie, meet a girl, spend their al-

22. New York *Times*, Jan. 9, 1938; *New Republic*, LXXXIII (June 12, 1935), 128.
23. Holland and Hill, p. 156; CCC Handbook, p. 120.
24. Holland and Hill, p. 157.
25. *Ibid.*, p. 41.

lowance, or just stroll around. Often, if no transportation was available and if it was not too far away, enrollees seeking entertainment would walk to the nearest community.[26] There was usually no restriction on their leaving camp after work, provided that they came back by lights out. If they were tardy in this respect, they were likely to lose their privileges.[27]

At 9:45 P.M. camp lights were flashed off and on, the signal to prepare for bed. Lights went out at 10 P.M. and taps was blown fifteen minutes later. If the boys had done a full day's work, many would have retired long before the official time, and quieting them at night was usually no problem at all. At 11 P.M. the camp commander made a brief bed check to see that no one was absent. Then the camp slept.[28]

It must not be thought that enrollees, after entering camp, did not see their families or home again until discharge day. Leave provisions were relatively generous, and enrollees were usually able to visit their families once a month if they so desired, though this, of course, was conditioned somewhat by the distance between the camp and the enrollee's home. It was the Corps' original intention to locate all youths about two hundred miles from their home districts, too far for weekly visits, yet close enough for monthly trips, but this provision was frequently neglected.[29] Obviously a New York boy in camp in Oregon was unable to get home regularly, but even he could get some leave should he decide to re-enrol at the end of his initial six-month stint. All re-enlisting enrollees were given a six-day leave of absence on full pay between tours of duty—time enough for most to get home, if only for a day or so.[30]

Besides normal leave provisions, there were other days when no work was done. The standard holidays, January 1, February 12, May 30, July 4, Labor Day, Thanksgiving, and Christmas were all observed, as were denominational religious holidays, be

26. *Report of the Director*, 1937, p. 3; 77th Cong., 2nd Sess., *Civilian Conservation Corps: A Monograph by the Legislative Reference Service, Library of Congress* (Washington, 1941); Senate Documents, No. 216, pp. 51-52.
27. Harper, p. 51.
28. *Report of the Director*, 1941, p. 9; Holland and Hill, p. 41.
29. Holland and Hill, p. 77.
30. CCC Handbook, p. 201.

they Jewish, Catholic, Greek Orthodox, or Protestant.[31] Moreover, all enrollees of voting age were given three days with pay to register and vote in primaries and local, state, and national elections.[32] Perhaps not surprisingly, the CCC vote tended to be solidly Democratic. Local Republicans, therefore, often challenged fruitlessly the right of enrollees to vote in other districts.[33] Indeed, some tried more direct methods. Testifying before a New York state commission investigating election irregularities, CCC enrollees in camp at Tuckahoe, New York, disclosed how they had been bribed by local Republicans to vote the GOP ticket in 1936. Having accepted the money, the enrollees proceeded to vote for F. D. R.![34]

Enrollees were also free on weekends, unless, of course, the weather during the week had been so bad that there was work to be made up.[35] If not, Saturday was often devoted to sports and to group activities such as drama and choral work. CCC boys were avid play producers, sometimes reaching quite high standards. A few CCC authors and actors, in fact, were able to get work with the Federal Theatre Project after leaving camp.[36] There were also camp dances. Most camps held about four dances annually, inviting girls from the local communities.[37] These were popular affairs with both the enrollees and their partners, the music more often than not being furnished by the camp swing band. On Sundays religious services were held in all camps. In June, 1941, for example, there were 154 full-time CCC chaplains on duty, as well as 189 part-time contract clergymen paid by Fechner's office, and five hundred volunteer, unpaid clergymen from neighboring towns. The chaplains preached to the enrollees, counselled them, visited the sick, buried the dead, and performed the few marriages contracted between enrollees and local girls.[38] These clergymen, unfortunately, were often of

31. *Ibid.*
32. *Ibid.*
33. New York *Times*, Oct. 23 and 29, 1936.
34. *Ibid.*, Dec. 15, 16, and 17, 1936.
35. Federal Security Agency, *The CCC At Work* (Washington, 1942), p. 40.
36. New York *Times*, April 3, 1937.
37. Holland and Hill, p. 204.
38. *Report of the Director*, 1941, p. 26.

limited ability and made little attempt to adjust the level of their services to the enrollees. They put more stress on preaching than on personal contact, and for this reason their work in the camps was not as effective as it could have been.[39]

A constant weekend activity among some youths was journalism, and most camps contributed regular activity reports to the national CCC newspaper, *Happy Days*.[40] In addition, many camps published their own newspapers. In August, 1935, there were 1,122 such journals, some bearing such esoteric titles as the *Flickertail Crier*, the *Gully Growler*, and the *Grapevine Send-off*. Most of the work was done by the enrollees themselves during journalism courses on weeknights and on the weekends.[41] For many enrollees, the weekend was emphatically not a time of relaxation.

Enrollees transferred the traditional camp practice of "hazing" to the CCC context. New enrollees were fair game, and many an unfortunate youth, sleeping deeply after his first day on the job, awoke to find himself in the center of the parade ground, having been carried there, bed and all, by his seasoned barracks companions. Dressing hurriedly in the morning, he might also have found his shoes nailed securely to the floor. This type of hazing was innocuous enough. More harmful was the bullying which took place in a few camps and which often worried new enrollees.[42] Hazing received official sanction in some camps, and "kangaroo courts" were established. In these, enrollees who had committed minor offences, or who had offensive personal habits, were tried and summarily, usually corporally, punished. The vehemence with which those delegated to do so carried out the sentences led to complaints, however, and the courts were soon abandoned in all but a very few camps. Discipline, even for minor offences, was again the prerogative of the camp commander.[43]

An interesting aspect of CCC life was that the enrollees

39. Holland and Hill, p. 214.
40. Harper, p. 52.
41. *Literary Digest*, CXXIII (June 16, 1937), 32; Records of the CCC, Educational Correspondence, CCC Activities in Nov., 1935 (typescript), p. 7.
42. Holland and Hill, pp. 129-130.
43. Harper, p. 45.

evolved their own language, a peculiar mode of speaking which was incomprehensible to the outside ear. Only a CCC enrollee, for example, could tell that "Hey, greaseball, got a stiffy? Well, sawdust and blankets will do," was simply a request for a cigarette, followed by an assertion that tobacco and paper would suffice. Enrollees referred to soft drink as "slough-water," a clergyman was a "sin-buster," and "submarine turkey" was a fish. CCC slang bore little resemblance to Army slang or to the language of the assembly line and the city street. It was something indigenous to the camps themselves and to the collective existence in the woods.[44]

There were critics of the tone of CCC camp life. Some directed their shafts at specific aspects of the camp existence. The Women's Christian Temperance Union, for example, while supporting the Corps in general, campaigned vociferously to have beer banned from camp canteens.[45] Townsfolk living near camps occasionally complained that the enrollees were making too free with their daughters.[46] Others were more generally critical, claiming, with some justification, that despite the education program, the camps did not do enough for the boys intellectually—that they did not give them any real interest in government, in public problems, or in American democracy itself. Nor were the boys sufficiently prepared for life outside the CCC existence.[47] There is truth in this complaint, yet in the long view the conclusion seems inescapable that the CCC was a vitalizing, not a stultifying force for most of the young men who passed through its forest portals. Work in the wilderness, as we have seen, gave to so many new health, new courage, and new faith in their country and its future.

44. New York *Times*, May 14, 1936.
45. *Ibid.*, Sept. 7, 1935.
46. CCC enrollees contracted venereal disease at the rate of 18.3 per 1,000. This compares very favorably with the Army rate of 87 per 1,000 in World War I, 140 per 1,000 in the Spanish-American War, and 90 per 1,000 in the Civil War. *Time*, XXXIII (Feb. 6, 1939), 11.
47. Holland and Hill, pp. 138-139, 226-227.

9. *The Fight for Permanence*

Scarcely had the CCC been established when individuals and groups began to discuss the possibility of its becoming a permanent federal agency. The secretary of the American Forestry Association, Ovid Butler, called as early as September, 1933, for a permanent organization,[1] and in November of that year the acting chief forester, C. M. Granger, asked regional foresters for their suggestions.[2] The President himself soon began to talk about a possible permanent organization, though on a smaller scale,[3] and by 1935 he was stating specifically that "these camps, in my judgment, are going to be a permanent part of the policy of the United States Government."[4] Indeed, by late 1935 the Forest Service even had a draft bill ready.[5]

It was in 1936, however, that plans for permanence began to take definite shape, and there are several reasons which explain this. First, the camps had obviously succeeded in their work and were firmly entrenched in popular favor. The climate of public opinion, therefore, was right for such a move.[6] Second, in accordance with the existing law, the CCC's activity would automatically terminate on March 31, 1937, unless congressional action assured its continuance. This seemed a fine opportunity, therefore, to propose legislation for permanence.[7] Third, investigation had indicated that there was enough conservation work to justify a permanent agency. Official surveys showed "that the annual work load ahead for a permanent CCC would increase rather than diminish during the next few years."[8] Finally, 1936 was an election year, and while the permanence of the CCC

1. Ovid Butler to Roosevelt, Sept. 20, 1933, Files of the Secretary of Agriculture–Conservation.

2. Granger to Regional Foresters, Nov. 4, 1933, C.R.M., No. 791, Permanent CCC. The chief forester, Major Stuart, had committed suicide in October, 1933, and was eventually replaced by Ferdinand A. Silcox. See Schlesinger, II, 340.

3. Roosevelt to Owen Winston, Jan. 25, 1934, in Nixon, I, 247.

4. Rosenman, ed., *Papers*, IV, 365.

5. C.R.M., No. 791, Permanent CCC.

6. Sen. Albert Thomas (Dem., Utah) to Roosevelt, March 18, 1936, Roosevelt Papers, P.P.F. 1454.

7. Roosevelt to Fechner, March 23, 1936, Roosevelt Papers, O.F. 268, Box 7; Rosenman, ed., *Papers*, V, 150-151.

8. Fechner to Roosevelt, Oct. 24, 1936, *ibid.*, O.F. 268, Box 7.

was never a major issue, it is possible, in view of the Corps' popularity, that Roosevelt's advocacy of it during the campaign redounded to his political benefit.[9]

In this expectant atmosphere the various co-operating bodies began to produce their own proposals for permanence, each one tending to reflect the particular interests of the agency concerned. The Forest Service, for example, wanted the existing organization of the Corps to be continued virtually intact, but with far greater emphasis laid on its conservation aspect.[10] The Office of Education, on the other hand, not altogether satisfied with what it had so far received, pressed for a radical and impractical restructuring of the whole CCC framework. Under its plan the Corps was to have two co-directors, one for work and one for recreation, the whole enterprise to be supervised by a federal board of educators. The role of the Army was to be severely limited, and enrollees were to be selected by state and local guidance councils. They would then go to one of two proposed camp types, depending on whether they were between seventeen and twenty years old or between twenty-one and twenty-four. The work program was to be an amalgam of physical labor, prescribed recreation, and education, with the emphasis laid on the third component. Enrollees, after identifying their educational needs, were to be dispatched to a camp of their choice.[11] The War Department had no detailed plans for permanence: it wanted out of the whole CCC arrangement. When it became clear that Roosevelt was opposed to this, the Army supported the Forest Service in advocating that the present organization be unchanged.[12]

As well as receiving detailed plans, Fechner, in accordance with the President's wishes, held informal discussions with the Advisory Council seeking further views on the best ways of approaching permanence. He was unpleasantly surprised to find that some took a cautious attitude. W. Frank Persons, in particular, while realizing that the imminent expiration of the orig-

9. New York *Times*, Oct. 28, 1936.
10. C.R.M., No. 791, Permanent CCC.
11. "Plan for a Permanent C.C.C.," Jan. 30, 1936, S.D., Education, Correspondence.
12. Advisory Council, Minutes, Dec. 22, 1936.

inal statute made some action inevitable, counseled against pressing for immediate permanence. Rather, he thought that the Corps should be continued on a temporary basis for another eighteen months, during which time the whole matter could be investigated thoroughly, alternatives could be considered, policy defined, and a well-rounded bill eventually presented to Congress. Hasty legislation, he believed, would surely be regretted.[13] Fechner, for his part, could see no reason for delay. He foresaw no congressional controversy whatsoever over the passage of the bill, as he considered that all political groups were "favorable to a permanent CCC organization. So far as I know, the Democrats certainly are, the Republicans certainly are, the Farmer-Laborites certainly are, and the Progressives—at least as exemplified by their present representatives in Congress. I do not know of a Congressman or Senator who is definitely opposed to the continuance of the CCC."[14] Fechner thought that Congress would back anything the Advisory Council recommended, and he strongly disapproved of any further holdup, yet he agreed to make known the views of Persons and his supporters to Roosevelt.

The President, however, paid little attention to the Advisory Council's opinions when Fechner brought them to his attention. He agreed with the Forest Service and War Department and decided to proceed immediately with a bill which would make the Corps permanent, but which would effect no change in administration. The Army, despite its protests, was to remain in charge of the camps, and the role of the technical services was to be unchanged. Camps were, however, to be reduced in number, the permanent CCC to employ no more than 300,000 youths in 1,456 camps.[15]

It was no surprise, therefore, when, in his annual budget message on January 7, 1937, President Roosevelt spoke on the future of the CCC. "The Civilian Conservation Corps has demonstrated its usefulness," he declared, "and has met with general public approval. It should be continued. I intend shortly to submit a supplemental estimate of appropriation to carry the Corps from March 31, 1937, to the end of the current fiscal year;

13. *Ibid.*
14. *Ibid.*
15. *Ibid.*

and I strongly recommend that Congress enact during its present session the necessary legislation to establish the Corps as a permanent agency of the Government."[16] There was little comment in the leading newspapers on the proposal, and what there was predicted an easy passage for the measure.[17] Permanence for the CCC seemed destined to be a routine affair.

It was not until April 5, however, that the Administration moved further. In a message to Congress on that day, the President called for legislation creating a permanent CCC of 300,000 youths and veterans, together with 10,000 Indians and 5,000 enrollees in the territories and insular possessions. He justified his report by pointing to the "physical improvement" of forest land as a result of the Corps' activities, by warning of the need for much more of the same type of work, and by stressing "the improvement . . . in the moral and physical well-being of our citizens who have been enrolled in the Corps, and of their families."[18]

Apart from making the CCC an independent agency and transferring all Emergency Conservation Work records and property to it, the proposed bill did nothing more than perpetuate the organizational and administrative traditions that had been used and developed during the past four years. The offices and functions of the director and the Advisory Council were to be preserved, and the President was "authorized to utilize the services . . . of such departments or agencies of the Government as he may deem necessary for carrying out the purposes of this Act." He was also given the responsibility of deciding on rates of pay and allotments. Among the few significant changes in policy was the ruling that all Corps employees would henceforth come under Civil Service provisions. Those presently holding positions had to take a Civil Service Commission non-competitive examination within twelve months or lose their jobs. Moreover, the maximum number of enrollees was fixed at 300,000, including no more than 30,000 veterans. Enrollees were now to be between seven-

16. Rosenman, ed., *Papers*, V, 645.
17. New York *Times*, Jan. 9, 1937; St. Louis *Post-Dispatch*, Jan. 9, 1937.
18. Nixon, II, 34. The bill had been drafted by Fechner, based on previously issued Executive Orders relating to the administration of the CCC.

teen and twenty-three years of age and should "at the time of enrollment be unemployed and in needy circumstances." No relief provision was specifically mentioned. Despite these few alterations, the intention was clearly to depart as little as possible from the basic practices and traditions of the CCC as they had evolved in the past four years.[19]

The Senate Committee on Education and Labor held hearings on the measure on April 9 and 13, 1937.[20] The bulk of the time was spent questioning Fechner on the specifics of administration, work, and opportunity in the Corps. Little of significance was discussed and no controversial issues were raised. The only Republican committee member who attended, Senator James J. Davis of Pennsylvania, confined his questions to particular details concerning his home state and seemed in no way to dispute the need for a permanent CCC at this time.[21] Only Senator Elbert D. Thomas of Utah attempted to draw attention to any of the broader issues involved in the transfer to permanent status. He thought that the whole work relief concept of the Corps should be discarded, and that it should become a place of rehabilitation for socially deprived young men, whatever their financial status. Millionaires' sons probably needed training in social responsibility more than anyone else, he surmised.[22] For the most part, however, the hearing was a formality. Passage of the measure was probably fully expected.

Of more substance were the House hearings, held before the Committee on Labor on April 14 and 15, 1937. Several congressmen took exception to Fechner's apparent lack of emphasis on the educational aspects of the CCC life and to his refusal to permit the shortening of the work day to allow more classes. Representative Albert Thomas, Democrat of Texas, opposed the lack of compulsory education in the camps and said that on-the-job training was insufficient. He claimed that the Corps merely took boys off relief and eventually discharged them without

19. *Permanency Hearings*, 1937, pp. 1-3.
20. *To Establish a Civilian Conservation Corps: Hearings Before the Committee on Education and Labor, United States Senate, 75th Congress, First Session, on S. 2102*, April 9 and 13, 1937 (Washington, 1937).
21. *Ibid.*, pp. 54-56.
22. *Ibid.*, p. 57.

having given them much of long-term value.[23] A permanent CCC, he asserted, should have a wider educative function. Representative Glen Griswold, Democrat of Indiana, also advocated compulsory education, disagreeing with Fechner's insistence that the two principal objectives of the Corps were relief of unemployment and the accomplishment of useful work.[24] Congressman James J. Scrugham, Democrat of Nevada, took issue with the clause limiting enrolment to 300,000 youths. He considered 350,000 to be an absolute minimum figure in view of the unemployment rate and the amount of conservation work yet to be done.[25] He was supported by Representative Walter M. Pierce, Democrat of Oregon, who contended that "the WPA money has not been nearly as successful or profitably spent" as the CCC appropriation. To cut the best of all the Administration's relief projects was indefensible.[26] There was, however, no serious opposition to the intent of the measure, with Republican committee members limiting their collective contribution to a few specific questions. The bill was reported favorably on April 21. Any serious criticism would now have to take place on the floor of the House; and though a group of House Democrats had indicated their dissatisfaction at the reduction of enrolment to 300,000, the prospects for passage were still excellent.[27] When the measure received an early clearance from the Rules Committee on May 3, a permanent CCC seemed only a matter of time.[28]

The House, acting as the Committee of the Whole, debated the measure on May 11, 1937. It was soon apparent that virtually no one wanted to end the CCC. What was surprising, however, and alarming to Administration leaders, was the strength of bipartisan support for a proposal that the Corps be extended for two years only. Announcing that he intended to offer an amendment to this effect, the House Minority leader, Representative Bertrand H. Snell of New York, while praising the good work of the Corps, declared he was "not ready to say that the U.S. will never again be able to take care of its boys from 17 to 25 years

23. *Permanency Hearings*, 1937, pp. 93-95.
24. *Ibid.*, p. 97.
25. *Ibid.*, p. 101.
26. *Ibid.*, p. 105.
27. New York *Times*, April 22, 1937.
28. *Ibid.*, May 4, 1947.

of age without putting them in the CCC camps."[29] Democrats who spoke early supported this point of view: they warned against hasty legislation and advocated a two-year extension period while the whole question of the role of a permanent CCC in American life was more thoroughly explored.[30] The Democratic leaders in the House soon realized, to their surprise, that all their skill would be required to keep the measure out of trouble.

The Administration's view was presented by Representative William P. Connery, who had introduced the bill, and Representative Jennings Randolph, Democrat of West Virginia. They rested their case on twin arguments of the Corps' popularity and proven worth, emphasizing that the President clearly desired that the measure should pass.[31] Randolph cited a recent public opinion poll which indicated that 87 per cent of all Americans, including a majority of registered Republicans, favored the Corps, and he dwelt on its success in building "not only better land, but better men."[32] These arguments were beside the point since few congressmen, Republican or Democrat, denied that the Corps had been anything but a success, and most of them wanted it to be continued.[33] Rather, the relevant issue was whether hasty legislation was warranted or whether an extension period of two years, during which time a thorough investigation of all aspects of the Corps could be made, would be a better way of insuring continuance. Moreover, the argument that the President wanted the bill passed intact was not calculated to overly impress congressmen, who were already sorely troubled and divided by his strong backing of the controversial Supreme Court reform plan.[34] They had had enough of presidential pressure for one session.

29. *C.R.*, 75th Cong., 1st Sess., Vol. 81, Pt. 4, p. 4351.
30. *Ibid.*, pp. 4350-4351, 4357.
31. *Ibid.*, pp. 4355, 4361-4362. This was the same Connery who had opposed the original measure in 1933. See chap. i, above.
32. *Ibid.*, p. 4361.
33. The only vocal opposition to continuance came from a long-time foe of the CCC, Rep. John Taber (Rep., N. Y.), who felt that the Corps did not teach the boys in "the old fashioned American way, how to make something of himself." He stood "absolutely square-toed opposed" to the bill. *Ibid.*, p. 4360.
34. See Burns, pp. 293-315.

There were several other specific objections to the Administration's measure, some of which had been explored previously at the hearings. Representative Arthur B. Jenks, Republican of New Hampshire, favored the bill but wanted provision made for ten hours of vocational training, to be taken out of the working hours. He was supported by Representative Arthur H. Greenwood, Democrat of Indiana.[35] Representative Randolph felt that the enrolment limit of 300,000 was too low and personally preferred a minimum of 350,000.[36] Representative Jack Nichols, Democrat of Oklahoma, pointed out that the Civil Service provision would mean the end of a good source of patronage for Democrats and accordingly he proposed that it be removed.[37] The bill as it stood was seriously in trouble, though the success of the CCC was never the point at issue.

Connery, probably sensing failure, made a strong plea for passage of the Administration's measure. Pointing out that Congress could abolish the CCC at any time, permanent or not, he stressed that "this is the pet project of the President of the United States; it is his baby if you please . . . he has asked it be made permanent." Snell immediately ridiculed him for insisting that the measure be passed "because it is the pet project of the President." It was, he asserted, a poor excuse for doing a foolish thing: the wisest policy was to extend the CCC for two years, then see if the need for permanence still existed.[38] Possibly to forestall a Republican move to this effect, Representative Fritz G. Lanham, Democrat of Texas, offered an amendment continuing the provision of the existing act for two more years, "till we can better know under what conditions it should be made permanent. It is an emergency measure," he said, and to make it permanent now would be to take a pessimistic view and admit that the emergency would never end.[39]

Democrats supported the Lanham Amendment strongly. Representative Samuel Hobbs of Alabama believed the CCC was

35. *C.R.*, 75th Cong., 1st Sess., Vol. 81, Pt. 4, pp. 4352, 4358.
36. *Ibid.*, p. 4363.
37. *Ibid.*, p. 4376.
38. *Ibid.*, p. 4379. This was one of Connery's last appearances in Congress, as he died in June, 1937.
39. *Ibid.*, p. 4379.

one of the "most splendid accomplishments of the New Deal," but that the proposed permanency bill was "hopelessly unconstitutional" in its unauthorized delegation of power to the director and to the President. Others spoke on similar lines and the Lanham Amendment passed the Committee of the Whole by 224 to 34.[40] The committee then further amended the Administration's bill. Educational and vocational training was made compulsory.[41] The Civil Service provision was removed, thus safeguarding congressional patronage;[42] and, unexpectedly, the committee voted to cut Fechner's salary from $12,000 to $10,000.[43] The relief provision, as it affected enrolment, was reinserted.[44]

On the following day, May 12, the House confirmed the amendments of the Committee of the Whole and then voted on the passage of the bill, which now extended the Corps for two years only. The measure was passed by the huge margin of 389 to 7, only two Democrats and five Republicans voting against it.[45] Nevertheless, the Administration's measure had been altered in its essentials. The CCC, though now independent, was not yet permanent.

Many newspapers interpreted the passage of the Lanham Amendment not as an expression of lack of confidence in the CCC but as a blow struck for congressional independence. The New York *Times* described it as "the largest Democratic defection in years," and thoroughly approved of the House's action.[46] The Chicago *Tribune* called the defeat the "most drastic since Roosevelt took office," but pointed out that "the merits of the CCC were not at issue" and that its success was beyond question. Nevertheless, the *Tribune* thought that, given the present trend to concentration of power in the presidency, a permanent CCC could have become "An American Black Shirt or Brown Shirt Army, a political agency dangerous to the Republic," and for this reason the paper supported temporary extension only.[47] Both the

40. *Ibid.*, p. 4383.
41. *Ibid.*, p. 4386.
42. *Ibid.*, p. 4390.
43. *Ibid.*, p. 4388.
44. *Ibid.*, p. 4384.
45. *Ibid.*, p. 4430. They were Reps. Ross A. Collins (Dem., Miss), Fred L. Crawford (Rep., Mich.), Francis D. Culkin (Rep., N.Y.), Martin J. Kennedy (Dem., N.Y.), Earl C. Michener (Rep., Mich.), John Taber (Rep., N.Y.), and James W. Wadsworth (Rep., N.Y.).
46. New York *Times*, May 12 and 13, 1937.
47. Chicago *Tribune*, May 12 and 15, 1937.

Boston Evening *Transcript* and the Baltimore *Sun* interpreted the action as a serious setback for the President.[48] The St. Louis *Post Dispatch* regretted the defeat while asserting that, though not yet permanent, "the CCC would remain a useful agency for giving young men healthful and morale-building work."[49]

Fechner had assumed that the debate would have been a formality only, and he was dismayed by the House's action. Bewildered and enraged, he threatened to resign. "I am ready to go back to the Machinists tomorrow," he stormed, "and when I come back from Alaska I may do that. I cannot understand how Congress ran away with this thing yesterday afternoon. There has been no opposition [to permanence] in the hearings."[50] The President, on the other hand, outwardly shrugged off the revolt. The refusal of the House to vote permanence was "a minor point," he considered, "so long as the CCC was extended." Moreover, the Senate Committee on Education and Labor had reported favorably on the plan for permanence. There was little point in talking about defeat until after the senators had considered the amended House measure.[51] The fight was not yet over.

The Senate debated the House measure on May 19, after Senator Hugo L. Black of Alabama had explained the importance of the House amendments.[52] Much of the time was devoted to the question of Fechner's salary. Senators Tom Connally, Democrat of Texas, and Champ Clark, Democrat of Missouri, led a determined drive to sustain the House cut from $12,000 to $10,000. Connally claimed that $12,000 was more than a senator, or even Harry Hopkins, was paid; moreover, Fechner, he contended, was trying to influence the CCC enrollees politically, especially on the matter of Supreme Court reform.[53] He was successful in bringing the matter to an early vote, which went against the director by 44 to 29.[54]

On the larger issue of permanence for the Corps, the senators

48. Boston *Evening Transcript*, May 13, 1937; Baltimore *Sun*, May 13, 1937.
49. St. Louis *Post-Dispatch*, May 17, 1937.
50. Advisory Council, Minutes, May 12, 1937.
51. New York *Times*, May 13 and 14, 1937.
52. *C.R.*, 75th Cong., 1st Sess., Vol, 81, Pt. 5, p. 4763.
53. *Ibid.*, p. 4768.
54. *Ibid.*, p. 4825-4826.

were much more inclined than the House to support the Administration. Though few went as far as Senator "Cotton Ed" Smith of South Carolina, who declared that the CCC was "the most marvellous piece of legislation that has been enacted during the present Administration, or any preceding one,"[55] most were inclined to favor a permanent agency. Indeed, Senator Carl Hayden, Democrat of New Mexico, declared that he "would like to see a million young men a year going through the camps."[56]

Senator William E. Borah led the forces against permanence. He yielded to no one in his appreciation of the benefits the CCC had brought to boys, local communities, and the nation, but to make it permanent was, he insisted, to admit that America would always have an unemployment problem, and this he was not prepared to do.[57] Yet, his was distinctly the minority view: an amendment to extend the camps for only two years was soundly defeated.[58] The vote on the Black Amendment to substitute the original bill for the House measure was a one-sided affair. The amendment was carried by a huge majority of 67 to 2, with Borah the only Republican voting against it. Thus, the Republican senators voted with the Administration and against the action taken by the House.[59] An impasse had been reached.

The inevitable conference was held between the labor committees of the two chambers. When the results of their deliberations were reported on June 7, they showed that on the major issue the Senate conferees had capitulated to House intransigence. The Corps was not to be permanent, but would be extended for three, not two, years. Fechner's salary was to be cut. Enrolment would not be limited to youths from families receiving relief, but to all young men between seventeen and twenty-three years of age who were unemployed and in need of employment. It was anticipated that those to whom the relief provision actually applied would be given first preference. The peak enrolment was to be 300,000, including veterans and Indians. The Senate gained two major points when the conference agreed to remove the House's clause authorizing ten hours of vocational training per week, substituting the wording "train-

55. *Ibid.*, p. 4830.
56. *Ibid.*
57. *Ibid.*, p. 4835.
58. *Ibid.*, p. 4841.
59. *Ibid.*, p. 4844. Twenty-seven senators did not vote.

ing for citizenship," and to reinsert the Civil Service provision that those presently employed would be given time to study for the mandatory examination.[60]

These amendments were still too much for the House to accept. Congressmen demanded that the vocational training clause be reinserted and the Civil Service provision be once more removed, thus safeguarding their source of patronage.[61] To these further changes the senators agreed, so that when the President signed the bill on June 28, 1937, it represented a victory for the House over both Administration and Senate.[62] Roosevelt's bid to make the Corps permanent had failed.

The failure of the CCC to become permanent in 1937 is all the more significant because it was so unexpected. At the beginning of the year it had stood at the zenith of its great popularity, drawing support from all sections of the community. Most officials were certain that congressional approval for the President's plan would have been little more than a formal action. What then were the reasons for the President's defeat, a reversal perpetrated by the large-scale defection of members of his own party?

The first argument against permanence brought forward in the debates was that a permanent CCC would be a gesture of pessimism, a recognition of defeat in the war against unemployment. No doubt this point has a certain validity, though Congress could always have abolished the CCC, permanent or not, once the unemployment situation had improved. Moreover, the argument ignored the urgent need for more conservation work, independent of the employment situation. Similarly, to stress the need for further study of the Corps was to ignore the fact that the CCC had been under observation for four years, and if any defects had subsequently been discovered in the legislation for permanence, they could easily be removed by congressional action. The fact that a permanent CCC with Civil Service provisions attached would have meant the end of a useful source of congressional patronage was no doubt important and must have loomed large in many a congressman's mind. Likewise, the

60. *Ibid.*, pp. 5371-5373.
61. *Ibid.*, pp. 6095-6102.
62. *Ibid.*, pp. 6203-6205; New York *Times*, June 29, 1937.

clause limiting enrolment to 300,000 would inevitably have meant the widespread closing of camps with the attendant local discontent. Nevertheless, it would have been possible to compromise on both these points and still make the CCC permanent. Of more substance, perhaps, was the feeling that the proposed legislation was somewhat hastily conceived, and that there had not been enough real consideration given to the future role of the CCC. The bill before Congress perpetuated almost intact the existing organization of the Corps, as well as its heavy emphasis on relief, and some congressmen were convinced that no proposal for permanence should be enacted until there had been much more discussion and reflection on just what broader functions a permanent agency could be expected to perform.

Probably just as important in explaining the defeat of the measure were the deep feelings of concern and uncertainty engendered in Congress and country by the President's Supreme Court reform plan. It is significant that the Corps itself was never under criticism. Democratic congressmen, however, may have sensed a need to affirm their independence after the trying early weeks of the session, when the court plan was bitterly debated and conscientiously opposed. There could hardly be a better way of protesting against what was considered to be the dangerous accretion of power by the Executive than to refuse to go along with the President on this issue, especially since the House Democratic leadership was making so much of the fact that the CCC was Roosevelt's "pet" and that he wanted the measure passed. To refuse this favor, while still extending the most popular New Deal agency, could well have been the House's way of reaffirming to President and people that it was not to be considered a rubber stamp.

The problem of Fechner's salary cut adds some substance to this hypothesis. Fechner had received since 1933 an annual salary of $12,000 without any criticism ever being uttered. Nothing at the hearings on the bill in April indicated that this amount was considered excessive; yet in May both Houses agreed that he should receive only $10,000 a year. Perhaps this reduction was due to an economy drive and a desire to bring his salary into line with those of congressmen and other federal officials, but it was probably reinforced by the fact that in the latter half of April, Fechner made a series of radio speeches in which he strongly advocated the adoption of the President's court reform plan.[63] For these he was publicly criticized by Senator Clark, who later injected the matter into the Senate debate on the director's salary.[64] Surely Fechner's pay cut can be explained in part by his support of court reform. Moreover, the editorial support given the House's motion, while disavowing any intention of criticizing the CCC, nevertheless indicated that the time was not ripe for the creation of further permanent federal bodies. In adopting this view, even normally friendly editors were possibly reflecting the fear of further Executive encroachment which the court reform furor had created.[65] It seems reasonable, therefore, to conclude that the plan for a permanent CCC failed not only for the reasons adduced in the House but also because of the vague uneasiness against increasing federal power which had been engendered by the court-packing issue. Indeed, it may well have met a better fate had it been dealt with before the court plan was made known. In any event, 1937 was a bad year for President Roosevelt. The court reform bill was only one in a series of measures defeated in the House because of increased congressional independence.[66] Failure to make the CCC permanent must be considered within this context.

The fight for permanence was not over, though never again did it attain such significant proportions. The President still aimed at a permanent Corps,[67] and the American Conservation Association, a group of former enrollees and other interested parties, was formed specifically to agitate to this end.[68] In January 1939, bills were introduced into the House and Senate. Their main provisions, apart from permanence, were once more to include Corps employees within Civil Service provisions and to

63. New York *Times*, April 22, 1937.
64. *Ibid.*; see also *C.R.*, 75th Cong., 1st Sess., Vol. 81, Pt. 5, pp. 4767-4768.
65. New York *Times*, May 12 and 13, 1937; Chicago *Tribune*, May 15, 1937.
66. Dexter Perkins, *The New Age of Franklin Roosevelt 1932-45* (Chicago, 1957), pp. 63-64.
67. New York *Times*, Sept. 22, 1937; Roosevelt to Gov. Prentice Cooper, Nashville, Tenn., Feb. 1, 1939, in Nixon, II, 297-298.
68. New York *Times*, Feb. 6, 1939.

increase Fechner's salary to $12,000. There were no other changes from the 1937 legislation.[69] Work would continue, as previously, under the auspices of the director, but it would be directly carried out by the co-operating federal departments.

The House Committee on Labor held hearings in February. While support for the CCC was as strong as ever, and while no one wanted the camps discontinued, members expressed the usual reservations about making the Corps permanent. For example, Representative Richard J. Welsh, Republican of California, said he had always felt that the establishment of the CCC "is one of the most outstanding, if not the most outstanding, Administrative and Congressional accomplishment since the depression," but he was nevertheless "not sold" on the wisdom of making it permanent at this time.[70] Moreover, there was enough discussion concerning the need for military training in the camps to indicate that a new CCC Act could be held up while congressmen debated this contentious issue.[71] Both Fechner and Brigadier General George P. Tyner, who attended the hearing, spoke strongly against making formal military training part of the Corps' curriculum, Tyner insisting that the War Department considered it to be quite unnecessary and, if CCC boys alone were to receive such instruction, quite unfair. He thought that the present situation was of positive value, even without formal instruction, in that the enrollees were learning to accept Army discipline and camp life, while the Reserve officers in charge of the camps were gaining valuable experience in command techniques. In his view, formal military training would be superfluous.[72] In spite of the War Department's explicit disavowal of the need for military training, however, many congressmen remained committed to it as a prerequisite for the passage of a permanent

69. See *To Make the Civilian Conservation Corps a Permanent Agency: Hearings Before the Committee on Labor, House of Representatives, 76th Congress, First Session, on H.R. 2990*, Feb. 9, 23, and 24, 1939 (Washington, 1939), p. 1. The President in his budget message had recommended that the Corps be made permanent. He had privately told Fechner, however, that he would be perfectly satisfied if all Congress did was to extend the present legislation. New York *Times*, Jan. 6, 1939; Advisory Council, Minutes, Nov. 29, 1938.

70. *Permanency Hearings*, 1939, p. 26.

71. *Ibid.*, p. 39.

72. *Ibid.*, p. 96.

CCC bill.[73] It was considered as well that the President's pending administrative reorganization plan might affect the CCC to such an extent that it would surely be better to study its provisions before discussing permanence.[74]

The report from the Committee on Labor to the House, therefore, did not advocate permanence for the CCC at this time. While pointing out that testimony before the committee had clearly shown that the Corps "operated effectively and efficiently," that its "social benefits" had been great, and that there remained much conservation work to be accomplished, the committee nevertheless recommended extension for five years only, from July, 1940.[75] It was considered too difficult at the time to study the unemployment situation and gauge its long-term implications, and until this was done it was deemed unwise to make the CCC permanent. This being the case, the committee decided it was better not to include the Civil Service provision nor to raise Fechner's salary. No mention was made of military training.[76]

Thus, the House Labor Committee, apart from increasing its time span, made no significant change in the act which had governed the Corps since 1937. Though the Senate Committee on Education and Labor favorably reported its bill to make the Corps permanent,[77] it was once more the House's decision which was followed. The House on July 31, 1939, by voice vote and without debate, extended the life of the Corps till July 1, 1943, but made no other changes in the bill of 1937.[78] The Senate followed suit the next day,[79] again without debate, and the President signed the measure on August 8, 1939.[80]

This was the final attempt to secure permanence for the CCC. It was but a pale echo of the 1937 campaign, arousing no press

73. *Ibid.*, p. 103.
74. *Ibid.*, p. 15.
75. Subsequently reduced to three, to July 1, 1943. *C.R.*, 76th Cong., 1st Sess., Vol. 84, Pt. 10, p. 10550.
76. *Amending an Act Establishing a Civilian Conservation Corps, House of Representatives, Report No. 447, 76th Congress, First Session* (Washington, 1939).
77. New York *Times*, July 23, 1939.
78. *C.R.*, 76th Cong., 1st Sess., Vol. 84, Pt. 10, p. 10550.
79. *Ibid.*, p. 10659.
80. New York *Times*, Aug. 9, 1939.

controversy or presidential statement, and provoking no congressional debate. The real fight for permanence had taken place two years previously, and the Administration had lost it. The significance of the CCC's failure to attain permanence should not, however, be overrated. Possibly large-scale planning was hindered, but this in itself was dependent on long-term budgeting, and nothing in the legislation indicated that Roosevelt intended to place CCC appropriations on such a footing. Since no change in structure was ever seriously planned, the failure of passage of these two bills meant very little. Indeed, it is hard to see how the CCC's future course could have been substantially different, even with permanence, so long as its organization, thrown together as it was in the Corps' first few frantic weeks and having slowly evolved a working equilibrium, remained unchanged.

10. *Progress, Consolidation, and Dissension, 1937-1939*

During the passage of the act of 1937, Congress had inserted a clause specifically encouraging vocational education and had criticized educational work in the CCC as it then stood. It was clear, therefore, that a pressing task for the director was to investigate thoroughly the whole training program. As a beginning, Fechner solicited the commissioner of education, J. W. Studebaker, for suggestions. Studebaker recommended that the work week be shortened, specifically that the Wednesday afternoons and Saturdays be devoted to education; instruction in the evenings would also be continued.[1] Studebaker was strongly supported by Ickes in advocating the change, but both Fechner and the President stood firm against it. "Of course I want the Office of Education to continue their fine work among the CCC boys," said Roosevelt, "but this work must be under the final control of the director, Mr. Fechner. In other words, Mr. Fechner is the responsible head and he must have the final say." Mr. Fechner said "no" most emphatically to any reduction in working hours for teaching purposes.[2]

The director was more receptive to another proposal from Studebaker. This was to remove the ultimate responsibility for education from the War Department, placing it in the Office of Education. The Office of Education would thus be on an equal footing with the Army and the technical services, each with its own particular sphere of responsibility.[3] Fechner greeted this suggestion with enthusiasm, and the Advisory Council soon evolved a new plan for the organization of educational work. The director of CCC education was to be directly responsible to Fechner's office, and the role of the War Department was correspondingly reduced. The Army now merely had to insure that floor space would be available for educational purposes in each camp and that all enrollees had the opportunity to attend classes.[4] Delighted, Studebaker exulted that the plan enabled

1. Studebaker to Fechner, July 8, 1937, Director, Correspondence.
2. Roosevelt to Ickes, July 17, 1937, Roosevelt Papers, O.F. 268, Box 8.
3. Studebaker to Fechner, July 20, 1937, Director, Correspondence.
4. Advisory Council, Minutes, Aug. 4, 1937; Fechner to Studebaker, Aug. 12, 1937, Director, Correspondence.

him "not only to place the full force of the U.S. Office of Education, but the whole educational system in the country, behind you and your efforts to give the enrollees the very best educational program possible." He eagerly awaited its early implementation.[5]

Unfortunately, the program was never to develop past the paper stage. As early as August 6, 1937, the Army officer in charge of CCC disbursement intimated to Fechner that the proposed scheme might run into constitutional difficulties. He doubted if the provisions of the act of 1937 would enable Fechner to bring the director of CCC education, Howard Oxley, into his office.[6] The blow fell on August 30. Assistant Director Taylor, after conferring with the comptroller general, bluntly informed Fechner that the new program would have to be dropped. There was no authority to transfer the funds needed for its implementation to the director's office, nor could the President do so by Executive Order.[7] Accordingly, Fechner, after confirming Taylor's message, advised all co-operating agencies that the old educational organization was still to be followed. He stressed, however, that because congressmen had shown so much interest in CCC education, it was incumbent upon all Corps officials to make serious efforts to improve the program wherever possible.[8] Thus ended abortively the most serious attempt to increase even slightly the emphasis on education in the CCC's activities and to bring to the teaching program a modicum of cohesion.

The failure of the new education plan brought not unification, but renewed criticism. Much of it was due to antagonism between the technical services and the Office of Education, dissension which had reached such a pitch by October, 1937, that McKinney, the CCC publicity director, complained that it was even intruding into official publications.[9] In December a long report prepared by Frederick Morrell of the Forest Service and Conrad Wirth of the National Parks Service sweepingly criticized the whole concept and orientation of education in the CCC.

5. Studebaker to Fechner, Aug. 29, 1937, Director, Correspondence.
6. Maj. Fred W. Boschen to Fechner, Aug. 6, 1937, *ibid.*
7. Taylor to Fechner, Aug. 30, 1937, *ibid.*
8. Fechner to Technical Agencies, Sept. 14, 1937, *ibid.*
9. McKinney to Technical Agencies, Sept. 14, 1937, *ibid.*

Morrell and Wirth advocated scrapping the existing program entirely and removing the educational advisers, substituting on-the-job training, which they thought to be the only type of education suitable in the camps. Men should be trained for work, they believed, not for high school diplomas.[10] The Director's Office was dismayed at the tone of the report, but recognized that it had some validity. Oxley, according to Taylor, had often treated the technical services cavalierly, and was now reaping the whirlwind. Still, such dissension, if left unchecked, could wreck the educational work entirely, dependent as it was on interservice co-operation.[11]

The Office of Education was equally dissatisfied with the current state of affairs. Studebaker was bitterly critical of the technical services. They were not pulling together, he claimed, and he indicated that he was not inclined to favor anyone "telling our men in the camps what they should do." Job training, while important, was, he believed, only part of the totality of CCC education, and he had no intention of increasing the emphasis on it.[12] Conditions were deteriorating steadily.

Confusion and conflict at the center were reflected in the camps. Educational advisers renewed their protests about unsatisfactory programs and technical service hostility. One of the most articulate of these was C. T. Clifton, of Camp SC-16, Yellow Springs, Ohio. His trenchant criticism of the program, adumbrated in a long letter to Fechner, was widely circulated among CCC officials[13] because it summed up forcefully the accumulated grievances of Corps educational advisers. Clifton paid tribute to the real accomplishments of CCC education, but he was more concerned with what it had failed to do, particularly in the field of vocational training which he categorized as "weak." He attacked Fechner for not having stimulated more interest in this aspect of the Corps' work. Clifton was also bitterly hostile to the Army, claiming that free discussion was effectively muzzled in the camps and with it any chance of

10. Morrell and Wirth to Fechner, Dec. 30, 1937, C.R.M., No. 790, Training.
11. Taylor to Fechner, Jan. 25, 1938, *ibid.*
12. Education, Minutes, May 21, 1938.
13. Clifton to Fechner, May 15, 1938, Director, Correspondence.

embarking on "the ambitious program of social and economic education" which the CCC was peculiarly fitted to supply. Education had become the "Cinderella" of Corps life, he complained, and few could miss his implication that the Director's Office and the War Department were the two "ugly sisters." In concluding, Clifton called for a "new liberal CCC program of work, study, and play," with more emphasis on training and less on relief.[14]

The dissension between the technical services and the Office of Education, the discontent in the camps, and the confusion about the education program's aims and methods could not continue unchecked. In June, 1938, therefore, Fechner appointed a special committee to investigate education in the CCC in the hope that its findings would provide guidelines for a revised program.[15] The six members included representatives from the technical services, the Department of Labor, and the Office of Education.[16] The committee reported to the director in January, 1939, after having studied camp education in four of the nine Corps areas. The report paid glowing tribute to certain facets of the work accomplished in the camps and to the dedication of most educational advisers, but it was sweepingly critical of the organization and objectives of the program as a whole. It stated that "the chief justification for a camp program was to make the boys more employable," and this it was often failing to do.[17] To reverse this tendency, the report advocated more emphasis on job training and urged that the foremen be given teacher-training courses in order to provide such instruction more efficiently.[18] Other specific shafts were aimed at the unsuitability of the hours allotted to instruction and at the dual administrative organization of the camp program, which rendered it difficult to define concise educational objectives.[19] The committee asserted that if the program were to be made more effective, classes should not be held in the evenings, as by then the enrollees, tired after their day's work, were least willing to co-operate.[20] Committee members found that educational advisers were all too

14. *Ibid.*
15. Snyder to Persons, June 7, 1938, S.D., Education, Correspondence.
16. Records of the CCC: Report of the Special Committee on Education in the CCC, 1939, mimeographed copy in National Archives, p. 1.
17. *Ibid.*, p. 14.
18. *Ibid.*, pp. 63-73.
19. *Ibid.*, pp. 185-186.
20. *Ibid.*, p. 186.

often grossly underpaid, overworked, and inadequately trained, while their freedom of action was circumscribed by Army control.[21] The whole import of the committee's findings was, first, to stress the need for a change of emphasis within the program, specifically a shift to vocational and on-the-job training, and second, to suggest that before educational work could be really successful the whole organization of the camps would have to be altered—the Army would have to be removed, and educational endeavor placed on an equal footing with the work program of the CCC.[22]

Similar shortcomings were described by the American Youth Commission, an agency established with Rockefeller Foundation money to study youth problems. It carried out a private investigation of CCC education at the same time as the special committee and, in its first report, also indicated the need for more vocational training, for better-paid advisers, and for less Army control.[23] The Youth Commission was at pains to point out, however, the "definite benefits" that the present system afforded enrollees, and in particular it praised the work done with illiterates. Furthermore, the commission believed that since 1937 greater emphasis had, in fact, been laid on training for employment, though such trends needed acceleration.[24]

The official response to these two reports was muted and generally unfavorable. The Selection Division considered them "misleading" and, while admitting that they contained some useful suggestions, thought they "were not based on careful study" and included too many generalizations "from a sample only."[25] Fechner made it clear that the special committee's recommendation had not changed his resolute opposition to shortening the hours of work. Likewise, he intended ultimate Army responsibility for education to continue.[26] Many of the main conclusions

21. *Ibid.*

22. *Ibid.*, p. 14.

23. Records of the CCC: Selection Division, Study of the CCC by the American Youth Commission, 1939, unpaged mimeographed copy in National Archives.

24. *Ibid.*

25. Rufus Miles, Division of Selection, to Persons, June 20, 1939, S.D., Education Correspondence. Miles had been detailed to analyze the reports.

26. Education, Minutes, March 8, 1939.

of the reports, proposals aimed at removing the basic grievances of educational officials, were thus disregarded or disavowed.

Some of the specific recommendations, however, were adopted. Serious attempts were made to improve the system of teacher training in camps,[27] and Fechner emphatically directed that more vocational education be included in camp programs.[28] A policy of directing enrollees to selected camps where they could best profit from the training opportunities was also instituted.[29] It is likely that even more of the recommendations would have been implemented had the CCC not been placed on a non-combatant footing in 1940, a move which changed completely the whole objective of CCC education and training.[30]

Many of the recommendations of both investigating bodies were indeed balanced and reasonable. Others took an unrealistic approach to the CCC situation. Suggested improvements within the existing organization were subordinated to sweeping denunciations of the whole structure of the Corps. The removal of the Army, or the shortening of the work week in order to add more classes, no matter how desirable in principle, would nevertheless have meant a radical reconstruction of the Corps' framework as delineated by statute and tradition. Such recommendations were thus beside the point, at least until the future of the Corps had been settled. What was now needed was improvement within the existing framework, not the abolition of the framework.

Furthermore, the reports of both the special committee and the American Youth Commission, through concentrating on the weakness of CCC education, tended to gloss over the very real areas of accomplishment. The special committee made little mention of the CCC's excellent work with illiterates, and neither body discussed the achievement in giving youths a second chance to complete their high school education or to continue with college work. In the fiscal year 1938-1939 alone, 8,445 enrollees were taught to read and write, and 763 were awarded

27. *Ibid.*, March 31, 1939.
28. Fechner to Adjutant General and Oxley, April 4, 1939, Director, Correspondence.
29. Education, Minutes, Aug. 14, 1939.
30. See chap. xi, below.

college scholarships.[31] Despite the fact that vocational training facilities were considered inadequate, the CCC still managed to produce 45,000 truck drivers a year, 7,500 bridge builders, 2,000 bakers, and 1,500 welders.[32] One cannot discount the real success of the Corps in providing a measure of useful training for at least some of its enrollees, and improving, even indirectly, the employment prospects of almost all.

Nevertheless, education must be counted one of the less successful fields of CCC endeavor. The program always suffered from its initial handicap of being a late starter in a competitive field. The Office of Education could never really convince the CCC authorities that its work was anything more than an afterthought, an extra to be accommodated if possible, but ignored if necessary. Neither the President nor Fechner, when it came to the pinch, was prepared to improve the position of the educational advisers in relation to the War Department or the technical services, either by giving them more money or by setting aside certain hours during the day for instruction. Moreover, though many of the problems plaguing CCC education were insoluble while the Corps retained its original form, it may fairly be said that, even in the limited sphere where it could operate effectively, the program often failed to meet fully the needs of the enrollees. Academic courses, while doubtless interesting in themselves, were of limited practical value to youths who would almost certainly lead non-academic lives, while one can legitimately question whether instruction in digging ditches and building dams was fitting the enrollees for life in an increasingly urbanized society. Though education in the CCC was emphatically not a total failure, its deficiencies were undoubtedly grave, and the blame must be shared by the President, the CCC organization, and the education officials themselves.

The organization of educational work was not the only policy matter called into question in 1937 because of the new legislation. Now that the relief provision was no longer a condition of enrolment, the President, in the interests of economy, wanted the base

31. Report of Education Activities in Junior CCC Camps, Fiscal Year 1938-1939, mimeographed, S.D., Education Correspondence.

32. *Report of the Director*, 1940, pp. 7-8.

monthly pay rate reduced from $30 if at all possible.[33] Fechner put the matter to the Advisory Council, where once again there was substantial disagreement. The technical agencies and the War Department supported a dual pay system, advocating that veterans should still receive $30 monthly, and all others should be cut down to $21.[34] The Selection Division could not support the idea of reducing the pay of all junior enrollees to $21 because of the opposition from state selecting agencies. It would mean the end of the $25 allotment to families. Snyder and Persons proposed instead that junior enrollees from families on relief should be paid the full $30 as before, but that those from families not on relief should receive only $15.[35] Both plans were sent to the President for perusal, but despite the fact that the suggestion to revise pay scales was his own, he changed his mind, discarded both, and decided to continue with the old scheme.[36] The $30 monthly pay rate lasted until the Corps was dissolved.

It was in 1937, too, that the first significant attempts were made to develop a workable re-employment service for discharged enrollees. The initial moves were made on the state level, the most important being the structure developed in Arkansas. Here the state director of CCC selection, Edward Bethune, co-operated with the Arkansas branch of the United States Employment Service in producing a monthly bulletin on discharged CCC enrollees, giving full particulars of height, weight, race, accomplishments, previous experience, interests, and reaction to camp life. These brochures were then sent to business firms and other prospective employers.[37] The arrangement was an outstanding success. By 1939 the Arkansas Employment Service was having little trouble in placing former enrollees.[38]

Officials of the Selection Division of the CCC were quick to see the merits of the Arkansas plan. They sent full details of its

33. Roosevelt to Fechner, July 12, 1937, Roosevelt Papers, O.F. 268, Box 8.

34. Advisory Council, Minutes, Aug. 16 and 20, 1937.

35. *Ibid.*

36. *Ibid.*, Sept. 13, 1937.

37. Edward Bethune to Snyder, July 15, 1937, Snyder to Bethune, Aug. 20, 1937, S.D., Policy.

38. Palmer Patterson, director, Arkansas State Employment Service, to Bethune, July 28, 1939, *ibid.*

operation to all state selection agents,[39] and by 1939 most of them had adopted it.[40] They were not always as successful as Arkansas, but where co-operation between selection director and employment agency was wholehearted, the prospect of former enrollees returning home to unemployment was greatly reduced.

Franklin Roosevelt had never sounded firmer in his desire to curb the spending policies characteristic of the early years of the New Deal than in the summer and fall of 1937. Even in the face of rising unemployment, he still spoke in terms of a balanced budget, an end to "pump priming," and a general reduction of federal expenditures.[41] The CCC inevitably felt the force of the economy drive. The director of the Bureau of the Budget advised Fechner in November, 1937, that the CCC's estimates for the 1938-1939 fiscal year had been slashed by $125 million.[42] Fechner vainly protested that this cut would mean the closing of 104 camps before December 30, and some 300 more by July 1, 1938, leaving only 1,200 in operation.[43] The President in his budget message of January 3, 1938, recommended that the CCC be reduced.[44] A few Democratic congressmen, led by Representative Jed Johnson of Oklahoma, attempted to bring about a revolt and restore the full appropriation, but the drive for economy was too strong and the House defeated their attempted amendment by voice vote.[45] In February, Fechner announced that more than one hundred camps had already been closed and that on March 1 he would begin to close three hundred more, until by July the reduced enrolment would stand at 250,000 men in 1,200 camps.[46]

The balanced budget, however, was sacrificed to the exigencies of the steadily worsening economic situation. The recession of late 1937 showed signs of developing into a full-scale depression. Stock prices plummeted, and unemployment rose from under five million in August, 1937, to more than nine

39. Snyder to Bethune, Aug. 20, 1937, *ibid.*
40. Persons to Charles Ketchum, Jan. 27, 1939, *ibid.*
41. Dexter Perkins, p. 66.
42. Fechner to James Roosevelt, Nov. 24, 1937, Roosevelt Papers, O.F. 268, Box 9; New York *Times*, Dec. 5 and 18, 1937.
43. Fechner to McIntyre, Nov. 30, 1937, Roosevelt Papers, O.F. 268, Box 9; New York *Times*, Dec. 29, 1937.
44. Rosenman, ed., *Papers*, VII, 28.
45. New York *Times*, Jan. 11, 1938.
46. *Ibid.*, Feb. 26, 1938.

million in May, 1938.[47] Faced with the starkness of a collapsing economy, the President abandoned deflation for the well-tried policies of increased federal spending.[48] On April 14 he went before Congress seeking additional money for work relief, for the WPA, the NYA, and the CCC. Specifically, he asked that $50 million be voted for the Corps to keep the three hundred camps from closing and to maintain the number of camps at 1,500.[49] A resolution to this effect, introduced by the chairman of the House Appropriations Committee, Representative Clifton A. Woodrum, Democrat of Virginia, on March 23,[50] had already passed the House by the lopsided majority of 326 to 6.[51] It was approved by the Senate on April 19.[52]

Thus, the recession, though it destroyed Roosevelt's hope for a balanced budget, saved the CCC from further reduction. The Corps remained steady at 1,500 camps and 300,000 enrollees for the rest of 1938, and no cuts were planned for the 1939-1940 fiscal year.[53] Numerically at least, it was maintaining its strength.

The same could not be said for the organization of the CCC. Serious disagreements between the director and the technical services threatened to disrupt the agency's high level of performance. For the first four years of the Corps' existence, Fechner had made little attempt to direct the policy of the co-operating agencies in any way; he had allowed them to function very much according to their own methods and traditions. Now, secure in his office and concerned with what he regarded as a challenge to his authority by men like Ickes, Tyner, Morrell, and Persons, he attempted to reverse this trend and began a policy of gradually extending his authority over the technical services and even the War Department. The first signs came in July, 1937, when Fechner announced to the Advisory Council that he had decided to

47. Dexter Perkins, p. 66; John M. Blum, *From the Morgenthau Diaries: Years of Crisis 1928-38* (Boston, 1959), pp. 380-451.

48. Blum, p. 425.

49. New York *Times*, April 15, 1938.

50. *Ibid.*, March 24, 1938. It was not favored by the director of the Bureau of the Budget. See Bell to Roosevelt, March 25, 1938, Roosevelt Papers, O.F. 268, Box 10.

51. New York *Times*, April 11, 1938. One of the six recalcitrants was Rep. Taber of New York, "faithful to the last" in his opposition to the CCC.

52. *Ibid.*, April 20, 1938.

53. Bell to McIntyre, Nov. 18, 1938, Roosevelt Papers, O.F. 268, Box 10.

transfer to his office the CCC's liaison officers, presently hired and paid by the technical agencies.[54] The decision was bitterly fought by the Departments of Agriculture, the Interior, and War, not so much because of its intrinsic significance, but because the transfer would constitute a precedent for further centralizing action. Fechner took little notice of their protests and proceeded with the arrangement. Only when it was pointed out that its cost would be excessive did he drop the matter, to the relief, though not to the satisfaction, of the co-operating departments.[55]

The attempted transfer of liaison officers set the stage for greatly increased tension between Fechner and the federal agencies. The director's relationship with the acerbic Ickes had always been uneven; now it became positively stormy. Ickes accused him of discriminating against the Department of the Interior in allotting camps and of attempting to "curtail" the secretary's authority.[56] Oscar L. Chapman, acting secretary of the Department of the Interior, claimed that Fechner was attempting to "take over responsibilities which are delegated to other departments and which rightfully belong to them."[57]

The director's clash with Department of the Interior officials was soon dwarfed, however, by a full-scale row which broke out when he attempted to dictate terms to the Department of War. The struggle, the only one of its kind during the whole of the Corps' existence, was precipitated by a difference of opinion over the rotation of Reserve officers in the camps. By 1937, high Army officers were convinced that the CCC experience was of real value to those Reserve officers who were used in the camps; therefore, in order to spread these benefits over as broad an area as possible, they decided to replace all those who had been on duty for more than eighteen months with a fresh batch of younger men.

This was an extraordinarily unpopular decision. Hundreds of those due to be replaced had learned to look on their CCC jobs as permanent, and they were not about to give them up lightly.

54. C.R.M., No. 780(3), Liaison Officers.
55. *Ibid.*
56. Ickes to Fechner, March 24, 1938, Secretary of Interior, Records.
57. Oscar L. Chapman to Clifton A. Woodrum, March 4, 1938, *ibid.*

A petition to Roosevelt praying for his intercession on their behalf spoke of "the brutal and we believe thoroughly unwarranted, unwise, and altogether unjust order issued by the War Department . . . this callously brutal attempt to throw out of employment over 6,000 officers, most of them with families. . . . in order that the Regular Army shall not be marred by a permanent or semi-permanent force of 'we temporary gentlemen.' "[58] Fechner strongly supported the officers in their complaints because he feared that the mass replacement of camp commanders would inevitably have a disastrous effect on CCC morale. His arguments seem to have influenced the President, who put pressure on the War Department to rescind the order. The wrangle was eventually resolved by a compromise, the War Department reluctantly agreeing to replace only 50 per cent of the officers concerned. But Army feelings had been thoroughly ruffled by what was considered to be Fechner's blatant influence in a strictly departmental issue. Further conflict became almost inevitable.[59]

Smoldering Army resentment flared violently to life early in 1938, following a series of complaints from Fechner on specific points of administration. He was still not satisfied about the rotation of officers. Further, he suspected that the Army officials were spending CCC funds in an unauthorized way; he insisted, therefore, that he be allowed to inquire into the details of their disbursement.[60] The War Department had had enough. In a strongly worded memorandum, the acting secretary of war, Louis Johnson, refuted Fechner's charges and angrily asked, "how far should the Director, CCC inject himself into the details of the administration of the War Department?" Denying that the cooperating agencies were in any way subordinate to the director, Johnson asserted that since July 1, 1937, Fechner had ignored the advice of his Advisory Council, and had arrogated as much power as he was able to his office. Johnson thought that, if

58. Reserve Officers on Duty to Roosevelt, May 27, 1937, Roosevelt Papers, O.F. 268–Misc., Box 19.

59. Col. Edward Watson to Roosevelt, May 29, 1937, *ibid.*, O.F. 268, Box 8; New York *Times*, July 21, 1937.

60. Fechner to Roosevelt, Jan. 17, 1938, Fechner to Tyner, March 16, 1938, Roosevelt Papers, O.F. 268, Box 8.

pursued further, this trend was bound to wreck the CCC as an efficient agency.[61]

No one doubted that such overt hostility between War Department and director could, in fact, paralyze the CCC. Accordingly, a conference, attended by Fechner, the new chief of staff, General Malin Craig, and members of the Advisory Council, was held on April 1 under the chairmanship of James Roosevelt. Roosevelt came down heavily on the side of the Army. He let it be known that the attorney general's opinion was that the co-operating departments were in no way subordinate to the director's office, and he strongly advised Fechner to concentrate on making policy and to leave its implementation alone.[62]

Fechner, for his part, had no intention of letting things end there. After being refused a copy of the opinion, he left the whole matter to the President. In a letter to Roosevelt, after emphasizing the need to maintain unity in the CCC, he asked for positive reaffirmation that final authority for all CCC matters, including the right to investigate and direct the policies of the technical services, lay with the director.[63] His request placed the President in a dilemma. Roosevelt balked at the idea of offending the Army, but he sensed that Fechner attached such importance to the issue that he would resign if his demands were not met. After a fruitless attempt to satisfy both sides by approving Fechner's request verbally only, he capitulated and in November put his signature to a document specifically stating that "All matters of policy will be initiated by, or approved by, the Director. The Director will satisfy himself, through such methods as he may deem appropriate, that his policies are being administered and executed as approved. If violations are established, corrective action thereon shall be taken at the request of the Director."[64] This authorization was all Fechner wanted. He was now able to stress to a chastened Advisory Council where power lay. Triumphantly, he asserted that "There is no higher authority than the Director except the President. I want that thoroughly

61. Louis Johnson to James Roosevelt, March 21, 1938, *ibid.*, Box 9.
62. Advisory Council, Minutes, Nov. 10, 1938.
63. Fechner to Roosevelt, June 6, 1938, in Nixon, II, 232.
64. Henry M. Kannee, assistant to McIntyre, memorandum for files, Sept. 28, 1938, in *ibid.*, II, 256.

understood—there is no higher authority above the Director other than the President in administering this Act."[65]

The outcome of the struggle between Fechner and the Army is important because of the light it throws on the whole question of the director's place within the CCC organization. It has been alleged that Fechner had no real power, that he was a public relations man only, and that the Army effectively controlled CCC policy.[66] While it is true that the Army ran the camps and that Fechner often accepted Army advice, it is equally true that in the last resort he, not the military, called the tune. That he normally chose to accede to the Army's wishes in the interests of harmony within the CCC organization did not mean that he was powerless to oppose them should he deem it necessary.

Once he had received presidential confirmation of his authority, Fechner embarked on the most ambitious centralization plan of all, again in the teeth of the strongest opposition from the co-operating services. The CCC used a vast amount of motorized equipment in the course of its extensive operations, the responsibility for repair and maintenance of which had always lain with the co-operating agencies. In 1939 Fechner decided to alter this policy, proposing to set up a huge chain of central machine repair shops directly under his control. All repairs of CCC machinery would henceforth have to be carried out there, and the director's office, not the technical services or Army, would hire and pay the mechanics and other employees.[67] Immediately there was a storm of protest from the technical agencies, directed at both the plan itself and at Fechner's decision to implement it without consulting the Advisory Council. The secretary of agriculture insisted that it be held in abeyance,[68] Ickes demanded an investigation by the Bureau of the Budget,[69] and Wirth, the Department of the Interior's Advisory Council representative, declared that the plan was "so decidedly adverse to departmental and CCC interests that every effort should be made to have it reversed. Since it is believed useless to request Director Fechner

65. Advisory Council, Minutes, Nov. 10, 1938.
66. Rawick, pp. 95-99.
67. Fechner to Roosevelt, May 1, 1939, Roosevelt Papers, O.F. 268, Box 10.
68. Wallace to Roosevelt, July 11, 1939, *ibid.*
69. Ickes to Roosevelt, July 11, 1939, *ibid.*

to reverse his decision, it is urgently requested that this matter be taken up with the President."[70]

The protests did convince Roosevelt to appoint a committee to investigate the efficiency and economy of Fechner's plan.[71] It was but a brief respite for the technical services, however, as the committee's report was highly favorable to the scheme, recommending its early adoption.[72] The plan was implemented almost immediately, a signal triumph for Fechner's centralization policies. It was also his last official act. His health had been poor throughout 1939, and in December he suffered a severe heart attack. He died in Walter Reed Hospital on New Year's Eve, after a three-week struggle for life.[73]

There were several applicants for the vacant position, with McEntee and Brigadier General Duncan Major, now retired, the two strongest candidates. McEntee was strongly supported by the AF of L, and was eventually selected for the post. It was probably the logical choice, for he had been Fechner's right-hand man since the Corps' earliest days, knowing both the details of the organization and the people who made it work. His thoroughgoing approval of Fechner's centralizing proclivities, however, were not calculated to endear him to the co-operating agencies, and administrative dissension was to plague the Corps for the rest of its existence.[74]

Fechner, in attempting his policy of centralization, was clearly acting within the limits of his authority. Nevertheless, he effectively damaged the easy relationship between director and federal agencies which had been a significant feature of the CCC's initial success. By exercising his authority to the full after four years in which he had been content to play a passive role, he encroached on areas which the technical services considered to be theirs by "right of occupation." It is hard to decide why Fechner embarked on his policy of centralization. One can only surmise that it was due to a clash of personalities rather than a

70. Wirth to Ickes, May 22, 1939, Secretary of Interior, Records.

71. Roosevelt to James A. Farley, Sept. 15, 1939, Roosevelt Papers, O.F. 268, Box 10.

72. Harold D. Smith, director of the Bureau of the Budget, to Roosevelt, Nov. 20, 1939, *ibid.*

73. New York *Times*, Jan. 1, 1940.

74. Saalberg, p. 118. See also chap. xii, below.

yen for administrative efficiency. Fechner, growing old and ill, was becoming increasingly protective of the prerogatives of his office, increasingly suspicious of the attitudes and intentions of his technical service colleagues, and increasingly determined to reassert himself as undisputed head of the CCC hierarchy. Perhaps his short-lived resignation in 1939 in protest at the creation of the Federal Security Agency adds credence to this assertion. Fechner's centralization schemes may well have brought increased efficiency, but they did so at the expense of morale. Extended by McEntee, they contributed to the decline of the Corps after 1940.

Not even the controversy over the central repair shops caused as much concern to CCC officials in 1939 as did the establishment of the Federal Security Agency. For some years the President had wanted to implement a plan of administrative reform, but his schemes had invariably been frustrated by a recalcitrant Congress, fearful of losing power over patronage.[75] Not until 1939 did the President achieve some measure of success. In May, Congress passed by substantial majorities a watered-down reorganization proposal, to take effect on July 1, 1939. The bill consolidated the complex of federal agencies into administrative groups according to function and authorized the appointment of six administrative assistants to the President.[76] The most important agencies created were the Federal Security Agency, the Federal Works Agency, and the Federal Loans Agency, each presided over by an administrator.[77] Most federal agencies were to be placed under the jurisdiction of one of these consolidating bodies. The CCC, because of its achievements in the promotion of the welfare and education of its enrollees, was to come under the "direction and supervision" of the Federal Security Agency, which also regulated the U.S. Employment Service, the Office of Education, the Public Health Service, the NYA, and the Social Security Board.[78] The grouping itself is significant, for it revealed that in Washington at least, it was now considered that the CCC had more sophisticated functions—tasks concerned with the wel-

75. Basil Rauch, *The History of the New Deal 1933-38* (New York, 1944), pp. 313-314; Dexter Perkins, p. 63.
76. Rauch, pp. 313-314; New York *Times*, May 4, June 2, 1939.
77. New York *Times*, April 26, 1939.
78. Rosenman, ed., *Papers*, VIII, 263-265.

fare and training of youth—than simply work relief, and that these were considered to be its most significant endeavors. If this were not so, the Corps would surely have been assigned to the Federal Works Agency, along with the PWA and the WPA.

Fechner protested both the change itself and the placing of the CCC in the "welfare group." He pleaded with Roosevelt to allow the Corps to continue as "an independent agency, responsible directly to the President." If this continuation were not possible, it should be placed in the work, not welfare, category. To Fechner, the more complex definitions of function were immaterial, for the Corps, as far as he was concerned, had always been, and still was, primarily a "self contained work agency."[79] Nor did he realize immediately that the Federal Security Agency administrator would have authority over him.[80] When it became clear that this would be the case and also that the President had no intention of transferring the Corps to the Federal Works Agency, Fechner angrily submitted his resignation, effective July 1.[81] In explaining his action to the Advisory Council, he revealed clearly his bitter disappointment and frustration, not only because his own authority was to be superseded, but also because the Corps to which he had devoted six years, and which he had grown to love, was to be changed so drastically. No matter who was selected as administrator, Fechner claimed, he would be unable to run the Corps "without messing the thing up." The whole situation was "in such a fix" that Fechner had "lost interest in it and [did] not care to go on with it. . . . I think the greatest reason or factor in the success of the Corps is because the President let us run it. A new man who will not only have the responsibility of a number of other agencies, and also of the CCC will make a mess of it." He told the council that he had made arrangements to go back to his old job, "which is still waiting for me."[82]

Yet Fechner did not resign, though his failing health meant that increasingly he was director in name only. No doubt he acceded to the President's determination that he withdraw his

79. Fechner to Roosevelt, April 14, 1939; Nixon, II, 321.
80. Advisory Council, Minutes, May 1, 1939.
81. *Ibid.*, May 26, 1939.
82. *Ibid.*

resignation,[83] and perhaps the selection of Paul V. McNutt, a man whom he respected, to be Federal Security Agency administrator helped him change his mind.[84] The handsome, articulate McNutt, formerly governor of Indiana and regarded as a possible presidential nominee in 1940,[85] brought a wealth of ability and experience to his new job. His very presence, however, was galling to men who for a long time had been used to running their own organization in their own way, responsible only to the President. With the bluff, stubborn McEntee soon to take the helm of the CCC, the possibilities of increased administrative tension were great.

One other policy change in 1939 exacerbated the difficulties within the CCC ranks. Thoroughly alienated by Fechner's centralization policy, the War Department had redoubled its demands to be removed from the CCC organization.[86] Fechner welcomed this. He "would have no hesitation in taking over the functions in the Corps now exercised by the War Department," he declared.[87] The President was less confident of the director's ability to do so, but a development within Congress had made some action necessary. On April 3, 1939, against Roosevelt's expressed wish, Congress gave full disability benefits to Reserve officers on duty with the CCC.[88] The cost of this move to the government would be so great, and the risks involved in CCC work so small when compared to service in the Regular Army, that Roosevelt decided to replace all Reserve officers in the camps with civilians. Accordingly, he directed the secretary of war to implement a policy of gradually removing Reserve officers from duty, and the transfer was completed by the end of the year.[89]

Actually, the change was more apparent than real. The of-

83. *Ibid.*
84. *Ibid.*, Aug. 3, 1939.
85. Burns, p. 412. Donald B. Johnson, *The Republican Party and Wendell Willkie* (Urbana, Ill., 1960), p. 40, states that the majority of a group of newspaper editors polled in 1939 thought that McNutt would be the Democratic party's nominee.
86. Gen. Tyner to Smith, May 4, 1939, Roosevelt Papers, O.F. 268, Box 10.
87. Fechner to Roosevelt, May 5, 1939, *ibid.*
88. Rosenman, ed., *Papers*, VIII, 235.
89. Roosevelt to Secretary of War, June 3, 1939, Roosevelt Papers, O.F. 268, Box 10; unsigned memorandum, Jan. 6, 1940, *ibid.*, Box 11.

ficers were replaced by civilians selected from Reserve officer lists by the War Department under the supervision of the director.[90] The War Department likewise remained in ultimate control of camp administration. Thus, it was merely a change in status, rather than personnel, but Army authorities were so bitterly hostile that another link in the chain of administrative dissension was forged.[91] Congressmen also added their protests, predicting dire consequences for the efficiency of the CCC.[92]

The CCC ended 1939 with little enough reason for self-congratulation. True, it was still very popular, but the death of the director, the truculent personality of his replacement, the loss of morale and enthusiasm among the co-operating agencies, the uncertainty due to the outbreak of war, and the slashing of the CCC budget for 1940-1941 in accordance with good election year practice[93]—all pointed to rocky days ahead.

90. Roosevelt to Secretary of War, June 5, 1939, *ibid.*, Box 10.

91. Tyner to Smith, May 4, 1939, *ibid.*

92. Sen. Theodore Bilbo (Dem., Miss.) to Roosevelt, June 12, 1939, *ibid.*

93. Advisory Council, Minutes, Dec. 5, 1939. McNutt informed the council that the President had made the cut "himself, in his own handwriting."

11. *The CCC Weakens*

On February 10, 1939, Director Fechner bluntly told his Advisory Council that the current rate of desertion from the CCC was far too high. In fact, he admitted, "it was the worst spot on the whole record of the camps."[1] Six weeks later he emphasized that the President had insisted that steps be taken immediately to deal with the problem, because the adverse publicity given the desertion rates was damaging to the CCC's public image.[2]

Fechner was not exaggerating. By April, 1937, 18.8 per cent of all enrollees who left camp were dishonorably discharged for desertion.[3] By December, 1938, the rate was more than 20 per cent.[4] In other words, by 1939, one out of every five discharged enrollees severed his connection with the camps illegally. Desertion cost the Corps money as well as prestige because it meant that food, clothing, and training had all been wasted. Consequently, CCC officials were assiduous during the Corps' final years in investigating the reasons behind the increased incidence.

To Fechner and McEntee the answers were simple enough. Both laid some blame on weak Army control. McEntee once said that "a large number of the officers now in camp are not competent to control the boys, and lack a proper understanding of the work."[5] Disgusted with the weak leadership, the youths quit the camps in droves. More important, according to Fechner, was the enrolment age limit of seventeen years. His claim was that at seventeen a boy was not "physically developed to do the work expected of him." Tired and discouraged, he therefore "went over the hill." If the age limit were once more raised to eighteen, Fechner guaranteed a significant reduction in the high rates of desertion.[6] These points of view were grossly oversimplified, yet both contained a strong element of truth. Unquestionably, weak camp leadership was a factor in explaining desertions, but it did not explain their sharp rise. Moreover,

1. Advisory Council, Minutes, Feb. 10, 1939.
2. *Ibid.*, March 28, 1939.
3. *Ibid.*, April 20, 1937.
4. *Ibid.*, March 20, 1939.
5. McEntee to Fechner, Nov. 24, 1937, Director, Correspondence.
6. Advisory Council, Minutes, Feb. 6, 1939.

though Fechner was partially right in assuming that the older the enrollee the less likely he was to desert, the raising of the age limit to eighteen would have resulted in no appreciable lessening of the problem. A study made in May, 1939, revealed that, in fact, almost twice as many eighteen-year-old enrollees deserted as did seventeen year olds, and that youths aged nineteen left at an even higher rate.[7] A detailed and prolonged study of the whole problem was required, and it was the Selection Division which provided it.

The Selection Division had been probing the desertion problem since its first manifestations. There was a practical reason for this interest, as too many desertions could indicate poor selection work. In addition, both Persons and Snyder were deeply concerned with the problem for its own sake, acting on behalf of the many boys who were voluntarily and foolishly depriving themselves of all the benefits the CCC could bring them.[8] Having no national organization of their own, however, Persons and Snyder were largely dependent on state directors of selection for their information, though they were certainly able to suggest methods of investigation. Thus, in 1937 they urged that all State directors institute a monthly study of desertions in an attempt to determine prevailing causes.[9] Some declined to make the study because of a lack of staff members,[10] but many others complied. By 1939 the Selection Division had amassed a considerable amount of data on the desertion problem. But unfortunately no clear answers were provided. The reasons given for desertion formed no single pattern, while the value of each state's material depended largely on the effort expended in collecting it.

Most State Directors found that the reasons for desertion lay either with faulty camp administration or with inadequate preparation for camp life. The Connecticut director considered homesickness to be the major cause and thought that little could be done about it.[11] The Iowa agent thought that increasingly "strict discipline" was responsible for the rising rates, and he

7. *Ibid.*, May 26, 1939.
8. Interview with Dean Snyder, Dec. 12, 1962.
9. Snyder to State Directors, March 16, 1937, S.D., Discharges.
10. Miss Gay Shepperson, supervisor, CCC Selection, Ga., to Snyder, March 20, 1937, *ibid.*
11. Connecticut Director to Snyder, March 1, 1937, *ibid.*

called on Army officers to modify their authoritarian approach.[12] Others stated that the boys were being given a false impression of camp life and deserted when their expectations were not realized.[13] A few reported that desertion increased when enrollees were sent to camp outside their home states after having been told that they would be stationed near their homes.[14] An investigator for the Missouri director wove many of these factors together. Increased desertions, he asserted, were "due to the type of enrollment selected . . . homesickness on the part of a few men, group transfers out of state for men who were told prior to transfer that they were not going to be sent out of the state, and lack of welfare equipment." Also, some parents advised their sons to desert, he contended.[15]

A few state officials found the fault to lie more with the enrollees than with the camp. J. Fred Kurtz, the Pennsylvania director of selection, who was more concerned than most with the problem, thought that while severe discipline and homesickness undoubtedly caused desertion, they did not explain adequately the sharply rising rates. He believed that he could detect, in his state at least, a progressive deterioration in the quality of boys offering themselves for selection. "Many lads join up with the frank and sole intention of getting a CCC outfit," he said. After receiving their clothing issue, they promptly deserted.[16]

Kurtz was unusual in attempting to explain the rising rates; most directors merely listed reasons why desertions had occurred. Their explanations were often equally applicable to the years up to 1937, when desertions rates were much lower. Thus, though the Selection Division officials by 1940 possessed a vast amount of material about desertions, they were little closer to understanding why the numbers had increased. Because of this, Persons sent a circular to all state directors in 1940, asking

12. A. C. G. Miller, supervisor of selection, CCC, Ia., to Persons, Sept. 28, 1937, *ibid.*
13. M. L. Cooper, state supervisor, CCC, N.Y., to Snyder, Aug. 23, 1939, *ibid.*
14. J. L. Hill, state supervisor, CCC Selection, Okla., to Snyder, March 16, 1939, *ibid.*
15. H. G. Chafey to William H. Stone, supervisor, CCC Selection, Mo., Jan. 25, 1940, *ibid.*
16. Kurtz to Snyder, May 24, 1937, *ibid.*

for a comprehensive and confidential survey of desertion in their states and giving operational directions aimed at gauging the reasons for the increase in rates.[17] Some directors disregarded his appeal,[18] but other replies did point to certain trends which indicated why so many recent enrollees had deserted. Fourteen states reported, for instance, that the growing international tension since 1937 had been in part responsible. Enrollees deserted because they feared they would be drafted and sent to fight overseas.[19] Others said that the European situation had caused the Army to drain the best officers from the camps back into regular service. Their replacements had neither the character nor the experience to prevent a deterioration of camp morale and conditions.[20] Some directors concentrated on the improving economic situation of the country. The ablest young men could now get jobs and had no need of the CCC. Thus, there had been a progressive deterioration in the last few years in the quality of youths enrolled. They were younger, less self-reliant, less developed physically, and more prone to homesickness or discouragement.[21] In addition, the removal of the relief provision in 1937 had permitted the enrolment of youths from more financially secure families than had formerly been the case. Not only did these enrollees tend to be "more critical of camp conditions,"[22] but also their families did not particularly need the $25 allotment.[23] There was probably not the same compulsion, therefore, to stay in camp. Another reason adduced was the competition of the NYA, where enrollees, without ever leaving home,[24] earned almost as much money as they would have in the CCC. Still another was the growing shortage of farm labor, which provided alternative employment.[25]

Thus, after four years of patient probing, the Selection Division had gained some insight into the reasons for the increase in desertions. Would they be able to use this knowledge to good effect in achieving some significant reductions in the rates? Obviously, much was beyond their capability. Persons and

17. Persons to State Directors, Oct. 14, 1940, *ibid.*
18. S.D., Digest of State Reports Concerning Non-Honorable Discharge for Desertion, 1940, typescript.
19. *Ibid.*, pp. 2, 4, 11, 16, 19, 23, 26, 27, 35, 39.
20. *Ibid.*, pp. 4, 11, 27, 40.
21. *Ibid.*, pp. 2, 4, 8, 23, 25, 43.
22. *Ibid.*, p. 8.
23. *Ibid.*, pp. 23, 36.
24. *Ibid.*, p. 30.
25. *Ibid.*, p. 32.

Snyder had no method of calming fears about the international situation or of persuading the War Department to leave its best officers in command of CCC camps. Moreover, the Selection Division had no coercive powers; it had to achieve the best results it could by moral suasion alone. Persons and Snyder constantly emphasized to selection agents the need both to screen all applicants carefully, accepting only those youths who seemed likely to become "mature and proficient" workmen, and to paint a realistic picture of the nature of life in the Corps.[26]

Even before the study in 1940, they had been successful in securing the adoption of three policies designed to reduce desertion rates. First, in 1937, at Persons' behest, Fechner recommended that the "buddy system" be introduced in all camps. Each new recruit was to have a "buddy," or experienced enrollee, assigned to him upon his arrival at camp, whose job was to show him round the site, make him feel welcome, and discourage any tendency to desert through homesickness.[27] Second, in 1938, acting on a recommendation from Indiana, Persons successfully sought a modification of CCC regulations which permitted deserting enrollees to return to camp without penalty. There are indications that this expedient was relatively successful.[28] Finally, in 1939, it was decided that henceforth youths who were under eighteen years of age were to be selected only when it was impossible to fill state quotas from older age groups.[29] The success of these three policies, however, depended on the interest and ability of local camp commanders and selection agents. There was little the Selection Division could do to insure their implementation. In any event, all that could be expected was a small reduction in desertions, for the main causes of the problem were still outside the Selection Division's compass. The desertion problem remained a pressing one for Corps officials until the agency's abolition in 1942.

The unpalatable fact that one in every five enrollees did not even think life in the Corps worthwhile enough to complete his

26. Snyder to Selection Agents, May 1, 1938, C.R.M., Appendix V.
27. Advisory Council, Minutes, Nov. 22, 1937.
28. Persons to Miss Helen Lowell, supervisor, CCC Selection, Ind., April 11, 1938, June 9, 1939, S.D., Discharges.
29. Persons to State Directors, Feb. 15, 1939, C.R.M., Appendix IV, Document 594.

enrolment was both frustrating and disappointing to CCC officials, and their attempts to find a solution were sincere and painstaking. Like many other problems, these high desertion rates were probably the product of the CCC's makeshift organization and its diverse aims. The Corps was not solely concerned with the rehabilitation of American youth; had this been so, perhaps the desertion problem would have come under even closer scrutiny. But the CCC had conservation and relief functions as well. Inevitably, therefore, adolescent boys, not all of them fitted for the experience, were going to be transported from their familiar, often urban, home environment into the strange, silent forests. There many of them encountered effective discipline for the first time, and others received their first taste of hard manual work. That a sizable minority of these boys would simply not be able to make the necessary adjustment seems scarcely surprising. The reasons for the increased desertion rates after 1938 are harder to identify. The loss of the best Reserve officers and their replacement by less experienced men, the attraction of the NYA, the fear of being drafted, the gradual upswing in the economy—all of these must have played a part.

The desertion rates undoubtedly damaged the CCC's image, but they were far from destroying it. Far more damaging publicly to the CCC was the increased incidence of unrest and mutiny in the camps. The Washington *Times* broke the story of the most spectacular revolt of all in November, 1937, when it reported that mutiny had broken out in five CCC camps operating in the Shenandoah National Park in Virginia. More than one hundred enrollees had been dismissed for refusing to work. The camp commander explained that the youths "had enlisted apparently under the impression they were going to a Southern resort for the winter. When they arrived to find snow and ice and plenty of work, the trouble started."[30] Most enrollees were disgusted by the mutineers' action, the report concluded.

Fechner, dismayed at such unwelcome publicity for the CCC, immediately instigated a full investigation and soon uncovered a multiplicity of causes for the unrest.[31] Most of the youths who

30. Washington *Times*, Nov. 18, 1937.

31. Commanding Officer, Third Corps Area, to Fechner, Nov. 22, 1937, Director, Correspondence.

participated were from the mining districts of Pennsylvania, where a strike was the normal method of achieving redress for grievances. Furthermore, neither local CCC officials nor the camp commander had made any attempt to prepare the lads for the transfer from their highly industrialized home communities to a completely rural environment. The situation was further complicated by the presence in the camps of a large contingent of Southern enrollees, with whom the Pennsylvania boys, completely different in background and outlook, clashed repeatedly. These were the factors which coalesced to produce one of the most publicized of all CCC mutinies.[32]

The Virginia revolt was but the first of a series of unpleasant incidents which plagued the Corps. In 1938, for example, enrollees in a New York camp were caught stealing CCC material and disposing of it locally.[33] In January, 1939, Pennsylvania and Southern youths clashed at Luray, Virginia, in a major riot. Several enrollees were badly beaten, and one suffered severe knife and ax wounds.[34] The commander of a camp near Lexington, Indiana, permitted the wide-scale distribution of liquor to enrollees, and brought "two girls into the camp, for immoral purposes."[35] There were many signs that the high morale of the first four years of the Corps was disintegrating.

CCC officials could do little to prevent the disturbances, apart from urging the commanders to closely supervise incoming enrollees and to generally "keep their fingers on the pulse of the camp."[36] Persons sought to prevent as much as possible the mingling of urban and rural enrollees in the same camps, while fully realizing that this approach was a stopgap measure only.[37] On the other hand, Major General Tyner insisted that only the granting of wider punitive powers to camp commanders could remedy the situation; "the main reason for the unrest," he said, was the lack of respect for military authority among the en-

32. *Ibid.*
33. Advisory Council, Minutes, Nov. 10, 1938.
34. J. Fred Kurtz to Commanding General, Third Corps Area, Jan. 31, 1939, S.D., Discharges.
35. Advisory Council, Minutes, March 20, 1939.
36. Commanding General, Third Corps Area, to Camp Commander, Oct. 22, 1937, Director, Correspondence.
37. Persons to McEntee, Jan. 13, 1938, S.D., Discharges.

rollees.[38] Fechner refused to grant additional power, however, on the grounds that "these camps are not military camps," and the Regular Army discipline would be out of place in them.[39] The mutiny problem continued to bother the CCC officials, not because of its extensiveness, but because of the publicity given each outbreak.

Misdemeanors on the part of the CCC employees and camp commanders also brought criticism to the agency. Fechner expressed great chagrin in 1939 when it was revealed that a camp commander in Maryland had been arrested for selling liquor to enrollees, and that a New York officer had embezzled $20,000 of the camp's money; he knew that the twin scandals would damage the CCC's image of efficiency.[40] Ever since the highly publicized trial of Reno C. Stitely, a CCC clerk who had defrauded the Corps of $84,000 as a result of lax disbursement procedures, Congress and the press had been watchful for further indiscretions.[41] Their hostile scrutiny was a new and unwelcome experience for officials used to basking in the sunlight of universal public acclaim.

To add to the discomfort of CCC officials, familiar problems reappeared, often in more acute form. Agitation for fairer treatment of Negroes had certainly not been quashed by Fechner's decision in 1935 to curb Negro enrolment, and white hostility to Negro camps had not ceased. A determined effort to locate a Negro camp at Georgetown, Delaware, was frustrated by residents of the city, who lobbied successfully against its establishment.[42] As this would have been Delaware's first Negro camp, the failure meant that no Negro from that state was yet able to enjoy the benefits of CCC life. Negro action groups now concentrated on another aspect of the problem. As Walter White, executive secretary of the NAACP indicated, there was a real need to adjust Negro CCC enrolment to a re-employment ratio. The new jobs created by the slowly improving economy went to

38. Advisory Council, Minutes, March 28, 1939.
39. *Ibid.*
40. Fechner to McKinney, May 22, 1939, Director, Correspondence.
41. New York *Times*, Jan. 14, 19, 20, and 22, 1938.
42. Gov. Richard C. McMullen, Del., to Taylor, June 23, 1937, S.D., Negro Selection.

white youths, not Negroes, he averred, and Negro enrolment in the CCC should be at least doubled.[43]

Fechner remained intransigent in face of such pressures. Not only did he flatly refuse to select more Negroes,[44] but he also directed that Negro camps should be cut in strict proportion to the reduction of white companies, despite the slower Negro re-employment rate.[45] Neither would he permit any compromise on camp segregation, even though he was forced to break another of his own injunctions in the process and send the Negroes out of their home states. Philip La Follette, governor of Wisconsin, requested in 1938 that Wisconsin Negroes be enrolled in integrated camps within the state rather than be sent to segregated camps in Illinois.[46] The Director's Office refused, claiming it would be "contrary to official policy,"[47] a reply which the executive secretary of the Milwaukee Urban League characterized as "a decided disappointment, coming as it did from a Federal agency." "To my knowledge," he wrote, "there are no units in Wisconsin designed as Italian, Polish, German or Jewish. Therefore we feel it well within the fitness of things to raise the question as to why Negroes are being set aside into so-called Negro units."[48] There was no acceptable solution to the problem. To the end, it was hard to locate Negro camps,[49] while there was little increase in the Negro selection rate, even after rising re-employment made it more difficult to secure qualified white applicants.[50]

Another aspect of the total pattern of CCC discrimination against Negroes became a matter of increasing urgency in the years after 1937. It concerned their use as supervisors in Negro camps. The question first arose quite early in the CCC's existence. In 1934, in response to pressure from the NAACP, General

43. Walter White, executive secretary, NAACP, N.Y., to Fechner, Dec. 28, 1937, Director, Correspondence.

44. Fechner to White, Dec. 29, 1937, *ibid.*

45. Fechner to Persons, March 23, 1938, *ibid.*

46. La Follette to Fechner, Dec. 19, 1938, *ibid.*

47. Taylor to La Follette, Feb. 21, 1939, *ibid.*

48. William Kelly, executive secretary, Milwaukee Urban League, to Taylor, Feb. 23, 1939, *ibid.*

49. Carl Martin, supervisor, CCC Selection, Ill., to Persons, March 4, 1941, S.D., Negro Selection.

50. George N. Sadka, supervisor, CCC Selection, Miss., to Persons, Feb. 4, 1941, *ibid.*

MacArthur and Fechner agreed to appoint Negro educational advisers whenever practicable; this soon became established policy.[51] Thus encouraged, Negroes began to seek appointments to other positions, including that of camp commander. The Army drew the line on this but Roosevelt, no doubt looking to the Negro vote, thought the idea had merit, and in 1936, at his direction, three Negro Reserve officers were each placed in charge of a Negro camp.[52] These appointments were given wide publicity, but the whole business was little more than a symbolic gesture. After re-election Roosevelt displayed no further interest in the question, and though Negroes pressed vehemently for increased openings, the Army, with Fechner's tacit consent, refused to call any more Negro Reserve officers to duty as camp commanders. Army authorities claimed that it was simply not possible to get a community to accept a Negro camp if it had a Negro in command.[53] They undoubtedly had a point, yet it is equally true that their efforts in this direction were extraordinarily halfhearted. With neither director nor War Department in any way committed to increasing the opportunities available to Negro officers, progress could hardly be expected.

Negroes, however, were used increasingly as project supervisors in Negro camps. An order of 1938 made this mandatory, and the policy was implemented and sustained in spite of the vigorous opposition of some selection agents and Army officers.[54] Moreover, Negroes continued to benefit mentally and physically from Corps life and still remained in the camps half as long again as white enrollees.[55] The failure of the CCC in aiding Negro enrollees was certainly not one of performance, but one of potential. Much was accomplished, but much more could have been done.

51. Louis Howe to Fechner, April 3 and 7, 1934, Fechner to Howe, April 4, 1934, Director, Correspondence. Howe confessed that he did not "give a damn about this thing."

52. Memorandum for Press, Aug. 7, 1936, Director, Correspondence.

53. Fechner to A. Williams, March 6, 1939, *ibid.*

54. Persons to Maj. C. C. Graham, district commander, CCC, Little Rock, Ark., March 16, 1940, *ibid.* See also chap. v, above.

55. *Emergency Relief Appropriation Act, Fiscal Year, 1941, Hearings Before the Committee on Appropriations, United States Senate, 76th Congress, Third Session, on H. J. Res. 544, A Joint Resolution Making Appropriations for Work Relief and Relief for the Fiscal Year Ending June 30, 1941* (Washington, 1940), p. 206 (hereinafter cited as *Relief Appropriation, 1941, Hearings*).

If the closing of the camps worried Negro leaders, it profoundly disturbed many congressmen. The pressure from politicians on the Director's Office in the final years of the CCC was no longer concerned with getting camps established in their districts, but with preventing their removal. This was a phenomenon as old as the Corps itself, but the protests intensified markedly as the rate of camp closings increased, and congressmen had to face the local political effects of the President's economy schemes.[56] Men like Senator "Cotton Ed" Smith started to demand full congressional investigations every time a camp was removed from their district.[57] Though insurgent congressmen did not have enough strength in 1938 to defeat the President's reduction plans, as they had done in 1935, their opposition was none the less bitter for that.[58] In fact, Fechner considered that the intense reaction by some congressmen to the closing of the camps endangered the whole image of the CCC. The situation had "become very bad," he thought.[59]

Behind the discomforts of congressmen was the vociferous anger of hundreds of local communities which had lost their CCC camps, and with them a strong aid to economic recovery. Many of these towns and villages did not even have the compensation of a completed work project to fall back on, so drastic had been the reductions. The Menominee, Michigan, Chamber of Commerce in protesting the closing of a camp there, said work had barely begun. Leaving it in such an embryonic state would represent an inexplicable waste of money, time, and effort.[60] In some districts specially constituted local organizations attempted to force the retention of camps. The North-Western Ohio Drainage Association, formed with the sole aim of preventing the abandonment of four CCC drainage camps, represented twenty

56. I.e., Rep. J. G. Scrugham to Ickes, April 1, 1938, Secretary of Interior, Records. Rep. Vincent T. Harrington (Dem., Ia.) wrote to 179 congressmen and forty-four senators in an effort to prevent the closing of drainage camps in his district. See McEntee to James Roosevelt, May 18, 1938, Roosevelt Papers, O.F. 268, Box 10; Advisory Council, Minutes, April 19, 1938.

57. Advisory Council, Minutes, Nov. 2, 1937.

58. New York *Times*, Jan. 11, 1938.

59. Advisory Council, Minutes, Nov. 2, 1937.

60. Menominee, Mich., Chamber of Commerce to Roosevelt, Feb. 28, 1938, Roosevelt Papers, O.F. 268–Misc., Box 19.

counties.[61] It held so many well-attended mass protest meetings that Senator Victor Donahey, Democrat of Ohio, nervously feared that its influence would determine the results, in three districts, of the 1938 congressional elections.[62] Other groups and individuals began to criticize aspects of CCC life. A special commission reported to the Massachusetts State Legislature that "Communists were creating dissatisfaction, unrest and class consciousness among the young men in the camps," a contention enthusiastically supported by Mayor Frank L. Hague of Jersey City. A Brooklyn County judge denounced it as a "haven for ex-convicts," yet the American Prisons Association upbraided it for not officially accepting parolees and probationers.[63] Increasingly, the Corps was feeling the lash of criticism from all sides.

Nevertheless, the fact of the CCC's popularity must never be obscured. Individuals and organizations ranging from the Catholic Social Action Congress to the president of the Latvian Republic still accorded it unreserved praise.[64] Richard St. Barbe Baker, a leading British conservationist, considered the CCC to be "the finest thing ever heard of," and hoped to bring one hundred Englishmen to the United States to study its workings.[65] One of the highlights of the American visit of the King and Queen of England in June, 1939, was their tour of a CCC camp in Virginia.[66] Newspapers also added their plaudits. The Washington *Times-Herald*, defiantly answering foreign criticism of the United States, cited the record of the CCC as proof of the country's greatness.[67] *Collier's* simply considered it indispensable."[68] Mothers still pleaded that their sons be enrolled,[69] and former enrollees continued to pay glowing tributes to the benefits of camp life.[70] Criticism of the Corps may have increased, but as

61. Earl H. Hanefield, director of agriculture, Ohio, to Henry Wallace, Feb. 4, 1938, *ibid.*, O.F. 268, Box 9.

62. Sen. Victor Donahey to James Roosevelt, March 14, 1938, *ibid.*

63. New York *Times*, Nov. 1, 1935, June 29, 1937.

64. Secretary of State to Fechner, Oct. 15, 1937, Director, Correspondence.

65. Advisory Council, Minutes, May 26, 1939.

66. Eleanor Roosevelt, *This I Remember* (New York, 1949), pp. 192-193.

67. Washington *Times-Herald*, July 16, 1939.

68. *Collier's*, Aug. 19, 1939, editorial.

69. Mrs. Cora Willis, Lonsdale, Ark., to Mrs. Roosevelt, April, 1938, Director, Correspondence.

70. Woodrow H. Hopkins to McKinney, March 13, 1939, *ibid.* As a

yet it had made little impression on the phalanx of favorable public opinion. This eventuality still lay in the future.

Casting its ominous shadow over much of American life in the late thirties was the steadily worsening international situation. As war in Europe drew nearer, Americans became progressively concerned about the state of their own defenses. Inevitably, the issue of military training in the CCC became an increasingly vital one, affecting many facets of Corps life. The military training controversy was not a factor in the fight for permanence of 1937 but it was brought squarely to the forefront of public concern at the end of that year by the director himself. Speaking at Miami, Fechner declared that the CCC boys, because of their camp training and discipline, were "85 per cent prepared for military life" and could be "turned into first-class fighting men at almost an instant's notice."[71] He went on to point out that the "military aspect" of CCC life was unintentional and formed but a very small part of the camp program, but his speech was interpreted in many quarters as supporting military training in the Corps. The Des Moines *Register* demanded that the CCC "stick to the civilian idea" and that Fechner eschew further discussion of the issue.[72] The Women's International League for Peace and Freedom angrily denounced "the use of the CCC as a means for training young men for war."[73] However, some Army officers connected with the Corps not only supported Fechner, but also demanded that a complete training program be instituted immediately.[74] Significantly, public opinion at last seemed to favor such a move. A Gallup Poll taken in August, 1938, revealed that 75 per cent of those polled supported military training in the camps, a startling increase from 1936 when no clear preferences could be discerned.[75] Though a substantial body of the press, particularly in Western states, remained

---

result of his camp experience, this youth had been able to get a newspaper job on leaving the CCC and was currently manager of the Springfield, Ill., circulation branch of the Chicago *Daily News*.

71. New York *Times*, Dec. 21, 1937.

72. Des Moines *Register*, Dec. 24, 1937.

73. Women's International League for Peace and Freedom to Ickes, Jan. 25, 1938, Secretary of Interior, Records.

74. New York *Times*, March 21, 1938.

75. *Ibid.*, June 2, 1940.

doggedly opposed to training,[76] and though Roosevelt in October, 1938, once more specifically disclaimed even considering the introduction of any such program,[77] the issue was bound to remain a live one.

A few of the largest daily newspapers helped to keep the question in the forefront by repeated editorial comment and news coverage. The New York *Times* proposed that CCC labor be used to man airplane plants. In this way the Corps could be "made an essential part of the national defense program."[78] The Washington *News* believed that the international situation rendered it essential to use CCC boys in defense work, and claimed that War Department officials unanimously favored military training in the camps.[79] To be sure, some Army officers were extremely vocal in pressing for training, and in May, 1939, an interdepartmental government committee urged that the CCC provide apprentices for aircraft mechanics as a defense measure.[80] Congressmen, mainly from Southern states, introduced legislation providing for military training in the Corps and spoke publicly in favor of it.[81] Worried CCC selection agents called for some slackening in the publicity given the issue because of its effect on selection rates. Dayton Jones, the California agent, in May, 1939, reported the wholesale withdrawal of applicants due to fear of becoming "cannon fodder."[82] Such pleas were in vain. By the outbreak of World War II, military training in the CCC had firm Army, press, and popular support.

The coming of the war in Europe brought increased demands for a military training scheme. The Chicago *Tribune* angrily declared that "we should not neglect the opportunity afforded by the CCC to prepare for any emergency which may arise."[83] The

76. I.e., San Diego *Sun*, Aug. 6, 1938. "It would be a denial of democracy to make only those men for whom the economic machine had not been able to find a use, subject to military training."
77. New York *Times*, Oct. 26, 1938.
78. *Ibid.*, Dec. 15, 1938, Jan. 5, 1939.
79. Washington *Daily News*, Dec. 6, 1938.
80. Dallas *News*, May 10, 1939; New York *Times*, May 14, 1939.
81. C.R.M., No. 784(7), Military Training. The first to introduce bills in 1939 were Rep. James P. Richards (S.C.), who wanted six hours of training a week, and Sen. Robert J. Reynolds (N.C.), who wanted two to five hours of training weekly. Six out of nine similar bills introduced between 1939 and 1941 came from Southern congressmen or senators.
82. Dayton Jones to Snyder, May 15, 1939, S.D., Military Aspects.
83. Chicago *Tribune*, Sept. 9, 1939.

attitude of some Army officers verged on the irrational. Addressing enrollees at the dedication of a CCC camp near Franklinton, North Carolina, Colonel C. L. McGee declared that "It's great to get into war. It broadens you." McGee insisted that "it is a glorious thing for an American youth to lay down his life in a foreign land for defense of his country," and he was hopeful that all CCC lads would be given first claim to this happy experience.[84] The effect of such histrionics on the camp desertion rate was not recorded. At the Capitol, the chairman of the House Military Affairs Committee, Representative Andrew J. May, Democrat of Kentucky, admitted that he might introduce a bill providing for five hours' military instruction a week in all camps. "We should give CCC boys an advantage in wartime that many of their wealthier fellows lacked," he said, in answer to critics who called the bill class legislation which "placed an unequal military burden on the poor youths forced to enroll in the camps."[85] The public was obviously solid in its support for training. The latest Gallup Poll revealed that 90 per cent favored military activity in the CCC.[86]

A few important newspapers stood firm against the majority. The New York *Herald Tribune* argued that the problem should not be approached from the standpoint of the European war, but in the light of how America would benefit. "The camps are in conception and execution essentially non-military,"[87] it declared. The St. Louis *Post Dispatch* firmly asserted that the CCC "should continue to be civilian"[88] in title and objectives. The official position was stated clearly in December, 1939, by Fechner when he appeared before the House Labor Committee. He asserted that many of the essentials of military life—discipline, hygiene, and leadership training—were already embodied in the CCC program. "I think it would be a grave mistake to go further and attempt to militarize what is essentially a civilian conservation corps," he said. "If the Congress and the people, in their wisdom determine that there exists a need for additional military forces in this country . . . we should very frankly provide

84. Greensboro, N.C., *News*, Nov. 11, 1939.
85. Washington *Post*, Nov. 16, 1939.
86. *Ibid.*, Oct. 1, 1939.
87. New York *Herald Tribune*, Sept. 12, 1939.
88. St. Louis *Post-Dispatch*, Sept. 16, 1939.

for additional military forces, and not attempt to gain this objective through making the Corps half civil and half military."[89] Ten days later, McEntee presented the same argument in a coast-to-coast radio debate with Raymond J. Kelly, national commander of the American Legion. He saw a dangerous parallel between a militarized CCC and the labor camps of Nazi Germany.[90]

By far the strongest argument against military training in the CCC however, was provided by the Army chief of staff, General George C. Marshall. In a press interview, he denied all reports that the Army wanted such training or was even considering immediate use of the Corps as a noncombatant auxiliary to Army troops, though he did concede that if any emergency should arise, then perhaps some CCC labor would be used on noncombatant work. Meanwhile, both he, as a former CCC commander, and other Army officials were perfectly satisfied with what the Corps was doing in introducing youths to a military mode of existence; they had no desire to interfere with the current program.[91]

Marshall's positive statement did much to stem the tide of agitation for formal military training in the CCC. Commenting on this in his first press conference as director, McEntee said "he did not anticipate the recurrence of a serious campaign to force military training on the Corps."[92] He was correct—for the moment. In his statement, General Marshall had given implicit approval to the future use of the Corps on noncombatant technical activity if the situation so warranted. Attention was now turned to this alternative. In an attempt to placate the proponents of full military training, Senator James F. Byrnes, Democrat of South Carolina, introduced an amendment to the 1940-1941 Relief Appropriation measure which provided for noncombatant military training in the CCC.[93] The Byrnes Amendment had the full support of the Federal Security Agency, the War Department, and the Administration. Testifying in its favor before the Senate Appropriations Committee, General Marshall

89. Washington *Daily News*, Dec. 7, 1939.
90. New York *Times*, Dec. 18, 1939.
91. Washington *Star*, Dec. 30, 1939; Schlesinger, II, 339.
92. Washington *Post*, Feb. 16, 1940.
93. *Relief Appropriation, 1941, Hearings*, pp. 186-206.

said that its passage would enable the Corps to provide specialized training in fields important to the Army. He mentioned specifically the need for cooks and engineers. There existed in the CCC, he said, "a set-up which would facilitate training in a number of specialized fields of a non-combative nature." Moreover, the camp system was such that "we would not have to go beyond their present activities to get the training that we need and want."[94] Though opposed by a few isolationists like Senator Gerald Nye, the amendment met few congressional barriers. An attempt by Senator Walter F. George, Democrat of Georgia, to authorize voluntary combat training was defeated, and the relief bill, with the Byrnes Amendment attached, had a clear passage.[95]

McEntee, Studebaker, and Frank J. McSherry, director of defense training, Federal Security Agency, working in consultation with Army authorities, drew up details of the plan. It provided for eight hours per week basic training for each enrollee in subjects such as hygiene, basic mathematics, or English, all already taught in the camps as part of the general education program; it also provided for twenty hours per week of general defense training, eight of which were deductible from the work hours. This section covered vocational subjects, such as blueprint reading, shop mathematics, and basic engineering. After completing general defense training, the ablest enrollees were to be moved to full-time defense work in specific areas geared directly to Army needs. The more important of these fields included cooking, first aid, demolition, road and bridge construction, radio operation, and signal communication.[96] The education program of the CCC was thus diverted toward fulfilling the needs of national defense.

The plan was fully operative by early September, 1940, and remained so until the abolishment of the Corps.[97] Though basic Army drill was eventually ordered for all enrollees,[98] it was in noncombative work that the CCC made its most significant contribution to national defense. Testifying before the Senate Labor

94. *Ibid.*, pp. 191-192.
95. *Ibid.*, p. 188; New York *Times*, June 13 and 21, 1940.
96. Advisory Council, Minutes, Aug. 26, 1940.
97. *Ibid.*
98. New York *Times*, Aug. 17, 1941.

Committee on a bill to terminate the CCC and the NYA, the adjutant general, Major General James A. Ulio, paid tribute to the Corps' noncombatant program, not only for its intrinsic worth, but also because the use of CCC labor had enabled the Army to release enlisted men from noncombat duties.[99] Furthermore, a number of CCC enrollees enlisted, or were drafted, after completing their Corps training. These men were often already well versed in specifically military occupations, as well as being familiar with Army discipline. This was but one instance, Ulio stated, of how the CCC had aided the war effort.[100]

The vexing question of military training was thus settled successfully by compromise, and the Corps co-ordinated its educational activities into the basic weave of the nation's defense policy. In retrospect, bearing in mind the state of America's military unpreparedness as war drew nearer, it is possible that some training scheme might have been introduced with profit earlier than 1940. Yet, as one surveys the various arguments for and against such an innovation, two facts emerge. The first is that, indisputably, the enrollees, by their very presence in camps run by the military, were receiving a valuable introduction to Army conditions, an experience that must have greatly aided many when they were eventually drafted. Second, given the emphasis on work, which was still the cardinal aspect of CCC life, any training which was introduced into the existing CCC program would have had to be of a limited nature only, probably confined to some marching or rifle shooting. In view of the controversy such a minor innovation would inevitably cause, the game was clearly not worth the candle. More was to be gained by allowing the present situation to continue, rather than risking strife over a limited scheme. In any event, the introduction of noncombatant training soon made the issue irrelevant.

Despite the successful settlement of the military training question, the pressing problems of administrative friction and

99. *Termination of the Civilian Conservation Corps and the National Youth Administration, Hearings Before the Committee on Education and Labor, United States Senate, 77th Congress, Second Session, on S. 2295. A Bill to Provide For the Termination of the National Youth Administration and the Civilian Conservation Corps*, March 23 to April 17, 1942 (Washington, 1942), pp. 254, 258 (hereinafter cited as *Termination of CCC Hearings*, 1942).

100. *Ibid.*, pp. 253-280.

sagging morale remained with the CCC. Furthermore, the war in Europe brought some measure of economic recovery to the United States. Though officials insisted that the CCC was no longer a relief agency but a means of "providing employment as well as vocational training for youthful citizens,"[101] the relief stamp would always remain with it, particularly as its enrollees still came primarily from the lowest income groups. With a reviving economy creating more jobs for everyone, the Corps was forced increasingly to compete for men with private employment. Its relief function was no longer needed. Could its continued existence, therefore, be justified? After Pearl Harbor, this question became: is the CCC necessary to the winning of the war?

101. Quarterly Selection Report of the CCC, Oct., 1939, p. 2; C.R.M., Appendix V, Document 668.

12. *The Final Years, 1940-1942*

The death of Fechner was the opportunity for Ickes, the secretary of the interior, to attempt to destroy the CCC director's power. In a letter to the director of the Bureau of the Budget, he proposed abolishment of the CCC Director's Office, the relief of the War Department from its duties, and the vesting of total power in the camps with the Departments of Agriculture and the Interior.[1] Disclaiming ulterior motives, Ickes said that Fechner's death provided a fine chance to reorganize the Corps. It is likely, nevertheless, that his dominant reason was to prevent McEntee from becoming director, as the centralizing proclivities of Fechner's assistant were thoroughly disliked and distrusted. Some Department of the Interior officials referred to him as "his august majesty."[2] The President had no intention of changing the existing organization, however, and McEntee was duly appointed, no doubt to Ickes's chagrin.[3] The increasing friction between the Department of the Interior and the Director's Office did not augur well for the difficult days ahead.

The first problem to be faced was familiar. The President, in his budget message, announced that the Corps was to be cut to 230,000 enrollees in 1,227 camps.[4] Once again the pattern of local protests and ill-feeling manifested itself.[5] In response, Congress was once more recalcitrant. The House, by 204 votes to 170, added $50 million to the CCC's appropriation, obviating the need to close any camps at all, and the Senate, defying its own Committee on Appropriations, followed suit.[6] The CCC was to remain at its current strength for the fiscal year 1940-1941. Republican votes were responsible for reversing the Administration's policy. It was one of the very few instances during the congressional session when Republicans deserted the party leadership, and the New York *Times* surmised that local re-election

1. Ickes to Harold D. Smith, Jan. 4, 1940, Secretary of Interior, Records.
2. See E. K. Burlew, first assistant secretary of the interior, to A. Weatherwax, assistant representative, Department of the Interior, Advisory Council, CCC, July 26, 1940, *ibid.*
3. Roosevelt to Ickes, Jan. 25, 1940, *ibid.*
4. New York *Times*, Jan. 5, 1940.
5. *Ibid.*, Feb. 4, 1940.
6. *Ibid.*, March 28, April 26, 1940.

considerations had probably prompted the move.[7] The parallel with the congressional revolt of 1936 is striking. Once again in an election year congressmen had defeated a presidential economy drive in the interests of their own political health. In 1940, as in 1936, the removal of a CCC camp from a constituency could spell political trouble for the incumbent.

The strength of support for the CCC in Congress must have been heartening to Corps officials. There were also other signs that the agency was in no immediate danger of losing its favored place with the people. It survived the election campaign unscathed, and the introduction of noncombatant training seemed a popular compromise.[8] Thus encouraged, the Corps took a further step in the attempt to shrug off its relief connections and adopt its new role as a reservoir for defense needs. Economic status was no longer to be considered the compelling factor in enrolments. Even youths whose parents were both employed could enlist if they possessed "good personal qualifications."[9] This was a revolutionary step. As McNutt said, the CCC was "now open to college boys." The declared aim, no longer connected with relief, was to prepare "young men for citizenship." The allotment was subsequently lowered due to the economic status of the new enrollees, and the emphasis shifted to the enrollees saving for themselves rather than giving to their families.

This broadening of function came far too late. By 1940 the CCC's identification with relief was too strong to permit any change in public attitudes. Few of McNutt's "college boys" were ever enticed to enter its ranks. They saw their destinies elsewhere. The CCC remained overwhelmingly the preserve of the decreasing numbers of unemployed young men.[10] Nevertheless, the Corps still received many public plaudits. William Green, the president of the AF of L, and a former critic of the CCC, referred in a speech to "this great movement designated the

7. *Ibid.*, March 28, 1940.

8. The Democratic party platform stated its intention to continue the CCC (see New York *Times*, July 18, 1940), while the Republican candidate, Wendell Willkie, based his appeal on issues far removed from the destruction of New Deal measures. See also Burns, pp. 442-451; Washington *Post*, June 2, 1940; Atlanta *Constitution*, June 26, 1940.

9. Persons to Selection Agents, June 26, 1940, C.R.M., Appendix VI, Document 701.

10. New York *Times*, Aug. 5, Nov. 24, 1940.

CCC camps of America." The director of the American Youth Commission termed it "a master plan for all service agencies."[11] Furthermore, McEntee was able to announce in November that no less than 306,500 enrollees were presently being trained for defense jobs.[12] The Corps, superficially at least, seemed in continued good health.

Still, signs of trouble were constantly present. McEntee was already receiving complaints that the CCC was competing with farmers for its work force, and he realized that increased antagonism could be expected from rural areas as the demand for labor increased.[13] The desertion rate showed little sign of decreasing,[14] and the tension between the Director's Office and the Department of the Interior was at a dangerous pitch. In a letter to Ickes, Wirth complained that the "morale of the CCC has deteriorated seriously during the past two years. This deterioration is definitely the result of the increased number of functions being taken over by the Office of the Director, CCC. . . . [The] mutual understanding essential to the coordination of such an enterprise is being destroyed due to the abandonment of the function of the Advisory Council." Finally, Wirth complained that only eight council meetings had been held between October 1, 1939, and October 1, 1940.[15]

To complicate further the already troublesome situation, the CCC, in late 1940, embarked on an experiment which was to cause it considerable public embarrassment. There were in the Department of Agriculture certain young idealists who were becoming increasingly interested in the creation of CCC "staff colleges." Convinced that the Army would soon have to sever all connections with the agency due to the tremendous increase in national defense requirements, an event to which they looked forward avidly, they envisaged the creation of a series of training camps where outstanding young men from the best universities, well imbued with a spirit of service, would be trained in the principles of CCC leadership, eventually to become camp

11. *Ibid.*, Sept. 12, Nov. 1, 1940.
12. *Ibid.*, Nov 24, 1940.
13. Advisory Council, Minutes, June 24, 1940.
14. Persons to State Directors, Sept. 16, 1940, C.R.M., Appendix VI, Document 716.
15. Wirth to Ickes, Nov. 5, 1940, Secretary of Interior, Records.

commanders.[16] In September, 1940, such ideas coincided with the desire of a similarly idealistic group of young men—graduates of Harvard and Dartmouth—to establish a work-service scheme near Tunbridge, Vermont. To this end they wished to use an old CCC camp at Mt. Sharon, near Tunbridge, from which they would issue forth each day to aid the nearby farmers. They also wanted to use CCC funds.[17]

The officials of the Department of Agriculture saw that these youths could form the nucleus of their staff training program, and they were able to persuade the President that the scheme was sound. Roosevelt, in fact, was enthusiastic. Writing to McNutt, he said that as the Army was withdrawing its best officers from CCC service: "I desire that there should be created in the Corps a special training agency to prepare for this leadership—perhaps in one or more of the camps now in use." He specifically stated that the Army was not to be involved with the experiment in any way, and he set up a committee to study the idea further.[18] Its members included Dean James Landis of the Harvard Law School, Professor Harold Lasswell of the Yale Law School, Dr. W. W. Alexander, chairman of the National Defense Commission, and Wayne Coy, the assistant administrator of the Federal Security Agency.[19]

The "staff college" experiment had caught the attention and interest of a nationally known newspaper columnist, Dorothy Thompson, then wife of the author, Sinclair Lewis. Miss Thompson, an important member of Roosevelt's election campaign team,[20] wrote to the President in October pressing for action on the Mt. Sharon camp and asking that he draft Eugene Rosenstock-Huessey, a German refugee and Dartmouth sociologist, to act as training consultant.[21] The President, probably conscious of Miss Thompson's political value, immediately complied. He

16. Frank Davidson to Paul Appleby, assistant secretary of agriculture, July 25, 1940, Files of the Secretary of Agriculture—Conservation.
17. New York *Times*, Sept. 22, 1940.
18. Roosevelt to McNutt, Sept. 18, 1940, Roosevelt Papers, O.F. 268, Box 11.
19. W. W. Alexander to Appleby, Sept. 30, 1940, Files of the Secretary of Agriculture—Conservation.
20. Saul A. Yager to Steve Early, Oct. 31, 1940, Roosevelt Papers, P.P.F. 6650: "Reaction to Dorothy Thompson last night tremendous . . . by all means keep Miss Thompson on the air."
21. Dorothy Thompson to Roosevelt, Oct. 18, 1940, *ibid.*

wrote to the secretary of agriculture to ask him to have Mt. Sharon opened as soon as possible and to get "Professor E. R. Huessey in some kind of supervisory or advisory capacity in the camp."[22] The Mt. Sharon experiment was under way.

All seemed imbued with the high ideals of the community service plan, all, that is, except the director, McEntee, whom Miss Thompson had summarily dismissed as "a dope" who would probably vote for Willkie.[23] He poured cold water on the whole idea, complaining that there had been insufficient time to consider all its implications, and he cast grave doubts as to its practicality.[24] Roosevelt airily disregarded McEntee's criticism as of no account. Writing to Miss Thompson, he sent a copy of the director's objections with the comment that "the enclosed from Mr. McEntee is not the least bit satisfactory. Please get for me a little more info. By gosh! the thing is going to go through! . . . My best wishes to you."[25] His enthusiasm for the plan could not be doubted, but his sagacity in permitting its implementation without adequate investigation can be questioned. Nor was it wise to write disparagingly of a high federal official to a newspaper columnist. As far as Mt. Sharon was concerned, Roosevelt's keen political acumen seemed to have left him.

Preparations at the camp continued. Its legal status was established by a co-operative agreement between McNutt and the Departments of War and Agriculture.[26] The Army agreed to eschew all responsibility in the camp, while McEntee was gently removed from the picture. McNutt gave assurances that because it was an experimental camp, there would be no objection to stretching CCC regulations a little.[27] Professor Huessey agreed to act as administrator of the camp, which was to open officially on January 1, 1941 with a company of college students in residence. Its aims were both numerous and nebulous, but the emphasis was on "indoctrination for democracy." Huessey wanted to make all enrollees "militant defenders" of the democratic process. To

22. Roosevelt to Secretary of Agriculture, Alexander, and Wayne Coy, Oct. 18, 1940, *ibid.*, O.F. 268, Box 11.
23. Miss Thompson to Roosevelt, Oct. 18, 1940, *ibid.*, P.P.F. 6650.
24. McEntee to Roosevelt, Oct. 17, 1940, *ibid.*, O.F. 268, Box 11.
25. Roosevelt to Miss Thompson, Oct. 29, 1940, *ibid.*
26. Appleby to Mastin G. White, solicitor, Department of Agriculture, Nov. 20, 1940, Files of the Secretary of Agriculture–Conservation.
27. R. W. Olmstead to Appleby, Dec. 16, 1940, *ibid.*

this end, every decision relating to camp life was to be by majority vote. There was to be no hint of Army authoritarianism at Mt. Sharon.[28] It was also planned to try and expedite Huessey's citizenship application in view of his new position.[29] A few federal officials had qualms about the venture. Harold D. Smith, director of the Bureau of the Budget, said that Mt. Sharon could "be susceptible to considerable criticism."[30] The President, however, strongly supported by his wife, was determined to carry it through.[31]

The public was first apprised of the Mt. Sharon experiment through the pages of the New York *Herald Tribune*.[32] There was violent reaction, particularly from congressional quarters. Representative Albert J. Engel, Republican of Michigan, a member of the Appropriations Subcommittee which handled CCC money, wrote to the new secretary of agriculture, Claude R. Wickard, asking what Harvard and Dartmouth students, members of the "more privileged" classes, were doing in a CCC camp.[33] Receiving what he considered to be an unsatisfactory reply and sensing the political possibilities in the issue, he pressed on with his investigations and excoriations. "It appears the pampered sons of rich families are usurping a form of relief meant only for the nation's underprivileged,"[34] he told the House of Representatives. He also revealed the haste with which Huessey's citizenship application had been processed.[35] Probably the most damaging disclosure of all was that Huessey, before fleeing Germany, had been instrumental in instituting the labor camps there. Though Huessey disclaimed any intention of starting a similar scheme in the United States and pointed out that his work in Germany had been completed before Hitler came to power, the revelation was enough to utterly discredit the Mt. Sharon experiment.[36] The House Appropriations Committee called for an immediate investi-

28. Olmstead to Appleby, Dec. 14, 1940, *ibid.*
29. Roy Hendrickson, chairman, Committee of Supervision, Mt. Sharon Camp, to Huessey, Dec. 19, 1940, *ibid.*
30. Smith to Roosevelt, undated, Roosevelt Papers, O.F. 268, Box 11.
31. Eleanor Roosevelt to Roosevelt, Dec. 26, 1940, *ibid.*
32. New York *Herald Tribune*, Dec. 28, 1940.
33. Rep. Albert Engel (Rep., Mich.) to Wickard, Jan. 4, 1941, Files of the Secretary of Agriculture—Conservation.
34. New York *Times*, Feb. 2, 1941.
35. Boston *Herald*, Feb. 12, 1941.
36. New York *Times*, Feb. 2, 1941.

gation, at which McEntee made quite plain his opposition to the whole undertaking,[37] and protesting citizens demanded the immediate abolishment of "Fascist and Nazi Camps."[38] Newspapers normally friendly to the CCC opposed the experiment. The New York *Times* called it "starry-eyed and impractical,"[39] and the Shreveport *Times* commented that "after seven years of tranquility, during which it received hearty support from Congress and the public," the CCC was now being harshly criticized: "Apparently the cause of it all is someone high in the CCC, who decided that a record of fine practical accomplishment was not enough and that some fancy experimentation should be added."[40] Despite the urging of Mt. Sharon's supporters that congressmen and newsmen should visit the camp before condemning the experiment,[41] it was clear that it should be closed before a major crisis developed, one which might call into question the whole record of the CCC.

Faced with the possibility of serious political trouble, the President, McNutt, and other Administration supporters of the scheme decided that discretion was the better part of valor. McEntee suddenly found himself with full powers again, and he lost no time in using them. On February 21 he placed the War Department in full charge of administration at Mt. Sharon, thus effectively ending the experiment.[42] By March 19, all the college students had left the camp, and regular enrollees had been moved in.[43] The CCC "staff college" was no more. Dorothy Thompson bitterly attacked McEntee for his action. "Nearly everything" was wrong with the CCC, she said. Out of the experimental camp "could have come a reawakening and a rebirth of freedom and democracy in this country." Instead, the Corps

37. Appleby to James H. Rowe, administrative assistant to the President, Feb. 6, 1941, Files of the Secretary of Agriculture–Conservation.

38. T. L. Danimen to Wickard, March 1, 1941, *ibid.*

39. New York *Times*, Feb. 9, 1941.

40. Shreveport *Times*, Feb. 12, 1941.

41. Appleby to Engel, Feb. 4, 1941, Files of the Secretary of Agriculture–Conservation.

42. McEntee to Morrell, Feb. 17, 1941, *ibid.*

43. Olmstead to James H. Rowe, March 19, 1941, *ibid.* The college students took over an abandoned farmhouse where they lived communally, while calling on the government for financial support. Lack of funds eventually forced them to disband.

"remains a charitable institution" with no wider purpose than to relieve want.[44]

The Mt. Sharon experiment was the first and only attempt by intellectuals to modify the CCC's basic structure. It turned out to be an embarrassment to the Corps. The idea certainly had some merit, but it was its impracticability and lack of planning which were more obvious. At a time when the need for the CCC was beginning to be questioned, it was politically naïve to draw unfavorable public attention to it in so spectacular a manner. For this blunder the President must be blamed. No doubt preoccupied with the election campaign, he had accepted the idea enthusiastically without sufficiently considering its practical implications. He had suggested the employment of Huessey without investigating his controversial background. His enthusiasm and idealism, exploited by his wife and his advisers, had temporarily overshadowed his political realism.

Certainly the Mt. Sharon experiment did not help the CCC. Indeed, it exposed the Corps to the most sustained public criticism it had yet experienced. Yet its crucial importance lay elsewhere. For all its mistakes and deficiencies, Mt. Sharon was the first real attempt to break away from the confines of the Corps' makeshift organization and to develop a base for a permanent body, a body with far wider aims than those heretofore most prominent. But it failed, its purpose quite misunderstood. The implications of the failure were not difficult to discern. It showed that very few people had yet thought constructively about the CCC's future. Despite stated changes in its aim, it was still not generally regarded as having any wider functions than the provision of relief and the performance of useful conservation work. The Corps was never able to outgrow its emergency stamp.

Mt. Sharon's failure and the accompanying criticism did not hurt the CCC too seriously, however, even though from 1941 on the agency was increasingly the subject of public concern. This attention, this questioning of the need to continue the Corps, was not the result of an unsuccessful experiment, but arose from the realities of swiftly rising employment rates and the single-minded concern of Americans with defense. How could a relief agency be justified in the transformed situation?

44. New York *Times*, March 4, 1941.

Newspaper comment provided one barometer of public opinion. A number of editorials, while paying the usual tributes to the CCC's splendid achievements, nevertheless wondered if it would be needed much longer. The Harrisburg *News* said that as jobs were currently plentiful, the CCC was becoming unnecessary. "To drain workers from industry rather than towards it in these urgent days seems as stupid as it is wasteful," the newspaper argued.[45] The Philadelphia *Ledger* denounced the "fight for recruits" between the CCC and the NYA "at a time when armament production centers are scouring the countryside for unskilled labor." The two "worthwhile agencies" had served their purpose and should be terminated.[46] The right-wing Indianapolis *Star* had lost all patience. Attacking "paid vacations" for the "Man Scouts," it spoke of the acute shortage of farm labor in the Midwest and demanded that the CCC boys be discharged to alleviate it.[47] The Des Moines *Register*, while praising the Corps' "magnificent job in conservation and in youth rehabilitation," nevertheless thought that the farm labor crisis now took precedence and that "a strong case could be made out for its abolition."[48] The CCC was also the object of vigorous Republican attacks in Congress, especially during the debate over the Federal Security Agency's appropriation. One of the CCC's most consistent foes, Representative Taber of New York, now spoke to a more receptive audience when he urged that Congress kill the agency. The Corps still had substantial bipartisan support, however, and though its appropriation for the 1941-1942 fiscal year was trimmed, the reduction was not drastic.[49]

Corps officials recognized that the CCC was "in a slump"; according to the New York *Times*, they were very puzzled by its "sudden loss of popularity."[50] Their diagnosis was not really accurate. The abuse of a few right-wing editors and the honest doubts of others did not represent a real loss in popular esteem but a simple recognition that times had changed. With employment rising, and the armed forces expanding, the CCC had lost

45. Harrisburg, Pa., *News*, June 10, 1941.
46. Philadelphia *Ledger*, Aug. 19, 1941.
47. Indianapolis *Star*, June 18 and 27, 1941.
48. Des Moines *Register*, June 11, 1942.
49. New York *Times*, June 3, 4, and 30, 1941.
50. *Ibid.*, July 15, 1941.

its main function. Corps officials were slow to recognize this fact. Instead, they made various attempts to combat what they thought was a recoverable loss in popular favor. The most significant ploy was to stress the vital role played by the CCC in national defense policy. To this end, as well as ordering basic Army drill for all enrollees,[51] the director placed a number of camps on military reservations. By December, 1941, fifty-five such companies were at work under military direction on a variety of projects, ranging from railroad construction to mosquito control.[52] In an effort to check the serious complaint that the Corps was causing a shortage of farm labor, McEntee permitted enrollees to leave camp temporarily to assist farmers and orchard growers during harvesting, while it was hoped that a vigorous publicity drive would boost sagging enrolment figures.[53] In further attempts to increase enrolment, a policy of continuous selection was instituted, with Army officers assisting the selection agents.[54] In September, 1941, McEntee even authorized increased Negro selection, a move which Persons long insisted was the only solution to selection troubles.[55] Thus, considerations of expediency and survival, not moral pressure, induced the CCC near the end of its life to provide some measure of equality in selection opportunity for Negro enrollees. Finally, responding to gathering pressure, plans were made to consolidate the CCC and the NYA. On December 10, Representative Lyndon B. Johnson, with Roosevelt's approval, introduced a bill into Congress to this end. The measure aimed to create an organization to be known as the Civilian Youth Administration. It was hoped that the consolidation would save the federal government $100 million in the current fiscal year alone.[56] Throughout 1941, Roosevelt had made no secret of his desire to retain the CCC. Opposing any cut in its appropriation, he

51. *Ibid.*, Aug. 17, 1941.

52. *Termination of CCC Hearings*, 1942, pp. 253-254.

53. New York *Times*, Aug. 13, Sept. 21, 1941.

54. Advisory Council, Minutes, Aug. 26, 1941. Selection agents disliked the new policy, which was not particularly successful.

55. *Ibid.*, April 22, Sept. 23, 1941. Most of the new Negro companies were put to work on military reservations.

56. See Roosevelt to Ickes, Dec. 6, 1941, Roosevelt Papers, O.F. 268, Box 11; New York *Times*, Oct. 9, 12, and 25, Nov. 16, 19, and 24, Dec. 10, 1941.

stressed its contribution to national defense and the continuing need for its conservation work.[57]

Nevertheless, neither presidential support nor expedients of policy could hide the fact that the Corps was in very serious difficulties. In October, 1941, McEntee predicted that he would be able to turn back $47 million of the CCC's current appropriation because of the drop in enrolment. At the beginning of 1941 the CCC had 300,000 enrollees. Ten months later there were only 160,000 left in nine hundred camps.[58] Moreover, youths were leaving at the rate of six thousand monthly to take jobs in industry as war conditions closed the unemployment gap.[59] There was no chance of replacing these men. Could the continued existence of the CCC, despite its undoubted contribution to defense needs, be justified? With its enrolment dropping steadily, the Corps seemed a dying organization. Could the federal government afford to continue pumping millions of dollars into it? Such questions demanded urgent answers, the more so because one of the provisions of the Appropriations Bill of 1941-1942 had authorized the creation of a Joint Committee of Congress, whose job was to investigate all federal agencies with a view to eliminating those not considered essential to the war effort.[60] The CCC was certain to come beneath its purview.

The *New Republic* angrily described the Joint Committee as having as its motive a "burning hatred of the New Deal."[61] While this accusation was an exaggeration, it is certainly true to say that in its membership the forces of conservatism were predominant. Six of its twelve members were from the South, including its chairman, Senator Harry F. Byrd, Democrat of Virginia, an outspoken opponent of Federal spending,[62] and the irascible, arch-conservative senior Senator from Tennessee, Kenneth Mc-

57. New York *Times*, May 17, 1941.
58. *Ibid.*, March 29, Oct. 5, 1941.
59. *Ibid.*, Oct. 5, 1941.
60. *Nonessential Federal Expenditures, Hearings, 1941*, frontispiece.
61. *New Republic*, CVI (May 25, 1942), 720.
62. *Nonessential Federal Expenditures, Hearings, 1941*, frontispiece. The full committee was Byrd, chairman, Rep. Robert L. Doughton (Dem., N.C.), vice chairman; Sens. Walter F. George (Dem., Ga.), Robert M. La Follette, Jr. (Ind. Rep., Wis.), Carter Glass (Dem., Va.), McKellar, Gerald P. Nye (Rep., N.D.); Reps. Thomas H. Cullen (Dem., N.Y.), Allen T. Treadway (Rep., Mass.), Clarence Cannon (Dem., Mo.), Clifton A. Woodrum (Dem., Va.), and John Taber (Rep., N.Y.).

Kellar.[63] Of the remainder, Representative John Taber had opposed the Corps since its inception, while the isolationist Senator Gerald P. Nye, Republican of North Dakota, was unlikely to favor its entry into the field of national defense. It was clear that Corps administrators would have to present a very strong case if they were to expect the committee to report in their favor.

The committee heard evidence concerning the CCC on November 28 and December 4, 1941. The first to testify was B. S. Beecher, an employee of the Bureau of the Budget.[64] Some congressmen criticized the standard of the work and the cost of the operation,[65] but the real attack came when McEntee testified the following week. The director frankly admitted that he did not think that "from a relief standpoint, there is a scintilla of reason for carrying on this Corps,"[66] but as a training agency, he insisted, its contribution was invaluable. Neither Byrd nor McKellar could accept this judgment. McKellar, declaiming that "you have not educated the boys at all,"[67] said the Corps could no longer be justified. Byrd had serious doubts about the value of the work to the country,[68] while McKellar insisted that "the principal activity of the boys was thumbing rides going to town." He did not believe that "there has been one single solitary cent of improvement of the national wealth or national economy in any shape or form" achieved by CCC work.[69] McEntee's task, that of justifying the Corps' operations, was rendered exceedingly difficult by Byrd's skepticism and McKellar's badgering and contempt. McKellar was sometimes positively insulting, referring to the director as "one of these new fellows" and accusing him of not giving "a tinker's hurrah" for any congressman or senator,[70] a somewhat illuminating insight into McKellar's attitude toward the New Deal. The trend of the hearing was clear. It could have been no surprise when on December 24, 1941, the committee recommended that the CCC "be abolished . . . not later than July

63. For information on McKellar, see Felix A. Nigro, "The Lilienthal Case," *Southwestern Social Science Quarterly*, XL (Sept., 1959), 147-158.

64. *Nonessential Federal Expenditures, Hearings, 1941*, pp. 1-20.

65. *Ibid.*, pp. 7-8. Taber insisted the boys only did three hours' work a day. Byrd said they did not "average anything like" forty hours a week.

66. *Ibid.*, p. 266.

67. *Ibid.*, pp. 274, 290.

68. *Ibid.*, p. 279.

69. *Ibid.*, p. 281.

70. *Ibid.*, p. 283.

1, 1942."[71] A strong minority report was filed by Senator Robert M. La Follette, Jr., who complained that the recommendations were "hasty and unwarranted." In his view, now that the country was at war, the CCC was more essential than ever.[72] His was a voice in the wilderness. The majority report was widely acclaimed. The New York *Times*, supporting its findings, said that the President held the key to further action.[73] The first step toward abolishing the CCC had been taken.

Roosevelt intended to fight for his pet project. In his budget message on January 7, 1942, he conceded that the Corps could well be cut, but he insisted that the state of war increased the need for the agency's noncombatant activities.[74] Later, he spelled this out at a press conference. The CCC, he said, was necessary to perform essential conservation work and also to serve as a predraft training organization for youths not yet old enough for the Regular Army.[75] When McKellar introduced a bill providing for the abolition of the Corps and the NYA, the President wrote him a letter asking that he reconsider his action in the light of the "essential war work" which the agency was performing.[76] He intended to make it quite clear that the elimination of the CCC "saves the nation no money," but that rather it would be a costly mistake.[77]

The Corps, too, made renewed attempts to convince the country of its indispensability. Stressing the need to do more "to justify our existence," Morrell, the Forest Service's representative on the Advisory Council, successfully proposed a broad "victory program" in which Corps work would be limited to fire protection, the development of Army camps, and the maintenance of military reservations, as well as supplying partially trained men to the Army. All camps which could not qualify under one of these categories were to be closed. It was decided eventually to

71. *Preliminary Report of the Joint Committee on the Reduction of Nonessential Federal Expenditures, Congress of the United States, 77th Congress, First Session, Document* 152 (Washington, 1941), p. 4.

72. *Ibid.*, pp. 11-16.

73. New York *Times*, Dec. 26, 1941.

74. *Ibid.*, Jan. 8, 1942.

75. Rosenman, ed., *Papers*, XI, 98.

76. Roosevelt to McKellar, March 16, 1942, in Nixon, II, 548.

77. Roosevelt to Harold D. Smith, June 17, 1942, Roosevelt Papers, O.F. 268, Box 11.

retain only 150 camps, mostly on military reservations or in vital forest areas.[78]

However, time was running out for the CCC. McKellar had no intention of postponing discussion of his measure, and he seemed to have the weight of public opinion behind him. For the first time, a Gallup Poll indicated a repudiation of the CCC, when in April, 1942, 54 per cent of those polled thought it should be abolished. Only 37 per cent favored its retention, and 9 per cent were undecided.[79] In the face of such an unfavorable reaction, morale among CCC officials reached its nadir. McEntee stated that in his opinion it "would be better to fold up the CCC" now, rather than wait for Congress to do so, and he opposed the President's determination to fight for its continuance. Dissension on the Advisory Council reached new heights; both Wirth and Morrell felt the Corps still had a future and they were disgusted by McEntee's defeatism.[80] The cracks in the CCC organization, visible since Fechner's time, had split wide open.

Meanwhile, from March 23 to April 17, the Senate Education and Labor Committee held hearings on McKellar's bill. An impressive array of witnesses testified in favor of retention. The adjutant general, Major General Ulio, spoke of the contribution that both the CCC's noncombatant program and its work on military reservations had made to the nation's defense preparedness. In his opinion, the CCC was a valued component of the war machine.[81] Earl W. Loveridge, assistant chief of the United States Forest Service, discussed the need for increased forest fire protection now that war had been declared because of the danger of sabotage or incendiary bombing.[82] J. C. Dykes, assistant chief of the Soil Conservation Service, described the work of the CCC camps under his control and showed that there was still a real need for their services.[83] Both McNutt and McEntee testified at length on the past successes of the Corps and its present contribution to the war effort.[84] McNutt even produced

78. Advisory Council, Minutes, Jan. 9 and 27, May 13, 1942; New York *Times*, April 26, 1942.
79. New York *Times*, April 18, 1942.
80. Advisory Council, Minutes, April 4, May 8, 1942.
81. *Termination of CCC, Hearings, 1942*, pp. 253-301.
82. *Ibid.*, pp. 333-336.
83. *Ibid.*, pp. 337-357.
84. *Ibid.*, pp. 70-116, 280-325.

a letter from the President in which Roosevelt specifically pronounced his opposition to the bill. "The Civilian Conservation Corps work on Army reservations is needed to prepare those reservations for full utilization," he wrote. "Likewise the remaining projects of the Corps which are now limited to those essential to the various phases of our war effort, and so located so as to provide protective services in vital areas should not be discontinued at this time."[85]

Against the weight of expert testimony, McKellar in his role of prosecuting attorney, harassed the witnesses, contradicted them, and occasionally insulted them. He never once relented in his self-appointed mission to rid the country of as much of the New Deal as he could. He contradicted General Ulio's statements that the CCC youths were performing essential defense work, and he asserted that Army privates were both capable and better qualified to do such jobs.[86] He ridiculed McEntee's description of the Corps' fire-fighting efforts, claiming that the Forest Service was well able to handle emergencies without its aid. He dismissed the formal education program as valueless and said that the noncombatant training program was duplicating Army schemes, thus serving no useful purpose.[87]

To support his argument, McKellar produced his own witnesses, perhaps less versed in the workings of the Corps than those who testified in its favor, but infinitely more colorful. George S. Benson, the president of Harding College, Searcy, Arkansas, an active anti-Roosevelt propagandist, declared that both the CCC and the NYA were "wasteful" and unnecessary, and that his college could perform their combined educative functions at one-third the cost. The revelation that Benson himself had made frequent use of NYA funds, however, and had protested vigorously when Harding College's quota was discontinued, cast doubts on the value of his testimony.[88] Ben H. Henthorne, president of the College of Commerce, Kansas City, thought that the "private business schools of America" could handle the type of work done in NYA, WPA, and CCC "more quickly, more efficiently, and more economically."[89] Leon C.

85. *Ibid.*, pp 72-73.
86. *Ibid.*, pp. 259-273.
87. *Ibid.*, pp. 41-42, 297-304.
88. *Ibid.*, pp. 523-540.
89. *Ibid.*, p. 568.

Phillips, governor of Oklahoma, said that the CCC was a contributing cause of juvenile delinquency in his state,[90] an assertion which was shown to be totally without justification.[91] Still, McKellar dominated the hearing, even though the chairman, Senator Elbert D. Thomas, Democrat of Utah, together with members like Senator Dennis E. Chavez, Democrat of New Mexico, and Senator Harry H. Schwartz, Democrat of Wyoming, endeavored to counteract the weight of his words with statements of support for the CCC.[92]

Anticlimactically, after the expense and publicity of the hearing, McKellar's bill was never reported from the committee. Congress found a new and perhaps swifter method of terminating the CCC. On May 4, 1942, defying public opinion, the President asked for an appropriation of $49,101,000 to maintain 150 CCC camps for the fiscal year 1942-1943.[93] Rather than proceed with formal legislation abolishing the Corps, it was simpler for Congress merely to decline to vote any more money for CCC work. Accordingly, the House Committee on Appropriations voted on June 3, by 15 to 12, not to comply with the President's request.[94] If this committee action were carried through, the CCC would have no funds after July 1, 1942, with which to perform its functions.

Friends of the CCC fought on the floor of the House to restore the appropriation. Representative Malcolm C. Tarver, Democrat of Georgia, stressed the increased need for forest protection because of the chance of Japanese attack and warned that a vote against the CCC was a vote against the President's war program. Representative John W. McCormack insisted that the War Department wanted the Corps retained. The fight for abolishment was led by Representative Albert J. Engel, Republican of Michigan. He said the Corps had once undoubtedly done

90. *Ibid.*, p. 569.

91. Roosevelt wrote to McNutt on April 1: "You have doubtless read the deliberately false statement of the Governor of Oklahoma, Mr. Phillips, in regard to CCC boys being in large proportion connected with crime and the courts. What do you think of your summoning or my summoning Governor Phillips to Washington to substantiate the charge? This would be fun as well as useful." Roosevelt Papers, O.F. 268, Box 11.

92. *Termination of the CCC, Hearings*, 1942, pp. 76-78, 278.

93. New York *Times*, May 5, 1942.

94. *Ibid.*, June 4, 1942.

good work, but that it had long been unnecessary. "Sacred cow" or not, it should clearly be abolished. Representative Taber, in opposition to the last, termed the agency "wasteful and destructive." On June 5, 1942, the House, by 158 to 151, voted not to appropriate further money for the CCC, but instead to provide $500,000 for its liquidation.[95]

Most newspapers hailed the House's action, though they were kind to a departing friend. The New York *Times* spoke of the great works the Corps had performed and the "fine spirit" of its enrollees, but the paper could see no reason for perpetuating the agency.[96] The Baltimore *Sun* expressed regret at the "ungraceful exit for one of the most successful of the old relief agencies," but conceded that it was no longer needed, especially since it had continued to recruit rural boys in the midst of a farm labor shortage.[97] Even the Chicago *Tribune*, jubilant at the action, still asserted that the Corps was the best of the New Deal agencies and had no criticism to make of its operations during the depression.[98] A few papers criticized the House for acting too hastily. The Republican New York *Herald Tribune* said the congressmen had used an ax instead of a pruning knife and denounced their inconsistency in singling out the CCC for abolition. "Why the CCC?" the paper demanded, noting that the Corps was "long considered the most sensible and effective of New Deal experiments."[99] Opinions such as the *Herald Tribune's*, however, were exceptional. Most editors said an honorable farewell to a trusted and competent servant whose services could now be dispensed with.

The general flavor of the newspaper opinion reinforces the argument that despite the spleen of a handful of conservative congressmen and the occasional excoriation of the right-wing press, the Corps never really became unpopular. Few denied its very real achievements or questioned its original worth. But it was still a relief agency, and despite recent attempts to do so it had never successfully sold itself as anything else. In an age of war, of the rapid mobilization of men, of burgeoning industrial

95. *C.R.*, 77th Cong., 2nd Sess., Vol. 88, Pt. 4, pp. 4927-4940.
96. New York *Times*, June 5, 1942.
97. Baltimore *Sun*, June 7, 1942.
98. Chicago *Tribune*, June 6 and 27, 1942.
99. New York *Herald Tribune*, June 6, 1942.

development, its clientele remained the unemployed. The problems of 1942, however, had very little resemblance indeed to those of 1933. The CCC had become outmoded

Even so, the fight to preserve it was not quite over. Interest shifted to the Senate floor, where that body prepared to pass on the House's action. The Corps' last days were fraught with drama. The Senate debate on the CCC's appropriation was held on June 26. The arguments were similar to those in the House, with Senators Elbert Thomas and Patrick McCarran defending the Corps' record against Byrd's and McKellar's attacks.[100] The vote was taken amid scenes of great excitement. When the yeas and nays were tallied, it was found that thirty-two senators had voted to retain the CCC, thirty-two to withhold its appropriation, and thirty-two had not voted. A second vote failed to break the tie; therefore, the vice president, Henry Wallace, used his casting vote to uphold the CCC.[101] The Senate had repudiated the House's action. Did the Corps still have a chance?

The respite was short-lived. The demise of the CCC was inevitable. There was newspaper criticism of the Senate's stand, while at the Senate-House conference it was apparent that the "House was overwhelmingly for abolition" and would not comply with the Senate's action.[102] On June 30, therefore, McCarran told the senators that the Senate conferees had decided to recede from their action of June 26; in return the House had agreed to provide $8 million for the liquidation of the CCC. He asked that the Senate confirm the action, and this they did by voice vote.[103] The Civilian Conservation Corps was dead.

100. *C.R.*, 77th Cong., 2nd Sess., Vol. 88, Pt. 4, pp. 5600-5602, 5604-5605.

101. *Ibid.*, p. 5612. Twenty-nine Democrats, two Republicans, one Independent, and Wallace voted for continuance. Eighteen Democrats and fourteen Republicans were ranged against continuance.

102. Chicago *Tribune*, June 27, 1942; *C.R.*, 77th Cong., 2nd Sess., Vol. 88, Pt. 4, p. 5789.

103. *C.R.*, 77th Cong., 2nd Sess., Vol. 88, Pt. 4, p. 5789.

13. *Conclusion*

In eulogizing the Civilian Conservation Corps, the *New Republic* spoke of its "immense contributions to the conservation of soils and forests [which] have enriched the national wealth far more than the sums spent on it, even if one overlooks the benefits on the health and morale of otherwise jobless young men." The Corps was still badly needed, the journal contended, assailing the "narrow-minded spleen which wiped it out in the interests of economy," thus committing "social sabotage."[1]

Superficially, such a judgment seemed reasonable. The Corps was in fact helping the war effort by performing useful work on military reservations, by protecting vital forest regions, and by supplying partially trained young men to the armed forces. Moreover, it may well have served the country beneficially immediately after the war. If the returning veterans had caused a temporary glut on the labor market, the CCC might have been used to relieve the situation. Its abolition in 1942, therefore, might have been untimely.

Yet it is difficult to see, given the labor situation in 1942, how in fact the Corps could have been continued. The agency was dependent for the bulk of its enrollees on the unskilled unemployed. In the full employment situation of the war, its source of supply no longer existed. It is true, too, that by 1942 the CCC as an organizational amalgam of federal departments was falling apart. Racked by internal dissension and apathy, its continuance as an effective agency would have been contingent on radical changes in organization, scarcely practical in the war situation. The reasons for this organizational deterioration were various. Undoubtedly personalities played an important part. Fechner's policy of increasing directorial control of CCC activities had upset the delicate balance existing between central organization and technical agencies, and McEntee's efforts had only exacerbated this trend. These and other specific examples of internal decay, however, were all merely symptoms of the fundamental cause of the agency's decline: the CCC had developed neither a permanent identity nor a permanent organization. It was never

1. *New Republic*, CVII (July 13, 1942), 39.

able to disavow its associations with relief. Its structure never lost its temporary look, and its machinery, though for a long time surprisingly efficient, was essentially makeshift, loose, and diffuse. Though its institutional momentum carried it on for nine years, the difficulties of the operation finally became too much. The Corps was never able to plan ahead financially with any degree of certitude, living virtually from hand to mouth throughout its existence. Clashes and wrangling among top officials, symptomatic of the slow breakdown at the center, were increasingly frequent in the CCC's final years.

Intimately connected with the Corps' failure to outgrow its temporary status was its inability to shake off the relief stamp. The CCC was never able to convince the Congress or the public that it had other functions besides the provision of relief and the performance of useful work. This was partly due, of course, to Fechner's reluctance to concede the need to develop a broader aim or to look ahead to a time when the situation which originally prompted the CCC's creation no longer existed. To be sure, McEntee did try to sell to the public the idea of the Corps as a work and training center, an agency which welcomed all young men without reference to their economic status, but by this time it was too late to change its original image. Most continued to consider the CCC as having primarily a relief function, and consequently, when rising re-employment rates made this irrelevant, the agency was bound to be stopped.

There is little need to dwell much longer on the specific results of the CCC's failure to develop wider aims. We have already noted its inability to grasp fully the golden opportunity given it to develop a thoroughgoing program of remedial education and vocational training, leading to eventual re-employment. Much good work was undoubtedly performed, yet in some respects the opportunity was squandered, due in large part to an absence of cohesive planning and basic confusion as to what the aims of CCC education should be. Many comprehensive schemes were advanced, but all foundered upon the rock of expediency and were judged impractical because of the agency's transient character. Unless and until the CCC lost its temporary basis, it was bound to suffer from an absence of direction, a confusion as to ultimate goals. This, perhaps, was the tragedy of the CCC. Despite its successes, its potential was never fully tapped.

A significant aspect of the CCC's existence, one which distinguished it from other relief agencies and which probably had some bearing on the lack of planning for the future, was the question of the CCC's conservatism. The CCC was not led by liberal intellectuals such as Aubrey Williams or Harry Hopkins, but by a conservative former trade-union official who boasted that his clerks had more formal education than he did. Moreover, responsibility for camp management was vested in the least radical body in the country, the Army. This, as has been mentioned, was undoubtedly a factor in explaining the CCC's relative popularity with even right-wing congressmen and commentators, who were further entranced with its possibilities as a political pork barrel. Add to this the fact that many saw in the CCC's activities some sort of return to an older and better America, an America of young men working close to the soil, and the sources of the Corps' popularity are explained. However, this also helps us to understand the lack of interest in charting a wider course for the agency's future. Congressmen never provided a framework for long-term development, while the Army did not consider its role to be a permanent one.

It is too easy, however, to accuse the CCC unfairly. Even if wider aims had been developed and the Corps placed on a permanent footing, it would have provided no immediate answer to the basic problems facing American youth. These could not be solved by moving boys from their homes to the woods, no matter how enlightened those responsible for the shift might be. Though the CCC could certainly have done more, it should not be treated as a scapegoat, a whipping boy for other more fundamental failures. Moreover, to talk of the CCC as conservative is to overlook the fact that the spirit which flowed through the whole New Deal program had clearly not passed it by. The CCC fitted squarely into the New Deal pattern. It is almost a cliché to describe the Roosevelt revolution as experimental, anti-ideological, essentially pragmatic, and, above all, humanitarian. Certainly, this was true of the CCC. It was frankly experimental, it had no real precedent to follow and no long-term goals to be reached. Its organization was essentially a makeshift response to the immediate problem of unemployed youth. Further, in its profound concern for the well-being of its enrollees, the CCC shared in the broadly humanitarian trends of the era, and this underlying principle was with it until the end.

In spite of the vicissitudes of its final years and the larger question of the lack of an overview as to its permanent function in the American social fabric, the Civilian Conservation Corps stood firmly upon its record. Immediately, to a country engaged in bloody war, it had provided the sinews of a military force. It had given young officers valuable training in command techniques, and the nearly three million young men who had passed through the camps had received experience of military life upon which the Army was well able to build.

Moreover, there is little need to dwell upon the vital contribution made by the CCC to the conservation of natural resources. The billions of trees planted or protected, the millions of acres saved from the ravages of soil erosion or the depredations of flooded rivers, the hundreds of parks and recreation areas which were developed, are a permanent testimony to the success of Corps work. They constitute a legitimate contribution to the heritage of every American.

Finally, the CCC had a lasting effect on its enrollees. Life in the camps brought tangible benefits to the health, educational level, and employment expectancies of almost three million young Americans, and it also gave immediate financial aid to their families. Equally important were the intangibles of Corps life. The CCC gave to its enrollees both a new understanding of their country and a faith in its future. Youths from the teeming cities learned something of rural America, boys from farms and country hamlets became acquainted with the complexities and ethnic variation of their land and its people. Both emerged from the camp experience with a greater understanding of America, and of Americans.

Despite its shortcomings, the CCC was of the profoundest importance. It was important because of its effect on the nation's national resources and the health of its enrollees, and it is important to the story of reform in the United States. It marked the first attempt by the federal government to provide some specific solution for the problems of youth in an increasingly urban society. In its makeshift, loose way it was a pathfinder, the precursor of more sophisticated programs and ideas. After the CCC came Roosevelt's National Youth Administration, the attempts at providing federal aid to education pursued by every postwar president, and the complex of youth agencies which form such an integral part of President Lyndon B. Johnson's war on poverty. Indeed, the parallels between one of these, the Job Corps, and the CCC are striking. To be sure, the Job Corps is a far more sophisticated agency than the old CCC, its functions at once more specialized and more diverse. Nevertheless, its enrollees, too, are unemployed young men between the ages of eighteen and twenty-five years; they, too, live in camps, sometimes old CCC sites first used over thirty years ago; they, too, work in the woods. By its successes as well as its shortcomings, the CCC has surely provided, in this instance, a concrete example for others to follow.

Though the CCC is dead, it has not been forgotten. As Arthur M. Schlesinger, Jr., wrote, it has "left its monuments in the preservation and purification of the land, the water, the forests, and the young men of America."[2]

2. Schlesinger, II, 340.

Selected Bibliography

1. Unpublished Documents

Records of the Civilian Conservation Corps, in National Archives.

Chronological Reference Material by Subjects.

780(a) Organization.
(c) Liaison Officers.
781 Special Enrollee Uniforms.
782(b) The Forest Service and ECW (typescript).
783 Soil Erosion.
784(1) Leaders and Assistant Leaders.
(4) CCC in Emergencies.
(7) Military Training.
785(5) CCC in the Territories.
787 Public Opinion.
788(1) Development.
790 Training.
791 Permanent CCC.

Appendices I through VI.
Correspondence of the Director, 1933-1942.
Minutes of the Advisory Council, 1933-1942.
Records of the Selection Division.

(a) Education, General Correspondence.
(b) Minutes of the Advisory Committee on Education.
(c) Policy.
(d) Discussion of Selection Policy, 1935.
(e) Negro Selection.
(f) Benefit Letters.
(g) Discharges.
(h) Digest of State Reports Concerning Non-Honorable Discharges for Desertion.
(i) Study of the CCC by the American Youth Commission, 1939-1942 (typescript).
(j) Military Aspects.

Public Relations File, Benefit Letters.
Report of the Special Committee on Education in the CCC, 1939 (typescript).

Franklin D. Roosevelt Papers, in Franklin D. Roosevelt Library, Hyde Park, N.Y.

(a) Official File.
(b) Private Personal File.

Louis Howe Papers, in Franklin D. Roosevelt Library.

Files of the Secretary of Agriculture, 1933-1942—Conservation, in National Archives.

Records of the Office of the Secretary of the Interior, 1933-1942, in National Archives.

II. Published Documents

Congressional

Amending an Act Establishing a Civilian Conservation Corps, House of Representatives Report No. 447, 76th Congress, First Session (Washington: Government Printing Office, 1939).

The Civilian Conservation Corps, a Monograph by the Legislative Reference Service, Library of Congress, 77th Congress, Second Session, Senate Document 216 (Washington: Government Printing Office, 1941).

Congressional Directory, 1933-1942.

Congressional Record, 1933-1942.

Emergency Relief Appropriation Act, Fiscal Year, 1941, Hearings Before the Committee on Appropriations, United States Senate, 76th Congress, Third Session, on H.J. Res. 544, A Joint Resolution Making Appropriations for Work Relief and Relief for the Fiscal Year Ending June 30, 1941 (Washington: Government Printing Office, 1940).

To Establish a Civilian Conservation Corps: Hearings Before the Committee on Education and Labor, United States Senate, 75th Congress, First Session, on S. *2102*, April 9 and 13, 1937 (Washington: Government Printing Office, 1937).

To Make the Civilian Conservation Corps a Permanent Agency: Hearings Before the Committee on Labor, House of Representatives, 75th Congress, First Session, on H.R. 6180, April 14 and 15, 1937 (Washington: Government Printing Office, 1937).

To Make the Civilian Conservation Corps a Permanent Agency: Hearings Before the Committee on Labor, House of Representatives, 76th Congress, First Session, on H.R. 2990, Feb. 9, 23, and 24, 1939 (Washington: Government Printing Office, 1939).

Preliminary Report of the Joint Committee on the Reduction of Nonessential Federal Expenditures, Congress of the United States, 77th Congress, First Session, Document 152 (Washington: Government Printing Office, 1941).

Reduction of Nonessential Federal Expenditures: Hearings Before the Joint Committee on the Reduction of Nonessential Federal Expenditures, Congress of the United States, 77th

Congress, First Session, Pursuant to Section 601 of the Revenue Act of 1941, Parts 1 to 4, Nov. 28, Dec. 1, 2, and 4, 1941 (Washington: Government Printing Office, 1942).

Termination of the Civilian Conservation Corps and the National Youth Administration, Hearings Before the Committee on Education and Labor, United States Senate, 77th Congress, Second Session, on S. 2295. A Bill to Provide for the Termination of the National Youth Administration and the Civilian Conservation Corps, March 23 to April 17, 1942 (Washington: Government Printing Office, 1942).

Unemployment Relief: Joint Hearings Before the Committee on Education and Labor, United States Senate, and the Committee on Labor, House of Representatives, 73rd Congress, First Session, on S. 598, March 23 and 24, 1933 (Washington: Government Printing Office, 1933).

Miscellaneous

Handbook of Civilian Conservation Corps, U.S. Department of Agriculture, Forest Service, Region VIII, 1938 (typescript in Duke University Library).

Official Handbook for Agencies Selecting Men for Emergency Conservation Work (Washington: U.S. Department of Labor, 1933-1942).

Report of the Secretary of War to the President, 1933 (Washington: Government Printing Office, 1933).

Summary Reports of the Director of Emergency Conservation Work (Washington: Government Printing Office, 1933-1943).

War Department Regulations, Relief of Unemployment (Washington: War Department, 1933-1937).

III. Newspapers and Periodicals

Baltimore *Sun*
Boston *Evening Transcript*
Chicago *Tribune*
Collier's
Des Moines *Register*
Greensboro, N.C., *News*
Happy Days
Literary Digest
New Republic
New York *Herald Tribune*
New York *Times*
Philadelphia *Ledger*
St. Louis *Post-Dispatch*
San Francisco *Examiner*
Time
Washington *Post*
Washington *Star*

Clippings on CCC in National Archives

Atlanta *Constitution*
Boston *Herald*
Dallas *News*
Harrisburg, Pa., *News*
Indianapolis *Star*
McKeesport, Pa., *News*
Madison, Wis., *Times*
New York *Daily News*
San Diego *Sun*
Shreveport, La., *Times*
Topeka, Kan., *Capital*
Washington *Daily News*
Washington *Herald*
Washington *Times Herald*

IV. General Works

Bellush, Bernard E. *Franklin D. Roosevelt as Governor of New York* (New York: Columbia University Press, 1955).

Blum, John M. *From the Morgenthau Diaries: Years of Crisis, 1928-1938* (Boston: Houghton Mifflin, 1959).

Bromley, Dorothy E. "The Forest Army that Lives by Work," *New York Times*, July 23, 1933, section viii, p. 2.

Brown, Nelson C. "The President Has Long Practiced Forestry," *New York Times*, April 30, 1933, section viii, p. 1.

Burns, James McGregor. *Roosevelt: The Lion and the Fox* (New York: Harcourt Brace, 1956).

Charles, Searle F. *Minister of Relief: Harry Hopkins and the Depression* (Syracuse: Syracuse University Press, 1963).

Chase, Stuart. "Where the Crop Lands Go: Spendthrift America's Dwindling Estate," *Harper's*, CXXV (Aug., 1936), 225-233.

The CCC and Wildlife (Washington: Government Printing Office, 1939).

The CCC at Work (Washington: Federal Security Agency, 1942).

Deering, Richard L. "Camps for the Unemployed in the Forests of California," *Journal of Forestry* (May, 1932), 554-557.

Forest Improvements by the CCC (Washington: Government Printing Office, 1938).

Forests Protected by the CCC (Washington: Government Printing Office, 1939).

Freidel, Frank. *Roosevelt*: Vol. I, *The Apprenticeship*; II, *The Ordeal*; III, *The Triumph* (Boston: Little, Brown, 1952, 1954, 1956).

Hands to Save the Soil (Washington: Government Printing Office, 1939).

Harper, Charles P. *The Administration of the Civilian Conservation Corps* (Clarksburg, W. Va.: Clarksburg Publishing Co., 1939).

Hill, Frank E. "The CCC Marches Toward a New Destiny," *New York Times*, Feb. 21, 1937, section viii, pp. 10-11.

———. *The School in the Camps: The Educational Program of the Civilian Conservation Corps* (New York: American Association for Adult Education, 1942).

Hofstadter, Richard. *The Age of Reform* (New York: A. A. Knopf, 1955).

Holland, Kenneth. *Youth in European Labor Camps* (Washington: American Council of Education, 1939).

Holland, Kenneth, and Frank E. Hill. *Youth in the CCC* (Washington: American Council of Education, 1942).

Ickes, Harold L. *The Secret Diary of Harold L. Ickes*: Vol. I, *The First Thousand Days*; II, *The Inside Struggle, 1936-1939* (New York: Simon and Schuster, 1953, 1954).

James, William. *Memories and Studies* (New York: Longmans, 1912).

Johnson, Donald B. *The Republican Party and Wendell Willkie* (Urbana: University of Illinois Press, 1960).

Leighton, George R., and Richard Hillman. "Half Slave, Half Free: Unemployment, the Depression, and American Young People," *Harper's*, CXXIII (Aug., 1935), 342-353.

Leuchtenburg, William E. *Franklin D. Roosevelt and the New Deal, 1932-1940* (New York: Harper and Row, 1963).

Lindley, Ernest K. *Half-way with Roosevelt* (New York: Viking Press, 1937).

Link, Arthur S. *American Epoch* (New York: A. A. Knopf, 1955).

McKinney, Guy D. "An Army in the Forests," *Natural History*, XXIV (Feb., 1934), 141-150.

Mitchell, Jonathan. "Roosevelt's Tree Army," *New Republic*, LXXXIII (May 29, 1935; June 12, 1935), 64-66, 127-129.

Moley, Raymond. *After Seven Years* (New York: Harper and Brothers, 1939).

Nixon, Edgar B. (ed.) *Franklin D. Roosevelt and Conservation, 1911-1945* (New York: General Services Administration, 1957).

Perkins, Dexter. *The New Age of Franklin Roosevelt, 1932-1945* (Chicago: University of Chicago Press, 1957).

Perkins, Frances. *The Roosevelt I Knew* (New York: Viking Press, 1946).

Rauch, Basil. *The History of the New Deal, 1932-1938* (New York: Creative Age Press, 1944).

Rawick, George P. "The New Deal and Youth: The Civilian Conservation Corps, the National Youth Administration, the American Youth Congress." Unpublished Ph.D. dissertation, University of Wisconsin, 1957.

Riesch, Anna L. "Conservation Under Franklin D. Roosevelt." Unpublished Ph.D. dissertation, University of Wisconsin, 1952.

Roberts, Stephen H. *The House that Hitler Built* (London: Methuen, 1937).

Rollins, Albert B. *Roosevelt and Howe* (New York: A. A. Knopf, 1962).

Roosevelt, Eleanor. *This I Remember* (New York: Harper and Brothers, 1949).

Rosenman, Samuel I. (ed.) *The Public Papers and Addresses of Franklin D. Roosevelt* (New York: Macmillan, 1938-1950).

Saalberg, John J. "Roosevelt, Fechner, and the CCC–A Study in Executive Leadership." Unpublished Ph.D. dissertation, Cornell University, 1962.

Schlesinger, Arthur M., Jr. *The Age of Roosevelt*: Vol. I, *The Crisis of the Old Order*; II, *The Coming of the New Deal*; III, *The Politics of Upheaval* (Boston: Houghton Mifflin, 1957, 1959, 1960).

Stiles, Leila. *The Man Behind Roosevelt* (Cleveland: World, 1954).

Tugwell, Rexford Guy. *The Democratic Roosevelt* (New York: Doubleday, 1957).

Wandall, Luther C. "A Negro in the CCC," *Crisis*, XLII (Aug., 1935), 244-253.

Wechter, Dixon. *The Age of the Great Depression, 1929-41* (New York: Macmillan, 1948).

Wirth, Conrad L. *The Civilian Conservation Corps Program of the United States Department of the Interior* (Chicago: Merchandise Mart, 1944).

Wolfskill, George. *The Revolt of the Conservatives: A History of the American Liberty League, 1934-1940* (Boston: Houghton Mifflin, 1962).

Index

Date Due

